MW00961329

Disclaimer:
This book is intended as a supplemental ⸻ engage their children in play therapy activities at home. It is **not a substitute for professional therapy** or medical advice. While the activities in this book can support your child's development, they are not designed to replace the individualized treatment plans provided by licensed therapists, occupational therapists, or healthcare professionals. For personalized guidance and professional evaluation, please consult with a qualified therapist or medical professional. Always follow the advice of your healthcare provider regarding your child's specific needs.

1. Create a Safe Sensory Time-Out Area

A sensory time-out area is a calming space where your child can retreat when they feel overwhelmed. It's a spot designed to help them self-regulate, relax, and process their emotions in a peaceful environment.

How it works:

- **Choose the right space:** Set up the area in a quiet corner or a place your child feels safe. Avoid busy parts of the home to ensure minimal distractions.
- **Customize the space:** Let your child help pick out comforting items like soft blankets, pillows, sensory toys, and calming lights. You can even add a music player with soothing tunes or white noise.
- **Sensory items:** Include fidget toys, weighted blankets, and calming sensory bottles. A large cardboard box can also be turned into a cozy nook with some duct tape and decorations.

Benefits for kids:

- Helps with **self-regulation** by offering a dedicated calming space.
- Encourages **independent emotional control** without needing to rely on external support.
- Provides **sensory stimulation** that helps reduce anxiety and stress.

Benefits for parents:

- **Reduces meltdowns** by providing a proactive solution for emotional management.
- **Empowers your child** to recognize when they need a break, fostering independence.
- **Easy to set up:** A time-out area can be created with everyday household items, making it a simple and effective tool.

2. Sensory Swings for Autism

Sensory swings are a fantastic tool for helping children with autism calm down and self-regulate. The gentle swinging motion provides sensory input that can be both calming and stimulating, depending on how it's used.

How it works:

- **Pick the right swing:** Compression swings, hammock swings, or platform swings can be set up in a doorway or outdoors.
- **Use it for different needs:** The swing can be used for calming when a child feels overwhelmed, or it can be turned into an active play tool for stimulating movement and balance.
- **Create routines:** Incorporating swinging into your child's daily routine can help improve focus and reduce anxiety.

Benefits for kids:

- **Calms the nervous system** through rhythmic, repetitive movement.
- **Improves balance and coordination** as they practice controlling their movements.
- **Increases focus** and attention by providing much-needed sensory input.

Benefits for parents:

- **Versatile tool:** Can be used for both calming and active play.
- **Reduces anxiety and stress:** Helps manage emotional meltdowns and self-regulation challenges.
- **Easy to incorporate into daily life:** Swings can be used during playtime or as part of a relaxation routine.

3. Visual Schedules

Visual schedules provide structure for children who benefit from seeing what comes next. These schedules outline daily tasks with pictures, helping children understand their routines and reducing anxiety over the unknown.

How it works:

- **Create step-by-step visuals:** Use pictures or symbols to represent each task or activity your child needs to do during the day (e.g., brushing teeth, getting dressed).
- **Post it where it's visible:** Hang the schedule in a place where your child can see it regularly.
- **Teach independence:** Encourage your child to follow the schedule themselves, marking off completed tasks.

Benefits for kids:

- **Increases independence** by allowing kids to follow routines without constant reminders.
- **Reduces anxiety** about transitions, as they can see what's coming next.
- Helps improve **time management skills**.

Benefits for parents:

- **Promotes routine adherence** without the need for verbal reminders.
- **Decreases power struggles** as children understand expectations through visual cues.
- **Eases transitions** between activities, making daily routines smoother.

4. Make an Obstacle Course

Obstacle courses are a fantastic way to get kids moving while working on gross motor skills and problem-solving. This activity can be done indoors or outdoors, depending on the space available.

How it works:

- **Create the course:** Use objects around the house like chairs, hula hoops, pillows, and painter's tape to create a course. Tape lines on the floor for balancing or jumping, set up chairs to crawl under, and use cushions as stepping stones.
- **Add challenges:** Include movements like jumping, crawling, and balancing to make the course more fun and challenging.
- **Time it for fun:** For an added element, you can time your child as they complete the course and challenge them to beat their best time.

Benefits for kids:

- **Improves gross motor skills** through jumping, crawling, and balancing.
- **Boosts problem-solving skills** as they figure out how to navigate each obstacle.
- **Burns off energy** in a productive and fun way.

Benefits for parents:

- **Encourages physical activity:** Keeps kids active, especially on rainy days.
- **Can be done with household items:** No need for expensive equipment.
- **Promotes creativity and teamwork:** Kids can help design the course and take pride in completing it.

5. Sensory and Calm-Down Bottles

Sensory bottles are a simple, yet highly effective tool for calming kids when they feel overwhelmed. These bottles are filled with water, glitter, and other small objects that move around when the bottle is shaken.

How it works:

- **Create your bottle:** Fill a clear plastic bottle with water, glitter glue, and small items like beads or sequins. The goal is to create a mesmerizing visual effect when the bottle is shaken.
- **Customize it:** You can change up the filler based on your child's preferences. For example, add a small toy or different colors to match a theme.
- **Use during stressful moments:** Encourage your child to shake the bottle and watch the contents settle when they need a break or are feeling overwhelmed.

Benefits for kids:

- **Calms the mind and body** through visual stimulation.
- **Improves focus and attention** by encouraging them to watch the slow-moving objects.
- **Promotes self-soothing** during moments of stress or sensory overload.

Benefits for parents:

- **Portable calming tool:** Can be used at home, in the car, or even at school.
- **Easy to make:** Requires minimal materials and effort.
- **Effective in helping kids regulate emotions** without the need for outside intervention.

---

6. Playground and Outdoor Activities

Outdoor play is essential for children's physical and emotional development. Engaging with playground equipment and outdoor activities helps kids develop their gross motor skills while providing fresh air and space to explore.

How it works:

- **Use playground equipment:** Encourage your child to climb, swing, or slide, which helps build strength and coordination.
- **Create outdoor games:** If playground equipment isn't available, create games like scavenger hunts or balance challenges using natural elements like rocks or sticks.
- **Barefoot play:** Let your child run or walk barefoot to engage their tactile senses and improve balance.

Benefits for kids:

- **Develops gross motor skills** through physical play like running, climbing, and jumping.
- **Boosts social skills** when playing with other children at the playground.
- **Increases sensory awareness** when playing in natural environments.

Benefits for parents:

- **Encourages outdoor play:** Getting children outside for physical activity helps with mood regulation and better sleep.
- **Easy setup:** Most outdoor activities require minimal or no equipment.
- **Promotes family bonding:** Parents can participate in outdoor games or observe their child's growth in confidence and physical ability.

7. Involve Your Child in Daily Decisions

Giving your child a role in making daily decisions helps boost their confidence, communication skills, and problem-solving abilities. Whether it's planning meals or picking out clothes, these moments are great opportunities for learning.

How it works:

- **Start with simple choices:** Ask your child to pick between two outfits or decide what they'd like to eat for lunch.
- **Incorporate decision-making into chores:** Involve them in grocery shopping by helping them pick out fruits or vegetables or choosing what items to add to the list.
- **Explain the consequences:** Talk about how different choices lead to different outcomes, helping them understand the value of their decisions.

Benefits for kids:

- **Boosts decision-making skills** and fosters independence.
- **Builds communication skills** as they explain their choices.
- **Increases confidence** in their ability to contribute to family activities.

Benefits for parents:

- **Encourages collaboration:** Children feel more invested in activities when they help make decisions.
- **Teaches responsibility:** Letting children make decisions helps them understand accountability.
- **Strengthens parent-child bonds** through shared responsibilities and conversations.

8. Add 'Brain Breaks' or Movement Activities

Incorporating short breaks throughout the day helps children reset, recharge, and refocus. Activities like yoga or simple movement exercises can be done between tasks to help children manage stress and stay engaged.

How it works:

- **Set a timer:** After 20-30 minutes of focused activity, take a 5-minute break for stretching or deep breathing.

- **Try yoga:** Guide your child through simple poses like "tree" or "child's pose" to help them relax.
- **Do quick physical exercises:** Encourage jumping jacks, hopping, or dancing to release energy and reset focus.

Benefits for kids:

- **Reduces stress and anxiety** through deep breathing and calming movements.
- **Increases focus and concentration** by giving the brain a short break.
- **Promotes physical activity**, which is essential for overall health.

Benefits for parents:

- **Easy to incorporate into daily routines:** No special equipment is needed.
- **Prevents burnout:** Keeps kids from getting overwhelmed or frustrated during longer activities.
- **Improves productivity and attention**, making the day run more smoothly.

9. Finger Painting

Finger painting is a great sensory activity that allows children to express themselves creatively while exploring different textures. It's a hands-on activity that encourages imaginative thinking.

How it works:

- **Set up a workspace:** Lay down newspaper or a plastic mat, and let your child choose the colors they want to use.
- **Encourage exploration:** Allow your child to use their hands and fingers to create shapes and patterns freely.
- **Talk about their creations:** Ask questions like "What are you making?" to encourage them to describe their artwork and feelings.

Benefits for kids:

- **Develops fine motor skills** as children manipulate the paint.
- **Encourages self-expression** through art.
- **Improves sensory processing** by engaging with different textures.

Benefits for parents:

- **Simple to set up:** Requires only basic art supplies.
- **Allows for creative freedom:** Kids can explore colors and textures at their own pace.
- **Promotes bonding:** Engaging in art activities together opens up opportunities for conversation.

10. Water Play

Water play is an excellent activity for sensory exploration and motor development. Children can pour, splash, and experiment with water, which helps improve coordination and sensory integration.

How it works:

- **Set up a water station:** Use a baby pool, a large plastic bin, or the bathtub. Add cups, funnels, and floating toys to enhance the experience.
- **Encourage experimentation:** Allow your child to pour, scoop, and splash water to explore its properties.
- **Add challenges:** You can turn water play into a learning game by asking your child to predict which objects will sink or float.

Benefits for kids:

- **Promotes sensory exploration** by engaging with water's tactile properties.
- **Improves motor skills** through pouring and scooping actions.
- **Encourages independent play** and experimentation.

Benefits for parents:

- **Simple and cost-effective:** Water play requires little preparation and minimal equipment.
- **Keeps children entertained** for long periods.
- **Provides educational opportunities** to talk about concepts like floating, sinking, and water movement.

11. Build with Blocks

Building with blocks is a classic activity that helps children develop fine motor skills, spatial awareness, and creativity. Whether you use wooden blocks, Legos, or foam blocks, this activity encourages problem-solving and imaginative play.

How it works:

- **Start with a simple challenge:** Ask your child to build something specific, like a tower, a bridge, or a house. This provides direction while still allowing them to be creative.
- **Encourage free play:** Let your child build whatever comes to mind. You can even join in to make it a collaborative effort.
- **Talk through the process:** Ask questions like, "How tall can you make the tower?" or "What's the strongest way to build a bridge?"

Benefits for kids:

- **Enhances problem-solving skills** as children figure out how to stack or connect blocks.
- **Improves fine motor skills** through grasping, balancing, and placing blocks.
- **Encourages creative thinking** by allowing children to design their own structures.

Benefits for parents:

- **Low-cost, high-reward activity:** Blocks are versatile and can be used for many different types of play.
- **Easy to set up and clean up:** No need for complicated preparations.
- **Promotes teamwork:** Building together strengthens parent-child relationships and encourages cooperative play.

12. Create a Story Together

Storytelling is a powerful way to enhance your child's language and communication skills. Creating a story together lets your child's imagination run wild while also teaching them about structure and sequencing.

How it works:

- **Start with a prompt:** You can say something like, "Once upon a time, there was a magical forest..." and let your child add to the story.
- **Alternate turns:** Take turns contributing to the story. This helps your child think on their feet and adds an element of surprise.
- **Illustrate it:** After the story is done, encourage your child to draw pictures that go along with the tale. This makes the story come to life in a visual way.

Benefits for kids:

- **Improves language development** as they create sentences and dialogues.
- **Enhances creativity** by allowing them to invent characters, plots, and worlds.
- **Boosts memory and sequencing skills** as they recall what happened in the story.

Benefits for parents:

- **Fosters communication** by creating a space where children feel comfortable expressing their ideas.
- **Promotes listening skills:** Children have to listen carefully to build on the story.
- **Fun bonding activity:** Creating a story together opens the door to laughter and shared creativity.

13. Play with Playdough

Playdough is a hands-on activity that's perfect for tactile exploration. Kids love to squish, mold, and create with it, which can improve fine motor skills and spark creativity.

How it works:

- **Set out tools and materials:** Provide playdough in different colors, along with simple tools like cookie cutters, plastic knives, and rolling pins.
- **Encourage open-ended play:** Let your child create whatever they want—animals, food items, or abstract shapes.
- **Make it educational:** Ask your child to mold letters, numbers, or shapes, combining play with learning.

Benefits for kids:

- **Improves fine motor skills** as they roll, squeeze, and shape the dough.
- **Encourages creativity** by allowing them to transform a simple material into different objects.
- **Calms and focuses the mind,** making it a great activity for relaxing.

Benefits for parents:

- **Easy to set up and clean up:** Playdough is a mess-free activity with minimal preparation.
- **Can be educational:** Parents can use the opportunity to teach letters, numbers, and shapes.
- **Helps with focus:** This is a great way to keep children engaged and calm.

14. Create a Sensory Walk

A sensory walk is a fun, engaging way for children to explore different textures and surfaces. This activity encourages children to focus on how their bodies and feet feel as they move through the sensory elements.

How it works:

- **Set up different textures:** Lay out various materials like bubble wrap, soft blankets, rocks, sand, or even grass. If indoors, you can use textured mats or materials from around the house.
- **Encourage barefoot walking:** Let your child walk or crawl over each surface, asking them to describe how it feels.
- **Add a challenge:** Blindfold your child and see if they can guess the surface based on touch alone.

Benefits for kids:

- **Stimulates the senses** by engaging the sense of touch and movement.
- **Improves balance and coordination** as they navigate through different textures.
- **Increases mindfulness,** teaching children to focus on how their bodies feel.

Benefits for parents:

- **Simple setup with household items:** No need to buy special materials; use what you have at home.
- **Encourages outdoor play:** You can easily take this activity outside to explore natural surfaces.
- **Provides sensory stimulation**, which is great for children with sensory processing challenges.

15. Build a Fort

Building a fort is a timeless activity that combines imagination, problem-solving, and gross motor skills. Whether it's made of pillows, blankets, or boxes, a fort provides a special place for children to hide, play, and dream.

How it works:

- **Gather materials:** Use pillows, blankets, sheets, and chairs to create a cozy hideaway. You can also use cardboard boxes for an extra sturdy fort.
- **Let your child lead:** Encourage your child to decide how they want the fort to look. They can even add fairy lights or decorations to personalize it.
- **Make it a special space:** Once the fort is built, it can be used for reading, relaxing, or other quiet activities.

Benefits for kids:

- **Enhances problem-solving skills** as they figure out how to build and structure their fort.
- **Encourages imaginative play**, where they can create different scenarios (like a castle or secret hideout).
- **Develops spatial awareness** as they navigate building the fort.

Benefits for parents:

- **Promotes independent play:** Kids can spend hours in their fort, allowing for self-directed activity.
- **No need for fancy materials:** Forts can be made from everyday household items.
- **Provides a quiet space** for children to read or relax in their own little world.

16. Balloon Games

Balloon games are a fun, energetic way to help kids release energy while working on coordination and teamwork. They're great for indoor play and can be tailored to children of all ages.

How it works:

- **Balloon volleyball:** Set up a "net" using a string between two chairs and encourage your child to keep the balloon in the air by batting it back and forth.
- **Balloon balance:** Challenge your child to balance the balloon on different body parts (e.g., head, hand, knee) and walk a short distance.
- **Keep it in the air:** Try to keep the balloon from touching the ground by using hands, feet, or even paper plates.

Benefits for kids:

- **Improves hand-eye coordination** and balance as they work to keep the balloon in the air.
- **Burns off energy** while engaging in a low-impact, fun activity.
- **Promotes teamwork** when playing with others, teaching cooperation and communication.

Benefits for parents:

- **Inexpensive and versatile:** All you need is a balloon to create multiple games.
- **Great for rainy days:** Perfect for indoor play when going outside isn't an option.
- **Provides light exercise**, helping children stay active and engaged.

---

17. Mirror Play

Mirror play is a wonderful activity for young children that promotes self-awareness and emotional development. It's also a fun way to explore facial expressions and body movements.

How it works:

- **Place a mirror at your child's level:** Let them watch themselves as they move, smile, or make different expressions.
- **Copycat game:** Encourage your child to make different faces and try to mimic each other's expressions.
- **Body part recognition:** Ask your child to point to different parts of their body while looking in the mirror (e.g., "Where's your nose?").

Benefits for kids:

- **Develops self-awareness** as they recognize their reflection.
- **Encourages emotional expression** by exploring different facial expressions and emotions.
- **Improves body awareness**, helping them identify body parts and movements.

Benefits for parents:

- **Simple to set up:** All you need is a mirror and your child's imagination.
- **Great for younger children:** It's an engaging activity for toddlers or children just beginning to develop self-awareness.

- **Promotes bonding** through interactive play that requires attention and participation.

18. Create a Weather Chart

A weather chart is a fun and educational tool that helps children observe and record daily weather conditions. It's a great way to introduce science concepts while also teaching routine.

How it works:

- **Create a chart:** Draw a simple chart with columns for each day of the week and rows for different weather types (sunny, cloudy, rainy, etc.).
- **Daily observation:** Each day, ask your child to look outside and decide what the weather is like. They can then draw or place a symbol (like a sun or cloud) on the chart.
- **Track patterns:** Over time, your child can notice weather patterns and changes.

Benefits for kids:

- **Introduces scientific thinking** by encouraging observation and recording data.
- **Builds routine and responsibility** as they update the chart daily.
- **Increases awareness of nature and the environment** through regular outdoor observation.

Benefits for parents:

- **Educational tool:** Teaches children about weather, patterns, and seasons.
- **Easy to implement:** Requires minimal materials and time.
- **Creates structure** by incorporating the activity into the daily routine.

19. Create a Nature Scavenger Hunt

A nature scavenger hunt is an exciting way to get kids outside and exploring their environment. It's a great opportunity for them to discover different plants, animals, and objects in nature while developing observational skills.

How it works:

- **Make a list:** Write down a list of things to find, like a leaf, a rock, a flower, or a bird. You can adjust the list based on your child's age and what's available in your area.
- **Go on an adventure:** Head outside to a park, backyard, or nearby trail, and encourage your child to find everything on the list.
- **Collect or photograph items:** For older children, you can add the element of photographing each item rather than collecting them.

Benefits for kids:

- **Encourages outdoor exploration**, fostering a connection with nature.
- **Develops observation skills** as they look for specific items.
- **Promotes physical activity** through walking and searching.

Benefits for parents:

- **Fun and educational:** Combines learning with physical activity in a natural environment.
- **Customizable:** Can be tailored to different age groups and outdoor settings.
- **Encourages family bonding** as you explore together.

---

20. Puppet Play

Puppet play is a fantastic way to help children express their emotions, develop language skills, and explore different scenarios. Using puppets allows kids to project their feelings in a non-threatening way.

How it works:

- **Choose or make puppets:** You can use store-bought puppets or create your own using socks or paper bags.
- **Act out scenarios:** Encourage your child to use the puppets to act out a story or conversation. You can guide them by setting up a theme, like "What did you do at school today?" or "How does the puppet feel right now?"
- **Create a puppet theater:** Turn a cardboard box into a small stage for the puppets to perform on.

Benefits for kids:

- **Improves language and communication skills** as they create dialogue for the puppets.
- **Encourages emotional expression** by allowing children to project feelings onto the puppets.
- **Boosts imagination and creativity** as they invent stories and characters.

Benefits for parents:

- **Helps children open up emotionally**, especially if they are shy or reluctant to talk.
- **Engaging and low-cost activity:** Puppets can be made from everyday household items.
- **Great for bonding:** Puppet shows can be collaborative, making it a fun family activity.

21. Sorting Games

Sorting games are a fun and simple way to develop your child's cognitive and fine motor skills. By sorting objects by color, size, or shape, kids learn important classification skills that will help them in school and everyday life.

How it works:

- **Gather objects:** Use household items like buttons, beads, or blocks. You can also use natural items like leaves, rocks, or sticks.
- **Create categories:** Ask your child to sort the items into groups. For example, they can sort by color, size, or type. You can make it more challenging by mixing criteria.
- **Use containers:** Provide small containers or trays for your child to place each sorted item, making it visually clear and organized.

Benefits for kids:

- **Enhances cognitive development** by improving categorization and classification skills.
- **Develops fine motor skills** as they manipulate small objects.
- **Boosts problem-solving skills** as they determine how to group items.

Benefits for parents:

- **Easy setup with everyday objects:** Sorting games require no special materials.
- **Supports early math skills** by introducing concepts like grouping and comparing.
- **Keeps kids engaged:** Sorting can be an independent or guided activity.

---

22. Create a Memory Box

A memory box is a wonderful way for children to store mementos that hold special meaning. It encourages reflection, emotional expression, and organization, helping kids preserve memories in a tangible way.

How it works:

- **Decorate the box:** Start by giving your child a plain box to decorate with stickers, markers, or paint. They can personalize it with their name or favorite colors.
- **Fill it with memories:** Encourage your child to collect items that are meaningful to them—photos, drawings, small toys, or even ticket stubs.
- **Storytime:** Every so often, have your child take out the items and share stories or memories about each one.

Benefits for kids:

- **Encourages emotional expression** by giving children a way to reflect on special memories.
- **Develops organizational skills** as they decide which items to keep in the box.

- **Promotes storytelling** as they share the stories behind each item.

Benefits for parents:

- **Fosters emotional bonding:** Sharing memories provides opportunities for deeper conversations.
- **Simple to create:** A memory box can be made from materials you already have at home.
- **Provides a calming activity:** Looking through memories can be a relaxing and reflective activity.

23. Simon Says

"Simon Says" is a classic game that helps children improve listening skills, impulse control, and physical coordination. This simple, yet entertaining game is perfect for group play or one-on-one interaction.

How it works:

- **Give commands:** One person plays Simon and gives instructions like "Simon says touch your toes" or "Simon says jump up and down." The catch is that players should only follow the commands when "Simon says" is stated first.
- **Incorporate variety:** Mix in commands for movement (e.g., hop, clap), body parts (e.g., touch your nose), and even silly actions to keep the game fun.
- **Take turns:** Let your child take on the role of Simon, which gives them the opportunity to lead the game.

Benefits for kids:

- **Improves listening skills** as they must focus on what Simon says.
- **Enhances impulse control** by encouraging them to wait for the correct prompt.
- **Boosts physical coordination** as they follow the different movement commands.

Benefits for parents:

- **Fun for all ages:** "Simon Says" can be easily adapted for younger or older children.
- **Requires no materials:** This game can be played anywhere, anytime.
- **Encourages family interaction** and can be played with multiple children or adults.

24. Create a Mood Chart

A mood chart is a helpful tool for children to track their feelings throughout the day or week. This simple visual aid helps them recognize and communicate their emotions, providing valuable insights for parents.

How it works:

- **Design the chart:** Create a simple chart with spaces for each day of the week or time of day. Include different moods (happy, sad, angry, calm) and let your child pick which one best represents how they feel.
- **Let them decorate:** Encourage your child to personalize the chart with colors, drawings, or stickers.
- **Daily check-in:** Each day, ask your child to check in with their emotions and update the chart. Over time, patterns may emerge that help identify triggers or emotional patterns.

Benefits for kids:

- **Encourages emotional awareness** as they learn to identify and name their feelings.
- **Promotes emotional regulation** by helping them recognize patterns in their moods.
- **Provides a visual tool** to express emotions when they may not have the words.

Benefits for parents:

- **Gives insight into your child's emotional state**, helping you understand their feelings better.
- **Easy to use** with a simple design that can be updated daily.
- **Can be a conversation starter**, encouraging more open communication about emotions.

---

25. Pillow Toss Game

The pillow toss game is a fun, physical activity that works on coordination, balance, and aim. It's perfect for indoors and provides an opportunity for children to practice motor skills in a playful setting.

How it works:

- **Set up a target:** Use a laundry basket or a cardboard box as the target. Place it a few feet away from your child.
- **Toss the pillows:** Give your child small pillows or stuffed toys to throw into the target. Start with an easy distance and increase it as they improve.
- **Make it a challenge:** Add rules like standing on one foot or tossing with their non-dominant hand to increase difficulty.

Benefits for kids:

- **Improves hand-eye coordination** through tossing and aiming.
- **Enhances balance and motor skills**, especially when challenges like one-legged tossing are added.
- **Boosts confidence** as they succeed in hitting the target and mastering new skills.

Benefits for parents:

- **Low-stakes, high-energy activity:** Great for burning off energy indoors.

- **No special materials needed:** Everyday household items like pillows and baskets work perfectly.
- **Provides positive reinforcement** through fun challenges that build confidence.

---

26. Color Matching Game

The color matching game is a great way to teach younger children about colors while improving their visual discrimination and fine motor skills. It's a simple, educational game that can be played with everyday objects.

How it works:

- **Gather colored items:** Collect small objects in different colors, such as toys, blocks, or crayons.
- **Create color zones:** Place sheets of colored paper or containers in different colors around the room.
- **Match the objects:** Have your child place each object in the corresponding color zone. For older children, you can time them to make it more challenging.

Benefits for kids:

- **Teaches color recognition** in a hands-on, engaging way.
- **Develops fine motor skills** as they pick up and sort the objects.
- **Encourages cognitive development** by helping them understand sorting and classification.

Benefits for parents:

- **No special materials needed:** This game can be played with items you already have at home.
- **Customizable:** You can adapt the difficulty by increasing the number of colors or adding time limits.
- **Keeps kids entertained** while teaching an essential skill.

---

27. Musical Chairs

Musical chairs is a fun, active game that teaches children about taking turns, listening, and following directions. It's perfect for group play but can also be adapted for smaller numbers.

How it works:

- **Set up chairs:** Arrange chairs in a circle or line, using one fewer chair than the number of players.
- **Play music:** Start the music and have the children walk around the chairs.
- **Stop the music:** When the music stops, each child must find a chair to sit on. The child who doesn't get a chair is out.

- **Keep playing:** Remove a chair after each round until one child is left.

Benefits for kids:

- **Improves listening and reaction skills** as they follow the music.
- **Teaches patience and turn-taking**, important social skills for group play.
- **Encourages physical activity**, helping kids burn off energy in a fun way.

Benefits for parents:

- **Great for parties or playdates**, keeping multiple children entertained.
- **Encourages teamwork and fair play**, valuable lessons for social development.
- **Simple and adaptable:** Can be played indoors or outdoors with any number of children.

---

28. Shadow Play

Shadow play is a creative and interactive way for children to explore light and shadows while developing their imagination and storytelling skills. All you need is a light source and a wall to create endless fun.

How it works:

- **Set up a light source:** Use a flashlight or lamp to project light onto a wall. Make sure the room is dim to enhance the shadows.
- **Create shadow figures:** Show your child how to use their hands to make shadow shapes like animals or people.
- **Tell a story:** Encourage your child to use the shadow figures to act out a short story. You can take turns adding to the narrative.

Benefits for kids:

- **Stimulates imagination** by turning shadows into characters and scenes.
- **Develops motor skills** as they manipulate their hands and fingers to create shapes.
- **Promotes creativity** through storytelling and role-playing.

Benefits for parents:

- **Easy to set up and cost-free:** Requires nothing more than a light and a wall.
- **Encourages creativity and bonding:** A fun, interactive activity to enjoy together.
- **Great for quiet time:** Shadow play can be a calming way to wind down before bedtime.

---

29. Bubble Wrap Stomp

The bubble wrap stomp is an exciting sensory activity that helps children release energy and improve coordination. The satisfying sound of popping bubbles adds an element of fun and sensory feedback.

How it works:

- **Lay out bubble wrap:** Place large sheets of bubble wrap on the floor in an open area.
- **Stomp and pop:** Encourage your child to stomp, jump, or walk on the bubble wrap, popping as many bubbles as they can.
- **Add challenges:** Make it a game by timing how fast they can pop all the bubbles or have them hop on one foot.

Benefits for kids:

- **Provides sensory stimulation** through tactile feedback and sound.
- **Encourages gross motor development** by promoting active movement.
- **Helps release energy** in a fun and satisfying way.

Benefits for parents:

- **Easy and cost-effective:** Bubble wrap is inexpensive and can be reused.
- **Keeps kids entertained indoors**, especially on rainy days.
- **Provides a sensory outlet** for children who enjoy tactile activities.

30. Create a Feelings Book

A feelings book is a personalized project where children can explore and document their emotions. This activity helps children better understand their feelings and provides a tool for expressing themselves in a creative way.

How it works:

- **Start with a blank notebook or paper:** Label each page with different emotions like happy, sad, angry, or scared.
- **Decorate and illustrate:** Encourage your child to draw pictures or cut out images from magazines that represent each emotion.
- **Discuss emotions:** As they create the book, talk with them about times when they've felt each emotion, helping them connect with their feelings.

Benefits for kids:

- **Promotes emotional intelligence** by helping children identify and express their feelings.
- **Encourages creativity** through drawing and storytelling.
- **Provides a healthy outlet** for processing emotions.

Benefits for parents:

- **Helps open up conversations** about emotions in a non-threatening way.
- **Provides insight into your child's emotional world**, allowing you to better understand their needs.
- **Simple and flexible project** that can be revisited over time as new emotions arise.

31. Paper Plate Masks

Creating paper plate masks is a fun and creative way for children to explore their emotions or pretend to be different characters. This activity promotes imaginative play and can also help children express feelings they may find difficult to verbalize.

How it works:

- **Provide supplies:** Gather paper plates, markers, glue, scissors, and any additional craft supplies like yarn for hair or glitter for decoration.
- **Create masks:** Encourage your child to draw faces on the paper plates. They can make silly faces, animal faces, or masks that represent different emotions like happy, sad, or angry.
- **Role-play:** Once the masks are made, use them in role-playing scenarios. You can act out different emotions or tell a story using the masks as characters.

Benefits for kids:

- **Encourages creative expression** through art and design.
- **Helps with emotional identification** as they create masks representing different feelings.
- **Develops fine motor skills** through cutting, gluing, and decorating.

Benefits for parents:

- **Simple and affordable:** All you need are basic craft supplies that are easy to find.
- **Fosters open communication:** Use the masks as a way to talk about different emotions and how they feel.
- **Promotes imagination and storytelling**, making it a versatile activity for play and learning.

32. Create a Dream Journal

A dream journal allows children to record and explore their dreams, encouraging self-reflection and emotional expression. This activity helps children process their thoughts and emotions, while also sparking creativity.

How it works:

- **Get a notebook or journal:** Give your child a special notebook where they can write or draw about their dreams.

- **Daily journaling:** Encourage them to jot down their dreams each morning, even if they only remember fragments. Younger children can draw their dreams if they prefer.
- **Discuss the dreams:** Talk with your child about their dreams, asking questions like, "How did you feel in the dream?" or "What do you think your dream was about?"

Benefits for kids:

- **Improves emotional awareness** by allowing them to reflect on their dreams and feelings.
- **Boosts creativity** through writing or drawing about imaginative dream worlds.
- **Enhances memory and reflection** as they recall and process their dreams.

Benefits for parents:

- **Encourages bonding conversations** about thoughts and emotions.
- **Provides insights into your child's inner world**, helping you understand their worries or excitements.
- **Simple and therapeutic activity** that can become part of a nightly or morning routine.

33. Dress-Up and Pretend Play

Dress-up and pretend play is an excellent way to foster creativity and imagination in children. By pretending to be different characters, children practice social skills, problem-solving, and emotional expression.

How it works:

- **Create a dress-up box:** Gather costumes, hats, scarves, and old clothing that your child can use to create different characters. You can even use household items like blankets for capes or towels for turbans.
- **Encourage storytelling:** Once your child is dressed up, ask them to tell a story or act out a scene. They can be a superhero, a teacher, or even an animal!
- **Join the fun:** Parents can join in by taking on a character role, which adds excitement and encourages collaboration in storytelling.

Benefits for kids:

- **Boosts imagination and creativity** as they create characters and scenarios.
- **Develops language and social skills** through role-playing and communication.
- **Helps with emotional expression** by acting out different feelings in a safe space.

Benefits for parents:

- **Encourages bonding** through shared play and storytelling.
- **Simple setup** with everyday clothing and household items.
- **Fosters self-confidence** as children take on different roles and explore new ideas.

34. Balloon Volleyball

Balloon volleyball is a fun indoor game that gets kids moving while improving coordination, balance, and teamwork. It's perfect for when children need to burn off energy without needing a lot of space or equipment.

How it works:

- **Set up a net:** Use a piece of string or a tape line on the floor as the net. Set it at a height appropriate for your child's age and size.
- **Play the game:** Use a balloon as the ball, and have your child hit it back and forth over the net. You can play with just one child or with a group of kids.
- **Make it challenging:** Add rules like using only one hand or setting a time limit for how long the balloon stays in the air.

Benefits for kids:

- **Develops gross motor skills** through hitting and balancing the balloon.
- **Improves hand-eye coordination** as they aim to keep the balloon in the air.
- **Encourages physical activity**, which is great for burning energy.

Benefits for parents:

- **Easy to set up and play indoors** without the need for special equipment.
- **Promotes teamwork and cooperation** when played with others.
- **Low-impact activity** that's safe for young children.

35. Nature Art

Nature art combines creativity with the outdoors, allowing children to use natural elements to create artwork. It's a wonderful way to connect kids with nature while fostering creativity and mindfulness.

How it works:

- **Gather natural materials:** Head outside and collect items like leaves, flowers, rocks, sticks, or pinecones.
- **Create art:** Use these materials to create pictures, sculptures, or even collages. You can glue the items to paper or arrange them on the ground for temporary art.
- **Discuss the process:** Ask your child to describe their artwork and what each piece represents. Encourage them to experiment with different patterns and textures.

Benefits for kids:

- **Encourages creativity** by using unconventional materials to create art.

- **Promotes mindfulness** as they engage with nature and focus on the process of creating.
- **Develops fine motor skills** as they arrange and manipulate the materials.

Benefits for parents:

- **Involves outdoor exploration**, which helps kids connect with nature.
- **Low-cost and eco-friendly:** No need for expensive art supplies.
- **Fosters creativity and reflection**, making it a great bonding activity.

36. Animal Walks

Animal walks are a fun, physical activity where children imitate the movements of different animals. This activity helps improve coordination, balance, and muscle strength while also encouraging imagination.

How it works:

- **Introduce animal movements:** Demonstrate how different animals move, like crawling like a bear, hopping like a frog, or waddling like a penguin.
- **Make it a game:** Call out different animals and have your child switch between movements. You can also create an obstacle course where they have to move like certain animals to get through.
- **Add sound effects:** Encourage your child to make the sounds of the animals as they move, adding to the fun and imagination.

Benefits for kids:

- **Improves gross motor skills** and coordination through active movement.
- **Encourages imaginative play** as they pretend to be different animals.
- **Helps with physical fitness** by engaging different muscle groups.

Benefits for parents:

- **Burns energy and keeps kids active**, especially on days when outdoor play isn't possible.
- **Easy to set up** with no equipment needed.
- **Encourages creative storytelling** through pretend play and sound effects.

37. Homemade Instruments

Making homemade instruments is a creative and musical activity that engages children's imagination and helps them explore different sounds. By creating their own instruments, children learn about music, rhythm, and the science of sound.

How it works:

- **Gather materials:** Use items like empty jars, rubber bands, spoons, and paper towel rolls to create instruments. For example, you can make a drum from a container or a guitar by stretching rubber bands over a box.
- **Decorate the instruments:** Let your child paint or decorate their instruments to make them personal and unique.
- **Play music:** Once the instruments are made, have a jam session! Encourage your child to experiment with different rhythms and sounds.

Benefits for kids:

- **Promotes creativity** through the process of building and decorating their own instruments.
- **Teaches basic music concepts** like rhythm, tempo, and sound.
- **Enhances fine motor skills** as they manipulate materials to create their instruments.

Benefits for parents:

- **Uses everyday household items,** making it a low-cost, eco-friendly activity.
- **Encourages musical exploration** in a fun and hands-on way.
- **Great for family bonding** as you play music together.

---

38. Ice Cube Painting

Ice cube painting is a sensory-rich activity that combines art and science. This activity involves using frozen, colorful ice cubes to create artwork, giving children a unique experience with textures, colors, and melting effects.

How it works:

- **Prepare the ice cubes:** Fill an ice tray with water, add a few drops of food coloring to each section, and freeze. For added fun, insert popsicle sticks into the cubes before freezing.
- **Create art:** Once the cubes are frozen, use the colorful ice cubes as "paintbrushes" on paper. As the ice melts, it leaves behind streaks of color, creating beautiful patterns.
- **Experiment with mixing colors:** Encourage your child to notice how colors blend as the ice melts and spreads on the paper.

Benefits for kids:

- **Engages the senses** through the combination of cold textures and colorful visuals.
- **Encourages creativity** with a unique painting medium.
- **Introduces basic science concepts,** like how ice melts and colors mix.

Benefits for parents:

- **Easy and inexpensive** with simple materials needed.
- **Promotes sensory exploration,** especially for children who enjoy tactile activities.
- **Fun outdoor activity,** especially on warm days when melting ice is faster.

39. Freeze Dance

Freeze dance is an exciting and energetic game that helps children develop listening skills, coordination, and self-control. It's perfect for rainy days or times when your child needs to get their wiggles out.

How it works:

- **Play music:** Start by playing upbeat music and have your child dance around.
- **Stop the music:** When the music stops, everyone must freeze in place. The goal is to stop dancing and hold their position until the music starts again.
- **Add challenges:** You can add variations like freezing in silly poses or freezing in specific positions, like balancing on one foot.

Benefits for kids:

- **Improves listening skills** by requiring them to stop when the music stops.
- **Encourages self-control** and focus as they practice holding still.
- **Boosts coordination and gross motor skills** through dancing and movement.

Benefits for parents:

- **Easy to play indoors** with just music and a space to dance.
- **Fun for group play**, making it great for siblings or playdates.
- **Burns off energy**, helping kids stay active and engaged.

40. Pasta Necklaces

Making pasta necklaces is a simple yet creative activity that helps develop fine motor skills while allowing children to express their artistic side. This hands-on craft is perfect for younger children and can be customized with different colors and designs.

How it works:

- **Prepare the pasta:** Use uncooked pasta with large holes like rigatoni or penne. For added fun, you can dye the pasta using food coloring and vinegar.
- **String the pasta:** Provide your child with yarn or string and have them thread the pasta pieces to create a necklace.
- **Decorate:** If desired, let your child paint or decorate the pasta before stringing it.

Benefits for kids:

- **Improves fine motor skills** as they thread the pasta onto the string.
- **Encourages creativity** through designing and decorating the necklace.
- **Teaches patience and focus**, as making a necklace takes time and attention.

Benefits for parents:

- **Affordable and easy setup** with materials you likely already have at home.
- **Encourages independent play** while still providing a structured craft activity.
- **Great for bonding** as you can create and design together.

41. Emotion Cards

Emotion cards are a simple yet effective tool to help children understand and express their feelings. By identifying and discussing emotions, children can build emotional awareness and communication skills.

How it works:

- **Create or buy emotion cards:** You can either purchase pre-made emotion cards or create your own by drawing different faces that represent various emotions (e.g., happy, sad, angry, excited).
- **Play identification games:** Lay the cards out and ask your child to pick a card that shows how they are feeling. You can also create scenarios and ask them which card matches how they think someone in the situation would feel.
- **Discuss the emotions:** Talk about each emotion and what might cause someone to feel that way. Encourage your child to think about their own experiences with each emotion.

Benefits for kids:

- **Builds emotional intelligence** by helping children recognize and label their emotions.
- **Encourages open communication** about feelings, which can help them manage emotions more effectively.
- **Improves empathy** as they think about how others might feel in different situations.

Benefits for parents:

- **Simple and engaging tool** for discussing emotions.
- **Great for emotional development** and can be used at various ages.
- **Easy to make at home** with basic materials like paper and markers.

42. DIY Slime Making

Slime is a fantastic sensory activity that's fun for kids of all ages. It allows children to explore different textures while also developing fine motor skills and creativity. Making slime together is a hands-on project that encourages curiosity and experimentation.

How it works:

- **Gather ingredients:** You'll need glue, baking soda, and contact lens solution. You can also add glitter, food coloring, or small objects for extra fun.
- **Mix it up:** Have your child help measure and mix the ingredients to create the slime. This is a great opportunity to teach them about how different substances combine to form a new texture.
- **Play with the slime:** Once it's ready, your child can stretch, squish, and mold the slime, exploring its texture and properties.

Benefits for kids:

- **Promotes sensory exploration** through hands-on play with unique textures.
- **Encourages creativity** as children experiment with different colors and add-ins.
- **Develops fine motor skills** through squeezing, pulling, and shaping the slime.

Benefits for parents:

- **Fun, interactive learning experience** that teaches children about science.
- **Affordable and easy to make** with basic household ingredients.
- **Keeps kids entertained** for long periods while promoting sensory development.

43. Simon Says with Emotions

This variation of the classic "Simon Says" game is designed to help children identify and express emotions. By incorporating emotional cues into the game, children practice recognizing and acting out different feelings, making it a fun way to boost emotional awareness.

How it works:

- **Give emotion-based commands:** Instead of physical actions, instruct your child to act out different emotions when you say, "Simon says." For example, "Simon says look surprised" or "Simon says act happy."
- **Alternate emotions and physical movements:** Mix in commands like jumping or clapping to keep the game exciting while still focusing on emotional expressions.
- **Let your child be Simon:** Give your child a turn at being Simon so they can think of creative ways to express emotions.

Benefits for kids:

- **Increases emotional awareness** by encouraging children to act out different feelings.
- **Improves listening skills** as they focus on following the correct commands.
- **Encourages empathy** by considering how different emotions are expressed.

Benefits for parents:

- **Teaches emotions in a playful setting**, making it more engaging for kids.
- **Promotes physical activity** along with emotional learning.
- **Great for group play**, whether at home or in a classroom.

44. Nature Rubbings

Nature rubbings are a simple and educational outdoor activity that helps children explore textures and patterns in the natural world. This hands-on craft allows children to connect with nature while developing their observational and fine motor skills.

How it works:

- **Gather materials:** Bring along paper and crayons on your nature walk. Look for interesting textures like tree bark, leaves, or rocks.
- **Create rubbings:** Place the paper over the textured surface and rub the side of a crayon across the paper. The texture of the object underneath will appear on the paper as a pattern.
- **Explore different textures:** Encourage your child to find a variety of natural items to make rubbings of, discussing the differences between each texture.

Benefits for kids:

- **Improves fine motor skills** as they hold the crayon and create the rubbings.
- **Encourages exploration of nature**, fostering a connection with the environment.
- **Develops observational skills** as they notice different textures and patterns in nature.

Benefits for parents:

- **Easy to set up** with basic materials.
- **Combines outdoor exploration with art**, making it a well-rounded activity.
- **Educational opportunity** to discuss nature and science while having fun.

45. Yoga for Kids

Introducing yoga to kids is a great way to help them learn about mindfulness, relaxation, and body awareness. It's a calming activity that helps children manage stress, improve flexibility, and build focus.

How it works:

- **Teach simple poses:** Start with basic yoga poses like "tree pose," "child's pose," and "cat-cow." You can demonstrate the poses and explain what they are supposed to mimic.
- **Focus on breathing:** Teach your child deep breathing techniques, which can help them relax and focus.
- **Create a routine:** Establish a short yoga routine that your child can do daily, either in the morning or before bedtime to wind down.

Benefits for kids:

- **Improves flexibility and balance** through gentle movements and poses.
- **Teaches mindfulness and relaxation techniques**, helping them manage emotions and stress.
- **Encourages focus and concentration**, which can carry over into other activities.

Benefits for parents:

- **Great for indoor play**, especially when children need to calm down or relax.
- **Promotes physical health and mental well-being** in a fun, approachable way.
- **Encourages healthy habits** that children can carry into adulthood.

46. Finger Puppet Theater

Finger puppets are a great way for children to explore storytelling, social interaction, and creativity. This activity lets children create characters and act out stories, helping them develop language and communication skills.

How it works:

- **Make or buy finger puppets:** You can make simple finger puppets at home using felt, paper, or old socks. Alternatively, you can purchase finger puppets.
- **Set up a stage:** Use a cardboard box or even a table as the puppet theater. Let your child decorate the stage to make it more personal.
- **Encourage storytelling:** Ask your child to create a story using the puppets. You can help them come up with a plot, or they can make it up as they go.

Benefits for kids:

- **Promotes creativity** by allowing them to invent characters and stories.
- **Improves language and communication skills** through storytelling.
- **Develops social and emotional skills** by exploring different characters and emotions.

Benefits for parents:

- **Encourages bonding through play**, especially when parents participate in the story.
- **Inexpensive and easy to set up**, with homemade puppets and simple materials.
- **Promotes independent play**, allowing kids to entertain themselves with their puppets.

47. Create a Personal Journal

A personal journal is a valuable tool for helping children express their thoughts, ideas, and emotions. It encourages self-reflection, emotional awareness, and writing skills. Children can use the journal to write about their day, draw pictures, or list things they're grateful for.

How it works:

- **Provide a notebook:** Give your child a notebook or journal that they can decorate to make it personal.
- **Daily or weekly entries:** Encourage your child to write or draw in their journal regularly. They can write about their feelings, what they did that day, or things they are looking forward to.
- **Optional prompts:** For children who may need some guidance, provide prompts like "What made you happy today?" or "Draw something that made you smile."

Benefits for kids:

- **Promotes self-expression** by giving them a private space to explore their thoughts and feelings.
- **Improves writing and drawing skills** through regular practice.
- **Encourages emotional awareness** and mindfulness by reflecting on their experiences.

Benefits for parents:

- **Helps open up conversations** about feelings when children share their entries.
- **Provides a calming activity** that can help children process emotions.
- **Encourages regular writing practice**, which helps with literacy development.

48. Create a Time Capsule

A time capsule is a fun and meaningful activity that encourages children to reflect on the present and think about the future. It's a great way for children to collect items that are important to them and "save" them for future discovery.

How it works:

- **Find a container:** Use a small box or tin to hold the items for the time capsule.
- **Collect items:** Encourage your child to gather meaningful objects like drawings, photos, toys, or notes that represent their current interests and experiences.
- **Bury or store the time capsule:** Decide together when and where to store the time capsule. You can bury it in the backyard or hide it in a closet to open in a few years.

Benefits for kids:

- **Encourages reflection and self-awareness** as they think about what is meaningful to them now.
- **Promotes creative thinking** about the future and what they hope to remember.
- **Provides a sense of anticipation** and excitement for the future when the capsule is opened.

Benefits for parents:

- **Creates a lasting memory** that both you and your child can enjoy years later.

- **Encourages organization and thoughtfulness**, helping your child decide what's important.
- **Fun and sentimental activity** that fosters bonding and shared reflection.

49. Create an Indoor Scavenger Hunt

An indoor scavenger hunt is a perfect way to keep children entertained and engaged on a rainy day. It encourages problem-solving, critical thinking, and physical activity as they search for hidden items around the house.

How it works:

- **Create a list:** Write down a list of items for your child to find around the house. These can be everyday objects like a red sock, a spoon, or a favorite toy.
- **Hide the items:** You can either hide the items around the house or simply ask your child to find things that are already out.
- **Add clues:** For an added challenge, give them clues or riddles to help them find each item.

Benefits for kids:

- **Improves problem-solving skills** as they search for hidden items and solve clues.
- **Encourages physical activity** by having them move around the house.
- **Promotes attention to detail** as they look closely for each item.

Benefits for parents:

- **Easy to set up** with items already in the home.
- **Keeps kids entertained indoors**, especially on rainy or cold days.
- **Provides a learning opportunity**, especially if you incorporate educational elements like colors, numbers, or letters.

50. Create Story Stones

Story stones are a fun and creative way for children to explore storytelling. By painting different pictures or symbols on stones, children can use them to create their own stories, fostering imagination and language skills.

How it works:

- **Gather stones:** Find smooth, flat stones that can easily be painted or drawn on.
- **Paint or draw on the stones:** Use paint, markers, or crayons to add images to the stones. These can be simple drawings like animals, houses, stars, or people.
- **Tell a story:** Once the stones are ready, have your child pick a few and use them as prompts to create a story. They can arrange the stones in different ways to come up with new tales.

Benefits for kids:

- **Encourages storytelling and creativity** by using the stones as prompts for imaginative stories.
- **Improves fine motor skills** through painting or drawing on the stones.
- **Develops language skills** as they narrate their stories aloud.

Benefits for parents:

- **Simple and inexpensive craft** that can be done with natural materials.
- **Encourages independent play** as children create their own stories.
- **Promotes language development** in a fun, hands-on way.

51. Obstacle Course

An obstacle course is a fantastic way to get kids moving while encouraging problem-solving, coordination, and balance. You can set one up indoors or outdoors using household items, making it adaptable and fun for all ages.

How it works:

- **Gather materials:** Use chairs, pillows, boxes, or hula hoops to create different obstacles. For example, your child can crawl under a table, jump over pillows, or balance on a line of tape on the floor.
- **Create a course:** Arrange the obstacles in a sequence, giving your child directions like "crawl under this," "hop on one foot," or "balance on this."
- **Time the course:** Make it more challenging by timing your child as they complete the course and encourage them to beat their best time.

Benefits for kids:

- **Improves gross motor skills** through jumping, crawling, and balancing.
- **Encourages problem-solving and creativity** as they figure out how to navigate each obstacle.
- **Builds confidence** as they complete the course and improve their time.

Benefits for parents:

- **Great for physical activity** and burning off energy indoors or outdoors.
- **Easy to set up with household items**—no special equipment needed.
- **Promotes independent play**, while still allowing for fun, collaborative challenges.

52. Memory Matching Game

Memory matching games are perfect for improving concentration, focus, and memory. This classic game can be played with cards, pictures, or homemade items, making it easy to adapt for any age.

How it works:

- **Create pairs of cards:** You can use playing cards or create your own by drawing pictures or printing out images. Make sure you have pairs of matching cards.
- **Lay the cards face down:** Spread the cards out in rows, face down, on a table or the floor.
- **Take turns:** Players take turns flipping over two cards at a time, trying to find a matching pair. If the cards match, they get to keep the pair. The game continues until all pairs are found.

Benefits for kids:

- **Enhances memory and concentration** by encouraging children to remember card placements.
- **Improves attention to detail** as they look for matching cards.
- **Teaches patience and turn-taking**, especially in group play.

Benefits for parents:

- **Easy to create with materials on hand**, such as paper or cards.
- **Can be played anywhere** and is adaptable for various skill levels.
- **Fun for family game time**, promoting bonding through a simple, interactive game.

---

53. Alphabet Scavenger Hunt

An alphabet scavenger hunt is a fun way to help kids learn their letters while engaging in an active, exploratory game. This activity helps children with letter recognition and vocabulary building.

How it works:

- **Choose a letter:** Start by selecting a letter of the alphabet. Ask your child to search for items around the house or outside that begin with that letter.
- **Make it a challenge:** You can give your child a list of letters or let them choose a new letter after finding an item for the previous one.
- **Time it for extra fun:** If you want to add a competitive element, time how long it takes them to find objects for a set number of letters.

Benefits for kids:

- **Boosts letter recognition** by associating letters with objects.
- **Encourages physical activity** as they move around searching for items.
- **Enhances vocabulary** as they discover new words during the scavenger hunt.

Benefits for parents:

- **Teaches letters in a hands-on, active way** that's more engaging than traditional methods.
- **Easy to set up** with no special materials needed.
- **Can be customized** for different age groups and learning levels.

54. Create a Collage

Collage-making is a creative activity that allows children to express themselves through art by combining different materials to create a larger picture. This project encourages fine motor development and self-expression.

How it works:

- **Gather materials:** Provide a variety of materials such as magazines, colored paper, scissors, glue, and markers.
- **Encourage creativity:** Let your child cut out pictures, shapes, or patterns from the magazines and arrange them on a piece of paper to create a unique collage.
- **Add a theme:** You can give your child a theme, such as "What makes you happy?" or "My favorite things," to inspire their creativity.

Benefits for kids:

- **Enhances creativity** by allowing children to combine different images and materials.
- **Develops fine motor skills** through cutting, gluing, and arranging pieces.
- **Promotes self-expression** as they create artwork that reflects their thoughts and emotions.

Benefits for parents:

- **Simple and low-cost activity** with items you likely already have at home.
- **Encourages independent play**, while also providing opportunities for collaboration.
- **Great for fostering communication**, as children often talk about the meanings behind their collages.

55. Dance Party

A dance party is a fun way to get kids moving while also improving coordination, rhythm, and body awareness. Dancing to their favorite music helps children express themselves physically and emotionally.

How it works:

- **Play your child's favorite music:** Choose upbeat, fun songs that will get your child excited to move and dance.

- **Encourage free movement:** Let your child dance however they want, encouraging them to use their whole body. You can also introduce simple dance moves for them to follow.
- **Add games or challenges:** Play freeze dance, where they have to stop moving when the music pauses, or challenge them to create their own dance routines.

Benefits for kids:

- **Improves coordination and balance** through rhythmic movement.
- **Encourages self-expression** by allowing them to move freely and interpret the music in their own way.
- **Provides physical exercise**, helping them burn off energy in a fun, engaging way.

Benefits for parents:

- **Simple, no-prep activity** that can be done anywhere.
- **Promotes bonding** as you dance and laugh together.
- **Great indoor activity**, especially for rainy days or when outdoor play isn't possible.

56. Sculpt with Clay

Clay sculpting is a hands-on activity that helps develop fine motor skills, creativity, and focus. It allows children to experiment with different shapes and textures, giving them a tactile way to express their imagination.

How it works:

- **Provide clay or playdough:** You can use store-bought clay or make your own homemade playdough.
- **Encourage free sculpting:** Let your child mold and shape the clay into whatever they want, whether it's animals, people, or abstract shapes.
- **Introduce tools:** Provide safe sculpting tools like plastic knives, cookie cutters, or rolling pins to help them create different textures and designs.

Benefits for kids:

- **Develops fine motor skills** as they roll, pinch, and shape the clay.
- **Encourages creative thinking** by giving them the freedom to create their own sculptures.
- **Promotes focus and concentration** through the calming, hands-on activity of molding clay.

Benefits for parents:

- **Low-cost, versatile activity** that provides hours of entertainment.
- **Helps with sensory development**, especially for children who enjoy tactile experiences.

- **Encourages independent play** while still offering opportunities for collaboration and conversation.

---

57. Mindfulness Breathing Exercises

Mindfulness breathing exercises are a great way to help children calm their minds and bodies. This practice teaches them how to focus on their breath, helping them manage stress and develop emotional regulation skills.

How it works:

- **Teach deep breathing:** Show your child how to take slow, deep breaths in through their nose and out through their mouth. Encourage them to count to 3 while inhaling and exhaling.
- **Use visuals:** You can use a visual aid, like a "breathing star" where they trace the points of the star with their finger as they breathe, or ask them to imagine blowing up a balloon as they exhale.
- **Practice regularly:** Incorporate breathing exercises into your child's daily routine, especially before bed or during moments of stress.

Benefits for kids:

- **Improves emotional regulation** by helping them calm down during stressful moments.
- **Teaches mindfulness,** which helps them stay present and focused.
- **Reduces anxiety** and encourages relaxation through controlled breathing.

Benefits for parents:

- **Easy to teach and practice** without the need for any special equipment.
- **Helps manage tantrums and emotional outbursts** by giving children a calming tool.
- **Great for bedtime,** helping children wind down and prepare for sleep.

---

58. Chalk Drawing

Chalk drawing is a versatile and creative outdoor activity that encourages children to express themselves artistically. Whether drawing on the sidewalk or a chalkboard, this activity helps develop fine motor skills and imagination.

How it works:

- **Provide chalk:** Give your child a variety of colorful chalk sticks and find a large outdoor surface like a sidewalk or driveway.

- **Encourage free drawing:** Let your child draw whatever they like, whether it's doodles, shapes, or full pictures. You can also suggest themes, like "draw your favorite animal" or "design your dream playground."
- **Play chalk games:** Use chalk to create hopscotch grids, mazes, or obstacle courses for an added layer of fun.

Benefits for kids:

- **Enhances creativity** by giving them a blank canvas to express themselves.
- **Develops fine motor skills** through the act of drawing and writing.
- **Encourages outdoor play**, combining artistic expression with fresh air and movement.

Benefits for parents:

- **Easy and inexpensive activity**, with chalk as the only needed material.
- **Encourages independent play** but can also be done collaboratively.
- **Promotes outdoor time**, allowing kids to enjoy nature while being creative.

---

59. Letter Tracing in Sand

Letter tracing in sand is a sensory-rich activity that helps children practice writing letters while also engaging their sense of touch. This activity is perfect for early learners who are working on letter recognition and fine motor skills.

How it works:

- **Set up a sand tray:** Fill a shallow tray or baking pan with sand. You can use colored sand or even salt or rice if you don't have sand on hand.
- **Practice tracing letters:** Show your child how to use their finger to trace letters in the sand. Start with simple letters like "A" and "B," then move on to more complex shapes.
- **Smooth it out and repeat:** Once they finish tracing, they can smooth the sand over and start again with a new letter.

Benefits for kids:

- **Improves letter recognition** through tactile learning.
- **Develops fine motor skills** as they practice writing in the sand.
- **Engages multiple senses**, making it a fun and effective way to learn.

Benefits for parents:

- **Simple setup** with just a tray and sand or similar material.
- **Reinforces learning** in a fun, hands-on way.
- **Perfect for early literacy development**, helping children master the alphabet in a new medium.

60. Shape Sorting

Shape sorting is a hands-on learning activity that helps children understand basic geometry while also improving their fine motor skills. This activity is ideal for younger children who are just starting to learn about shapes.

How it works:

- **Gather shapes:** Use shape-sorting toys or create your own by cutting out different shapes from colored paper or cardboard.
- **Sort the shapes:** Ask your child to sort the shapes into groups based on their type (e.g., circles, squares, triangles). You can also have them sort by color or size for an added challenge.
- **Talk about the shapes:** As your child sorts the shapes, discuss their names and characteristics, like how many sides a square has or how a circle is round.

Benefits for kids:

- **Teaches shape recognition** through hands-on play.
- **Improves fine motor skills** by encouraging them to manipulate and sort the shapes.
- **Builds problem-solving skills** as they figure out how to categorize the shapes correctly.

Benefits for parents:

- **Easy to set up** with basic materials like paper or store-bought toys.
- **Supports early math learning** by introducing shapes and geometry concepts.
- **Engaging and educational**, helping children learn while having fun.

61. Create a Family Tree

Building a family tree is an educational and meaningful activity that helps children learn about their family history and understand relationships within their family. This activity encourages conversations about family roles and connections.

How it works:

- **Draw the tree:** Start by drawing a simple tree shape with branches that represent different family members.
- **Add family members:** Help your child fill in the names of immediate family members (parents, siblings) and then extend to grandparents, aunts, uncles, and cousins.
- **Decorate the tree:** Encourage your child to decorate the tree with drawings, photos, or symbols that represent each family member.

Benefits for kids:

- **Teaches family relationships** and helps children understand where they come from.
- **Enhances memory and storytelling skills** as they learn and recall family history.
- **Promotes a sense of belonging** by helping them visualize their place within the family.

Benefits for parents:

- **Encourages family bonding** through conversations about family members and stories.
- **Provides a great way to introduce family history**, teaching children about their heritage.
- **Simple and meaningful project** that can be revisited and expanded over time.

62. Create a Sensory Path

A sensory path is an engaging activity that allows children to explore different textures and movements. It helps with coordination, balance, and sensory processing by encouraging children to use their bodies to interact with various materials.

How it works:

- **Design the path:** Use items like foam mats, bubble wrap, pillows, or fabric with different textures. Lay them out in a sequence to create a path for your child to walk, crawl, or jump on.
- **Add instructions:** Incorporate movements like hopping, balancing on one foot, or tiptoeing as they move along the path.
- **Encourage exploration:** Let your child walk along the sensory path barefoot or in socks to fully experience the different textures.

Benefits for kids:

- **Improves balance and coordination** by challenging them to move in different ways.
- **Encourages sensory exploration** through different textures and movements.
- **Helps with motor skill development** and body awareness.

Benefits for parents:

- **Easy to create at home** with everyday items.
- **Great for indoor play**, especially on rainy days or when outdoor space is limited.
- **Promotes sensory regulation**, especially for children with sensory processing issues.

63. Story Dice

Story dice are a fun way to encourage creativity, storytelling, and language development. By rolling dice with pictures on them, children can use the images as prompts to create unique stories.

How it works:

- **Create or buy story dice:** You can purchase story dice or make your own by drawing simple pictures on small cubes (like dice). Each side of the cube should feature a different image.
- **Roll the dice:** Let your child roll the dice and use the images that appear to create a story. For example, if they roll a cat, a house, and a tree, they might tell a story about a cat who lives in a treehouse.
- **Take turns:** You can make it a group activity by taking turns adding to the story based on the dice rolls.

Benefits for kids:

- **Boosts imagination and creativity** by encouraging children to invent stories based on random prompts.
- **Improves language and communication skills** through storytelling.
- **Teaches sequencing and narrative structure**, helping them organize their thoughts.

Benefits for parents:

- **Encourages family bonding** as you create stories together.
- **Simple to play anywhere**, with no need for special setup.
- **Promotes independent play**, allowing children to make up stories on their own.

64. Create an Obstacle Course for Hands and Fingers

This activity focuses on improving fine motor skills by challenging children to navigate small objects or complete tasks using only their hands and fingers. It's perfect for strengthening dexterity and hand-eye coordination.

How it works:

- **Set up the course:** Use small objects like buttons, beads, or marbles. Create tasks that involve picking up, stacking, or moving these objects using fingers or tweezers.
- **Add challenges:** Include obstacles like threading a string through beads, balancing marbles on a spoon, or stacking small blocks into a tower.
- **Time it:** Make it more fun by timing your child as they complete the course, encouraging them to beat their own time.

Benefits for kids:

- **Improves fine motor skills** and dexterity through precision tasks.
- **Encourages problem-solving** as they figure out how to complete each obstacle.
- **Boosts focus and concentration** as they work through the course.

Benefits for parents:

- **Uses simple materials** like household items for an easy setup.

- **Promotes independent play** and learning through hands-on challenges.
- **Helps develop skills needed for writing and other fine motor tasks**.

65. Create a 'Feelings Thermometer'

A feelings thermometer is a visual tool that helps children gauge the intensity of their emotions. By identifying where they are on the thermometer, children learn to recognize and regulate their feelings more effectively.

How it works:

- **Draw the thermometer:** On a piece of paper or poster board, draw a large thermometer with different levels ranging from "calm" at the bottom to "very upset" at the top.
- **Label the emotions:** Assign each level a feeling, such as "calm," "frustrated," "angry," or "furious." Let your child help choose the words or phrases that describe different intensities of emotions.
- **Use it daily:** Encourage your child to check in with their emotions throughout the day by pointing to where they are on the thermometer. Discuss what steps they can take to move down the thermometer if they're feeling upset.

Benefits for kids:

- **Increases emotional awareness** by helping them identify and label their feelings.
- **Promotes self-regulation** by encouraging them to recognize when they need to calm down.
- **Teaches problem-solving** by helping them think of ways to manage intense emotions.

Benefits for parents:

- **Easy to make at home** with just paper and markers.
- **Provides a visual tool** for discussing emotions in a non-threatening way.
- **Helps manage meltdowns** by giving children a way to communicate their feelings.

66. Ball Toss Game

The ball toss game is a simple and fun way to develop hand-eye coordination, balance, and motor skills. Whether played indoors or outdoors, it's a great activity for keeping kids active and engaged.

How it works:

- **Set up a target:** Use a laundry basket, cardboard box, or bucket as the target.

- **Throw the ball:** Give your child a soft ball or bean bag and have them toss it into the target. You can make it more challenging by moving the target further away or adding obstacles.
- **Add variations:** Challenge your child to throw the ball with their non-dominant hand or while standing on one foot for an extra balance challenge.

Benefits for kids:

- **Improves hand-eye coordination** and motor skills through tossing and aiming.
- **Encourages physical activity,** helping children stay active while indoors or outdoors.
- **Boosts confidence** as they successfully hit the target and improve their aim.

Benefits for parents:

- **Simple to set up** with common household items like baskets and soft balls.
- **Perfect for burning off energy** in a fun, structured way.
- **Easy to adapt** for different skill levels by adjusting the target distance or difficulty.

67. Freeze Dance with Emotions

This version of the classic freeze dance game adds an emotional twist, helping children practice identifying and expressing different feelings. It's a fun way to combine movement with emotional awareness.

How it works:

- **Play music:** Start by playing upbeat music and have your child dance around the room.
- **Pause the music:** When the music stops, call out an emotion (e.g., happy, sad, surprised) and have your child freeze in a pose that expresses that feeling.
- **Continue dancing:** Restart the music and repeat the process, encouraging your child to show different emotions each time.

Benefits for kids:

- **Encourages emotional expression** by acting out different feelings.
- **Improves listening and self-control** as they freeze when the music stops.
- **Promotes physical movement,** making it a great way to burn energy.

Benefits for parents:

- **Engages kids in both emotional and physical play,** teaching them about emotions in a fun way.
- **Simple to set up,** requiring only music and space to dance.
- **Perfect for group play** or individual activity, making it versatile for different settings.

68. I Spy Game

"I Spy" is a classic game that encourages observation and language development. It's easy to play anywhere, whether indoors or outdoors, and can be adapted for different age groups.

How it works:

- **Choose an object:** The person who is "It" silently picks an object within view and says, "I spy with my little eye, something that is [color/shape/size]."
- **Guess the object:** The other players take turns guessing what the object is based on the clues given. The first person to guess correctly becomes the next "It."
- **Make it more challenging:** For older children, you can use more complex descriptions, such as "I spy something that starts with the letter C" or "I spy something that can move."

Benefits for kids:

- **Improves observation skills** as they look closely at their surroundings to find the object.
- **Boosts language development** through descriptive clues and conversation.
- **Encourages critical thinking** and problem-solving as they use the clues to make educated guesses.

Benefits for parents:

- **No materials needed**, making it perfect for spontaneous play.
- **Great for travel or waiting times**, as it requires no setup and keeps kids entertained.
- **Engages the whole family**, promoting bonding through a simple, interactive game.

---

69. Color by Numbers

Color by numbers is a relaxing and educational activity that helps children practice number recognition, color identification, and fine motor skills. It's a great way to combine art and learning in one fun project.

How it works:

- **Provide color-by-number sheets:** You can print out free color-by-number pages online or purchase a coloring book with pre-designed pages.
- **Follow the code:** Each area on the picture has a number, and your child uses the corresponding color to fill in that space.
- **Watch the picture come to life:** As your child colors, the image gradually comes together, providing a sense of accomplishment.

Benefits for kids:

- **Improves number recognition** and understanding of color relationships.
- **Develops fine motor skills** through careful coloring within the lines.

- **Boosts patience and focus** as they work through the picture step by step.

Benefits for parents:

- **Engaging and educational** activity that reinforces early math skills.
- **Promotes quiet, focused play**, perfect for when you need a calm activity.
- **Easy to find**—there are countless free or affordable color-by-number resources available.

70. Sponge Painting

Sponge painting is a fun, messy art activity that encourages children to experiment with textures and colors. It's a great way to foster creativity while helping children develop fine motor skills.

How it works:

- **Provide sponges and paint:** Cut sponges into different shapes or sizes, and give your child non-toxic paint to dip the sponges into.
- **Let them create:** Encourage your child to stamp the sponges onto paper, creating patterns, shapes, or abstract art.
- **Mix colors and textures:** As they paint, talk about how different sponges create different textures and how colors mix together.

Benefits for kids:

- **Enhances creativity** by allowing children to explore different textures and colors.
- **Develops fine motor skills** as they hold, dip, and stamp the sponges.
- **Promotes sensory exploration**, especially through the tactile nature of the activity.

Benefits for parents:

- **Easy to set up** with minimal materials required.
- **Encourages independent artistic expression**, while still being simple enough for young children.
- **Perfect for outdoor play**, where the mess can be easily managed.

71. Paper Airplane Contest

A paper airplane contest is a fun, interactive way to boost children's creativity, problem-solving skills, and hand-eye coordination. This activity can be done indoors or outdoors, offering endless entertainment with a simple piece of paper.

How it works:

- **Create the planes:** Show your child how to fold a basic paper airplane or let them experiment with different designs. You can use online templates for more complex planes.
- **Test them out:** Once the planes are ready, have a contest to see whose plane can fly the farthest, stay in the air the longest, or perform the most loops.
- **Add challenges:** You can create targets or landing zones for the planes to hit for extra difficulty and fun.

Benefits for kids:

- **Develops fine motor skills** as they fold and shape the paper.
- **Encourages creativity** through experimenting with different plane designs.
- **Promotes problem-solving** as they test and adjust their designs for better performance.

Benefits for parents:

- **Inexpensive and easy setup** with just paper required.
- **Fosters friendly competition** and family bonding.
- **Encourages outdoor play**, allowing kids to run around while testing their planes.

72. Create a Gratitude Jar

A gratitude jar is a simple and meaningful activity that helps children focus on the positive things in their life. It encourages mindfulness and emotional well-being by teaching kids to recognize and appreciate the good moments each day.

How it works:

- **Find a jar:** Choose a jar or container that your child can decorate with stickers, paint, or ribbons to make it special.
- **Write down moments of gratitude:** Each day, ask your child to write down something they are grateful for on a small piece of paper. They can also draw pictures if they prefer.
- **Fill the jar:** Drop the notes into the jar. At the end of the week or month, take time to read through the notes together and reflect on the positive things that have happened.

Benefits for kids:

- **Promotes emotional well-being** by focusing on gratitude and positive thoughts.
- **Encourages mindfulness**, helping them appreciate the small, everyday moments.
- **Improves writing and reflection skills** as they jot down their thoughts.

Benefits for parents:

- **Great way to foster family bonding**, especially when reading the notes together.
- **Helps create a positive atmosphere at home**, by focusing on gratitude.
- **Simple and inexpensive activity**, requiring only a jar and paper.

73. Create a DIY Puzzle

Creating a DIY puzzle is a fun way for children to engage their creativity and problem-solving skills. This activity allows kids to design their own artwork and then turn it into a puzzle to challenge themselves or others.

How it works:

- **Draw a picture:** Have your child draw or paint a picture on a piece of sturdy paper or cardboard.
- **Cut it into pieces:** Once the artwork is complete, cut the paper into puzzle-like pieces. You can start with simple shapes for younger children or make the puzzle more challenging for older kids by cutting more complex pieces.
- **Put it back together:** Let your child or a sibling try to put the puzzle back together, or swap puzzles with someone else for added fun.

Benefits for kids:

- **Enhances problem-solving skills** as they work to fit the pieces together.
- **Boosts creativity** by allowing them to design their own puzzle.
- **Improves fine motor skills** through cutting and assembling the pieces.

Benefits for parents:

- **No need to buy puzzles**—a DIY version is simple and customizable.
- **Promotes creativity and cognitive development** in one engaging activity.
- **Provides an ongoing challenge**, as the puzzle can be used again and again.

74. Play with a Water Table

A water table is a fun sensory play activity that encourages hands-on exploration of water, textures, and floating objects. This simple setup offers endless possibilities for imaginative play, scientific discovery, and motor skill development.

How it works:

- **Set up the table:** Fill a shallow container or outdoor water table with water. Add toys like cups, boats, spoons, or sponges for your child to experiment with.
- **Encourage exploration:** Let your child pour, scoop, and splash the water, or challenge them to see what objects float or sink.
- **Add a theme:** You can create themed play sessions like a "pirate adventure" or a "floating race," encouraging even more imaginative play.

Benefits for kids:

- **Improves sensory awareness** through tactile interaction with water.

- **Develops fine motor skills** as they scoop, pour, and manipulate objects in the water.
- **Encourages scientific thinking**, as they experiment with concepts like floating, sinking, and pouring.

Benefits for parents:

- **Keeps children entertained** for extended periods, especially on warm days.
- **Simple and low-cost setup**, using items you already have at home.
- **Promotes outdoor play**, which helps with sensory and physical development.

75. Create a 'Feelings Wheel'

A feelings wheel is a visual tool that helps children identify and express their emotions. It promotes emotional literacy and self-awareness, making it easier for kids to understand and communicate their feelings.

How it works:

- **Draw the wheel:** On a large piece of paper, draw a circle and divide it into sections. Each section should represent a different emotion, such as happy, sad, angry, excited, or nervous.
- **Color the emotions:** Let your child color each section and label it with a feeling. You can add pictures or faces to represent each emotion.
- **Use it daily:** Throughout the day, encourage your child to point to the section of the wheel that matches how they're feeling. This helps them recognize and communicate their emotions more clearly.

Benefits for kids:

- **Teaches emotional awareness** by helping them identify and label their feelings.
- **Promotes self-regulation**, as children can visually track their emotions.
- **Encourages open communication** about emotions in a non-threatening way.

Benefits for parents:

- **Simple to create** with paper and crayons or markers.
- **Helps open up conversations** about feelings and emotional well-being.
- **Provides a visual tool** to help manage emotional outbursts or confusion.

76. Nature Walk Journal

A nature walk journal combines the benefits of outdoor exploration with creative reflection. Children can use their journal to document what they see, hear, and experience while on a walk, turning the simple act of walking into an educational adventure.

How it works:

- **Give your child a journal:** Let your child carry a small notebook and some crayons or pencils during the walk.
- **Observe nature:** As you walk, encourage your child to notice the trees, plants, animals, or weather around them. Ask questions like, "What do you see?" or "What do you hear?"
- **Document findings:** Have your child draw or write about what they see in their journal. They can collect leaves or flowers and glue them in for added fun.

Benefits for kids:

- **Encourages mindfulness** and observation of the natural world.
- **Promotes creativity** by combining nature and journaling.
- **Enhances writing and drawing skills** as they document their findings.

Benefits for parents:

- **Provides a calming, educational activity** that combines outdoor play with creativity.
- **Easy to implement** with just a journal and some basic art supplies.
- **Encourages family bonding** as you explore nature together.

77. DIY Marble Run

Creating a DIY marble run is a hands-on activity that challenges children's engineering and problem-solving skills. Using materials found around the house, kids can design their own marble run and experiment with different paths for the marbles to take.

How it works:

- **Collect materials:** Use cardboard tubes, paper towel rolls, tape, and a box or board to set up the marble run.
- **Build the run:** Help your child create ramps, tunnels, and pathways for the marbles to roll through. Encourage them to experiment with angles and height to see how the marbles move.
- **Test and adjust:** After building the marble run, drop in a marble and see how it flows. Adjust the course to make it faster or more challenging.

Benefits for kids:

- **Enhances problem-solving skills** by encouraging them to test and adjust their designs.
- **Promotes creativity and engineering** as they build and experiment with different paths.
- **Improves fine motor skills** through cutting, taping, and assembling the run.

Benefits for parents:

- **Simple and inexpensive,** using household materials for an engaging activity.
- **Encourages STEM learning** through hands-on experimentation and design.

- **Great for indoor play**, keeping children entertained while developing important skills.

78. Sensory Bag Play

Sensory bags are sealed bags filled with materials like water beads, glitter, or small toys. They provide a mess-free way for children to explore textures and practice fine motor skills, making them a perfect sensory activity for younger kids.

How it works:

- **Create the sensory bag:** Fill a zip-lock bag with materials like water beads, glitter, rice, or small plastic toys. Seal the bag tightly, ensuring no leaks.
- **Let your child explore:** Encourage your child to squish, squeeze, and move the items around in the bag. You can even add letters or numbers for educational play.
- **Add themes:** Create themed sensory bags based on holidays, seasons, or your child's interests by including relevant objects or colors.

Benefits for kids:

- **Engages their sense of touch** without the mess, making it perfect for sensory play.
- **Develops fine motor skills** as they manipulate the contents of the bag.
- **Promotes focus and calm**, making it a great activity for children who need sensory regulation.

Benefits for parents:

- **Quick and easy to create** using items you already have at home.
- **Provides a portable, mess-free sensory experience** that's perfect for travel or quiet time.
- **Helps manage sensory processing challenges**, giving children a way to calm down and focus.

79. Create a 'Worry Box'

A worry box is a helpful tool for children to express their worries and anxieties. By writing down or drawing their concerns and placing them in the box, kids learn to externalize their fears and feel a sense of relief.

How it works:

- **Find or decorate a box:** Let your child decorate a small box or container that will serve as their worry box.
- **Write down worries:** When your child is feeling anxious or upset, encourage them to write or draw their worries on small pieces of paper and put them in the box.

- **Review together:** At the end of the week or month, sit down together and go through the box. Discuss any worries they still have and how they can cope with them.

Benefits for kids:

- **Provides a safe outlet** for expressing fears and worries.
- **Promotes emotional awareness and coping skills** by externalizing feelings.
- **Helps reduce anxiety,** giving children a sense of control over their worries.

Benefits for parents:

- **Creates a space for open conversations** about emotions and fears.
- **Simple to set up** with just a box and paper.
- **Helps you understand your child's emotional world,** providing insight into their concerns.

---

80. Create a Treasure Map

Creating a treasure map is a creative and adventurous activity that encourages children to use their imagination, map-reading skills, and problem-solving abilities. It can be part of a larger treasure hunt, turning a simple game into an epic adventure.

How it works:

- **Draw the map:** Help your child create a treasure map of your home or backyard. Include landmarks like trees, furniture, or special spots that lead to the treasure.
- **Hide the treasure:** Hide a small toy, treat, or special item as the "treasure," marking the location with an X on the map.
- **Go on the hunt:** Use the map to guide your child to the hidden treasure. You can make the hunt more exciting by adding clues along the way.

Benefits for kids:

- **Encourages imaginative play** by creating a story around the treasure hunt.
- **Teaches basic map-reading and problem-solving skills** as they follow the clues.
- **Promotes outdoor exploration,** combining creativity with physical activity.

Benefits for parents:

- **Encourages physical and imaginative play,** keeping kids engaged for longer periods.
- **Simple to set up with just paper and a hidden item.**
- **Great for family bonding,** as everyone can participate in the hunt together.

81. Create a Shadow Box

A shadow box is a small, three-dimensional display that allows children to create a scene or tell a story inside a box. This hands-on craft combines creativity, storytelling, and fine motor skills.

How it works:

- **Find a box:** Use a shoebox or any shallow box as the base of the shadow box.
- **Create a scene:** Let your child decorate the inside of the box with drawings, small toys, or cut-out pictures to create a scene. They can use materials like paper, glue, and markers to bring their ideas to life.
- **Add depth:** Encourage your child to layer objects at different depths to create a 3D effect, adding elements like trees, buildings, or characters.

Benefits for kids:

- **Promotes creativity** by allowing them to design and build a unique scene.
- **Enhances fine motor skills** as they cut, paste, and arrange materials.
- **Encourages storytelling**, helping them express their ideas through art.

Benefits for parents:

- **Inexpensive and easy to create** using items around the house.
- **Encourages quiet, focused play**, making it a great rainy day project.
- **Fosters imaginative thinking**, allowing children to explore different themes and stories.

82. Create a DIY Sensory Bottle

A sensory bottle is a calming and visually stimulating tool that helps children relax, focus, and explore different sensory experiences. These bottles are filled with liquid and small objects that move around when shaken, providing a mesmerizing effect.

How it works:

- **Fill a bottle:** Use a clear plastic bottle and fill it with water, glitter, beads, and small objects like buttons or sequins. You can also add food coloring to the water for extra visual interest.
- **Seal the bottle:** Make sure the cap is tightly sealed with glue or tape to prevent leaks.
- **Explore the effects:** Encourage your child to shake the bottle and watch the objects move. They can also turn the bottle upside down and observe how the glitter and beads settle.

Benefits for kids:

- **Provides sensory stimulation**, especially for visual and tactile learners.
- **Helps with emotional regulation** by offering a calming, repetitive activity.
- **Encourages focus and attention** as they watch the objects move in the bottle.

Benefits for parents:

- **Easy to make with household materials**, requiring minimal effort and cost.
- **Portable calming tool**, perfect for helping children manage stress or anxiety.
- **Great for sensory play**, especially for children who benefit from tactile and visual experiences.

83. Scarf Dancing

Scarf dancing is a creative movement activity that helps children express themselves through dance while improving coordination and rhythm. Using lightweight scarves or fabric pieces, children can twirl, wave, and toss them to the rhythm of music.

How it works:

- **Provide scarves or fabric pieces:** Lightweight scarves or even strips of fabric work well for this activity.
- **Play music:** Choose some upbeat music and encourage your child to move the scarves to the beat. They can twirl, wave, or throw the scarves in the air.
- **Add instructions:** Give your child challenges like "wave the scarf in circles" or "toss it as high as you can," helping them explore different movements.

Benefits for kids:

- **Improves coordination and rhythm** as they move in time with the music.
- **Encourages physical activity** and self-expression through creative movement.
- **Develops gross motor skills** as they engage in large movements like twirling and throwing.

Benefits for parents:

- **Low-cost activity**, requiring only scarves or fabric.
- **Great indoor exercise**, especially on days when outdoor play isn't possible.
- **Encourages free-form movement**, allowing children to express themselves creatively.

84. Memory Scrapbook

A memory scrapbook allows children to document special events, memories, and milestones in a creative and personal way. This activity encourages reflection, emotional expression, and creativity through art and writing.

How it works:

- **Provide a scrapbook or notebook:** Let your child decorate the cover and make it their own.
- **Add memories:** Encourage your child to fill the scrapbook with photos, ticket stubs, drawings, and stories about special events, holidays, or everyday moments.
- **Reflect on the memories:** As they add to the scrapbook, ask your child to reflect on what made each memory special and how they felt at the time.

Benefits for kids:

- **Encourages emotional expression** by allowing them to document and reflect on important memories.
- **Promotes creativity** through drawing, writing, and decorating.
- **Improves fine motor skills** as they glue, cut, and arrange items in the scrapbook.

Benefits for parents:

- **Helps open up conversations** about emotions and memories.
- **Encourages family bonding**, especially when working on the scrapbook together.
- **Creates a keepsake** that your child can treasure for years to come.

85. Chalk Maze

A chalk maze is an engaging outdoor activity that combines creativity and problem-solving. Children can design their own maze on the sidewalk or driveway and then challenge themselves or others to complete it.

How it works:

- **Draw the maze:** Use sidewalk chalk to create a simple or complex maze on the ground. Encourage your child to think about where they want the start and finish to be and what obstacles or paths they want to include.
- **Navigate the maze:** Once the maze is complete, challenge your child to find their way through it. You can add extra rules, like hopping on one foot or walking backward through the maze.
- **Invite friends or family:** Let others try the maze, making it a fun group activity.

Benefits for kids:

- **Improves problem-solving skills** as they design and navigate the maze.
- **Encourages outdoor play**, combining physical activity with creativity.
- **Develops fine motor skills** through drawing and planning the maze.

Benefits for parents:

- **Inexpensive and simple**—all you need is chalk.
- **Encourages independent play** while also offering opportunities for family participation.
- **Promotes outdoor activity**, helping children stay active while engaging their minds.

86. Nature Bracelet

A nature bracelet is a simple craft activity that combines creativity with outdoor exploration. Children collect small natural items like flowers, leaves, or pebbles and attach them to a sticky bracelet, creating a unique piece of nature-inspired jewelry.

How it works:

- **Make the bracelet:** Wrap a piece of masking tape or double-sided tape loosely around your child's wrist, sticky side out.
- **Go on a nature walk:** Take a walk outside and let your child collect small items like leaves, flowers, grass, or tiny pebbles to stick to their bracelet.
- **Create the bracelet:** As they find items, they can attach them to the tape to create a unique nature bracelet.

Benefits for kids:

- **Encourages outdoor exploration** by turning a simple walk into a creative adventure.
- **Develops fine motor skills** as they pick up small items and attach them to the tape.
- **Promotes creativity** through the process of designing their own bracelet.

Benefits for parents:

- **Simple and cost-effective activity**, requiring only tape and natural materials.
- **Great for outdoor bonding**, encouraging family walks and exploration.
- **Provides a sensory experience**, allowing children to interact with different textures and materials.

87. Create a Vision Board

A vision board is a creative way for children to set goals, dream big, and visualize their future. By gathering pictures, words, and drawings that represent their hopes and aspirations, kids can build confidence and focus on what they want to achieve.

How it works:

- **Gather materials:** Provide magazines, newspapers, markers, glue, and a poster board for your child to use.

- **Create the board:** Encourage your child to cut out pictures and words that represent their dreams and goals, such as hobbies they want to try, places they want to visit, or skills they want to develop.
- **Reflect on the vision:** Once the vision board is complete, talk with your child about their dreams and what steps they can take to achieve them.

Benefits for kids:

- **Encourages goal-setting** and helps them visualize their future aspirations.
- **Boosts self-confidence** by focusing on what they want to achieve.
- **Promotes creativity and self-expression** through cutting, arranging, and designing the board.

Benefits for parents:

- **Great opportunity to discuss dreams and goals**, fostering open communication.
- **Encourages positive thinking** by focusing on what excites and inspires your child.
- **Simple and adaptable**, using everyday materials like magazines and paper.

88. Sock Puppet Show

A sock puppet show is a creative way for children to explore storytelling, social interaction, and imagination. By making their own puppets and acting out stories, children can practice language skills, emotional expression, and creativity.

How it works:

- **Make the puppets:** Use old socks and decorate them with markers, yarn, buttons, and fabric to create different characters.
- **Create a stage:** Use a table or a cardboard box as the puppet stage. Let your child decorate it to match the theme of their show.
- **Put on a show:** Encourage your child to come up with a story for the puppets to act out. You can even join in as a co-performer or audience member.

Benefits for kids:

- **Encourages imaginative play** by allowing them to create their own characters and stories.
- **Improves language and communication skills** through storytelling.
- **Promotes social and emotional development** as they explore different characters and emotions.

Benefits for parents:

- **Simple and inexpensive craft**, using materials already at home.
- **Promotes family bonding** through collaborative play and storytelling.
- **Great for independent play**, allowing children to entertain themselves with their puppet creations.

89. Color Sorting

Color sorting is a simple and educational activity that helps younger children learn about colors, patterns, and categorization. This hands-on game improves cognitive development and fine motor skills by encouraging children to sort objects based on color.

How it works:

- **Gather colorful items:** Use toys, buttons, blocks, or paper cutouts in different colors.
- **Create color zones:** Place colored paper or containers around the room that correspond to the items' colors.
- **Sort the objects:** Ask your child to sort the items into the correct color zones, encouraging them to recognize and group items by color.

Benefits for kids:

- **Teaches color recognition** and sorting skills in a hands-on way.
- **Improves fine motor skills** as they pick up and sort objects.
- **Boosts cognitive development** by encouraging classification and organization.

Benefits for parents:

- **Easy to set up** with items you already have at home.
- **Reinforces early learning concepts** in a fun, interactive way.
- **Can be adapted for different skill levels**, making it a versatile activity for various ages.

90. Tactile Sensory Bin

A tactile sensory bin is a hands-on, sensory-rich activity that helps children explore different textures and materials. It's perfect for sensory development, fine motor skills, and imaginative play, especially for children who enjoy tactile experiences.

How it works:

- **Fill the bin:** Use a large container and fill it with materials like rice, beans, sand, pasta, or cotton balls. Add small toys, spoons, and scoops to the mix.
- **Encourage exploration:** Let your child dig, scoop, and pour the materials in the bin. You can also hide objects for them to find, turning it into a mini treasure hunt.
- **Add a theme:** You can create themed sensory bins by using items that match holidays, seasons, or your child's favorite topics (e.g., dinosaurs, ocean animals).

Benefits for kids:

- **Promotes sensory exploration**, helping children engage with different textures.
- **Develops fine motor skills** through scooping, pouring, and manipulating objects.

- **Encourages imaginative play**, allowing them to create stories and scenarios with the objects in the bin.

Benefits for parents:

- **Simple and inexpensive**, using materials you likely already have.
- **Keeps children engaged and entertained** for long periods.
- **Helps manage sensory processing issues**, providing a controlled way for children to experience different textures.

91. Musical Instrument Parade

A musical instrument parade is a fun and energetic activity that encourages children to explore sounds, rhythm, and movement. By making their own instruments and marching in a parade, children can engage their creativity and improve coordination.

How it works:

- **Make instruments:** Create homemade instruments using everyday items like pots and pans for drums, rice in a bottle for maracas, or rubber bands stretched over a box for a guitar.
- **Form a parade:** Once the instruments are ready, have your child march around the house or yard while playing their instrument. You can add rhythm by playing music or setting a beat.
- **Take turns leading:** Let each child or family member take a turn as the leader, guiding the parade in different directions or changing the rhythm.

Benefits for kids:

- **Encourages creativity** by making and playing homemade instruments.
- **Improves rhythm and coordination** through marching and playing music.
- **Boosts confidence** as they take turns leading the parade.

Benefits for parents:

- **Simple and fun to set up**, with materials already at home.
- **Great for physical activity**, keeping kids moving while having fun.
- **Encourages family bonding** through a playful group activity.

92. Nature Bingo

Nature Bingo is a fun way to encourage outdoor exploration while teaching children about plants, animals, and other elements of nature. This activity combines a traditional bingo game with a scavenger hunt to engage children in discovering the world around them.

How it works:

- **Create bingo cards:** Make bingo cards with different nature items to find, such as "bird," "tree," "flower," "rock," or "cloud." You can either draw or print the images.
- **Go on a nature walk:** Take your child outside and encourage them to find the items on their bingo card. As they spot each one, they can mark it off.
- **Call out 'Bingo!':** Once they find a full row or column of items, they can shout "Bingo!" and win the game.

Benefits for kids:

- **Encourages outdoor exploration**, fostering a connection with nature.
- **Improves observational skills** as they look for specific items.
- **Teaches about the environment** through hands-on discovery.

Benefits for parents:

- **Simple and educational**, combining fun with learning about nature.
- **Encourages outdoor play**, which is great for physical and mental health.
- **Easy to adapt** for different environments and seasons, making it versatile.

93. Balance Beam Challenge

The balance beam challenge is a physical activity that helps children improve their balance, coordination, and concentration. It can be easily set up indoors or outdoors, making it a great way to get kids moving.

How it works:

- **Set up a beam:** Use painter's tape on the floor, a long piece of wood, or a low curb as a balance beam.
- **Walk the beam:** Encourage your child to walk across the beam without falling off. For an added challenge, ask them to balance an object (like a beanbag) on their head while walking.
- **Add variety:** Make the activity more fun by having them walk backward, sideways, or hop across the beam.

Benefits for kids:

- **Improves balance and coordination** as they walk across the beam.
- **Enhances focus and concentration**, especially with added challenges.
- **Boosts physical fitness** through active play and movement.

Benefits for parents:

- **Simple setup**, requiring minimal materials like tape or wood.
- **Promotes physical activity**, helping children stay active indoors or outdoors.
- **Encourages independent play**, allowing children to challenge themselves.

94. Sticker Storytelling

Sticker storytelling is a creative and imaginative activity that encourages children to use stickers to create scenes and tell stories. It's a great way to boost language skills, fine motor development, and creativity.

How it works:

- **Provide stickers and paper:** Give your child a variety of stickers (animals, people, objects) and blank paper.
- **Create a scene:** Encourage your child to arrange the stickers on the paper to create a scene or story.
- **Tell the story:** Ask your child to describe what's happening in the scene or act out a short story based on the stickers.

Benefits for kids:

- **Develops storytelling and language skills** through creative play.
- **Improves fine motor skills** as they peel and place stickers.
- **Encourages imagination**, allowing them to create their own narratives.

Benefits for parents:

- **Easy to set up**, requiring just stickers and paper.
- **Promotes quiet, focused play**, making it a great activity for downtime.
- **Encourages family bonding**, especially when working together to create stories.

95. Treasure Hunt in a Box

A treasure hunt in a box is a mini scavenger hunt that takes place inside a sensory bin or box. This activity combines sensory play with problem-solving, as children search for hidden objects among different materials.

How it works:

- **Fill the box:** Use a large bin and fill it with materials like rice, sand, or shredded paper. Hide small toys, coins, or themed objects inside.
- **Create clues:** Write simple clues or create a list of the items your child needs to find inside the box.
- **Hunt for treasure:** Encourage your child to dig through the box, using their hands or small tools, to find all the hidden items.

Benefits for kids:

- **Encourages sensory exploration** by engaging their sense of touch.
- **Develops problem-solving skills** as they search for hidden objects.
- **Boosts focus and attention**, especially when following clues.

Benefits for parents:

- **Easy to customize** based on themes or interests (e.g., pirate treasure, dinosaurs).
- **Simple setup** with materials like rice or sand.
- **Keeps kids engaged**, providing a fun and tactile way to play.

96. Rainbow Rice Sensory Play

Rainbow rice is a colorful sensory activity that engages children's sense of touch and sight. By playing with the bright, textured rice, children can improve their fine motor skills and explore different textures and patterns.

How it works:

- **Make rainbow rice:** Dye uncooked rice in different colors using food coloring and vinegar. Spread the rice out to dry before using.
- **Fill a sensory bin:** Place the colored rice in a bin or container and add small toys, spoons, and cups for your child to explore.
- **Encourage play:** Let your child scoop, pour, and mix the rice, creating patterns or using it to fill small containers.

Benefits for kids:

- **Engages their sense of touch** through tactile play with the textured rice.
- **Develops fine motor skills** as they manipulate the rice and tools.
- **Stimulates creativity** by allowing them to experiment with colors and patterns.

Benefits for parents:

- **Easy to make with basic ingredients** like rice and food coloring.
- **Provides a calming, sensory-rich activity**, perfect for children who benefit from sensory play.
- **Can be reused for multiple play sessions**, making it a long-lasting activity.

97. Cardboard Box City

Cardboard box city is a large-scale creative project where children use boxes to build an entire miniature city. This activity fosters creativity, problem-solving, and teamwork as kids work to design and construct their own cityscape.

How it works:

- **Collect boxes:** Gather small, medium, and large boxes from around the house or recycle old ones.
- **Build the city:** Let your child use the boxes to create buildings, roads, and other parts of the city. They can decorate the boxes with markers, paint, or stickers.

- **Add vehicles and people:** Use toy cars and figures to bring the city to life, allowing for imaginative play once the city is built.

Benefits for kids:

- **Promotes creativity** as they design and construct their city.
- **Encourages problem-solving** through figuring out how to build and connect different structures.
- **Enhances fine motor skills** as they decorate and arrange the city.

Benefits for parents:

- **Recycles old materials**, making it an eco-friendly project.
- **Keeps kids engaged for hours**, offering a large, imaginative play area.
- **Great for teamwork**, allowing siblings or friends to collaborate on the project.

98. Freeze a Toy in Ice

Freezing a toy in ice is a hands-on science experiment and sensory activity that encourages children to think critically as they work to free the toy. This simple experiment teaches children about temperature and patience.

How it works:

- **Freeze the toy:** Place a small toy in a container of water and freeze it overnight.
- **Challenge your child:** Give your child tools like spoons, cups of warm water, or salt, and challenge them to figure out how to free the toy from the ice.
- **Discuss the science:** As they work, talk with your child about how ice melts and the role of heat and salt in speeding up the process.

Benefits for kids:

- **Encourages scientific thinking** as they experiment with different ways to melt the ice.
- **Develops problem-solving skills** by figuring out how to free the toy.
- **Promotes sensory exploration**, especially with the cool, slippery texture of ice.

Benefits for parents:

- **Simple setup** with just water, a toy, and a freezer.
- **Educational and fun**, combining science with hands-on play.
- **Engages children for an extended period**, as melting ice takes time and patience.

99. Building with Popsicle Sticks

Building with popsicle sticks is a creative and engineering-focused activity that allows children to design and construct different structures. This hands-on project encourages fine motor skills, problem-solving, and imagination.

How it works:

- **Provide popsicle sticks and glue:** Give your child a set of popsicle sticks, glue, and markers or paint to decorate the sticks.
- **Design a structure:** Let them use the popsicle sticks to build simple structures like bridges, houses, or towers. They can glue the sticks together or use tape for temporary creations.
- **Experiment with stability:** Encourage your child to experiment with different designs and test the stability of their structures.

Benefits for kids:

- **Improves fine motor skills** as they manipulate and glue the sticks.
- **Boosts creativity** through designing and building their own structures.
- **Enhances problem-solving** as they figure out how to make their creations stable.

Benefits for parents:

- **Affordable and easy to set up**, with popsicle sticks and glue.
- **Encourages independent play**, allowing children to experiment with different designs.
- **Teaches basic engineering principles**, making it an educational activity.

100. Create a Wind Chime

Creating a wind chime is a fun, crafty activity that allows children to explore sounds, textures, and patterns. This hands-on project combines art, music, and science, as children make a chime that produces soothing sounds when the wind blows.

How it works:

- **Gather materials:** Use items like old keys, bottle caps, shells, beads, or small pieces of metal or wood. You'll also need string and a base, such as a stick or ring.
- **Assemble the chime:** Help your child attach the objects to the string and then tie the strings to the base. Encourage them to experiment with different materials to create a variety of sounds.
- **Hang it up:** Once the wind chime is complete, hang it outside and listen to the different sounds it makes in the wind.

Benefits for kids:

- **Encourages creativity** through designing and assembling the wind chime.
- **Teaches about sound and vibration**, introducing basic science concepts.
- **Develops fine motor skills** as they string together the materials.

Benefits for parents:

- **Simple and eco-friendly**, using recycled or found materials.
- **Fosters family bonding** through a collaborative craft project.
- **Creates a long-lasting decoration**, providing both beauty and sound.

101. Balloon Tennis

Balloon tennis is a fun, indoor game that combines physical activity with coordination and balance. It's a safe, low-impact game that's perfect for burning energy while staying active.

How it works:

- **Create rackets:** Use paper plates attached to wooden sticks or spoons as makeshift tennis rackets.
- **Blow up a balloon:** The balloon serves as the tennis ball. Since it moves slowly and is lightweight, it's easy for kids to hit without the risk of damage.
- **Play the game:** Set up a small "net" using a string between two chairs, and take turns hitting the balloon back and forth over the net.

Benefits for kids:

- **Improves hand-eye coordination** by hitting and controlling the balloon.
- **Encourages physical activity** through jumping and moving to hit the balloon.
- **Promotes teamwork and cooperation**, especially in a group setting.

Benefits for parents:

- **Safe and low-cost activity**, perfect for indoor play.
- **Easy to set up with household items**, requiring minimal preparation.
- **Great for burning off energy**, keeping kids active and engaged indoors.

102. Create a Paper Chain Countdown

A paper chain countdown is a fun craft that helps children visualize and anticipate an upcoming event. It's especially useful for counting down to holidays, birthdays, or special trips.

How it works:

- **Make the chain:** Cut strips of colorful paper and loop them together, securing each link with glue or tape to form a chain.
- **Start the countdown:** Each day, your child removes one link from the chain, counting down the days until the special event.
- **Decorate the chain:** You can add numbers or drawings on each link to make the countdown more personalized.

Benefits for kids:

- **Teaches time concepts**, helping children understand days and countdowns.
- **Encourages creativity** as they decorate the chain.
- **Promotes excitement and anticipation** for the upcoming event.

Benefits for parents:

- **Simple and quick craft** that keeps children engaged.
- **Provides a visual tool** for helping kids manage their excitement and understand time.
- **Great for teaching patience** in a fun, interactive way.

---

103. Felt Board Stories

Felt board stories are a creative way for children to explore storytelling and improve their language skills. By using felt pieces to act out stories, kids can express their imagination while building narrative and sequencing skills.

How it works:

- **Create the board:** Use a large piece of felt or a poster board covered in felt as the background. You can also use a smaller felt board from a craft store.
- **Make felt characters:** Cut out shapes of characters, animals, and objects from colorful felt pieces.
- **Tell the story:** Encourage your child to use the felt characters to tell a story on the board, moving the pieces around as the story unfolds.

Benefits for kids:

- **Develops storytelling skills** by acting out narratives with felt pieces.
- **Improves fine motor skills** as they manipulate the felt shapes.
- **Encourages creativity and imagination**, allowing them to create their own worlds.

Benefits for parents:

- **Simple to create** using inexpensive materials like felt and scissors.
- **Promotes independent play**, while also offering opportunities for collaborative storytelling.
- **Helps with language development**, especially for younger children.

---

104. Indoor Bowling

Indoor bowling is a fun and active game that can be set up using everyday household items. It's a great way to improve hand-eye coordination while offering a friendly competition that gets kids moving.

How it works:

- **Create the pins:** Use empty plastic bottles or paper towel rolls as bowling pins.
- **Find a ball:** Use a soft ball, like a foam ball or rolled-up socks, as the bowling ball.
- **Set up the game:** Arrange the "pins" in a triangle at one end of the room, and take turns rolling the ball to knock them down. Keep score to make it more competitive.

Benefits for kids:

- **Improves coordination and motor skills** as they aim and roll the ball.
- **Encourages physical activity**, even indoors.
- **Teaches turn-taking and sportsmanship**, especially in a group setting.

Benefits for parents:

- **Easy to set up with household items**, requiring no special equipment.
- **Perfect for indoor play**, especially on rainy days.
- **Fun for all ages**, making it a great family activity.

105. Magic Milk Experiment

The magic milk experiment is a simple science activity that allows children to explore the interaction between liquids and soap. This mesmerizing experiment engages their curiosity and teaches them about chemical reactions.

How it works:

- **Pour milk into a dish:** Use a shallow dish and pour enough milk to cover the bottom.
- **Add food coloring:** Drop a few different colors of food coloring into the milk.
- **Watch the reaction:** Dip a cotton swab in dish soap and then touch the surface of the milk. The colors will swirl and mix in magical patterns as the soap breaks the surface tension of the milk.

Benefits for kids:

- **Encourages scientific thinking** by observing chemical reactions.
- **Promotes curiosity** through hands-on experimentation.
- **Teaches basic science concepts** like surface tension and molecular interaction.

Benefits for parents:

- **Quick and easy setup** with common kitchen ingredients.
- **Provides an educational and fun experiment**, sparking interest in science.
- **Offers a calming and visually engaging activity** for young children.

106. Create a Weather Journal

A weather journal is a simple and educational tool that helps children observe, record, and learn about daily weather patterns. It encourages curiosity about nature and teaches children how to track and understand the weather.

How it works:

- **Set up a journal:** Provide your child with a notebook or journal to record daily weather observations.
- **Observe the weather:** Each day, have your child look outside and note the weather conditions (sunny, cloudy, rainy, etc.). They can also draw pictures or add words to describe the temperature and any other details.
- **Track patterns:** Over time, help your child identify patterns in the weather, such as changes in seasons or weekly cycles.

Benefits for kids:

- **Teaches observation skills** by encouraging them to notice daily weather changes.
- **Promotes understanding of nature and science**, especially weather patterns.
- **Enhances writing and drawing skills** through daily journal entries.

Benefits for parents:

- **Great educational tool** for teaching kids about weather and seasons.
- **Encourages a daily routine**, which promotes discipline and curiosity.
- **Simple and low-cost activity**, requiring only a notebook and time outside.

---

107. Pom-Pom Sorting

Pom-pom sorting is a fun and simple activity that helps younger children develop fine motor skills, color recognition, and sorting abilities. This hands-on game is perfect for toddlers and preschoolers.

How it works:

- **Provide pom-poms:** Use colorful pom-poms and small containers or cups.
- **Sort by color:** Ask your child to sort the pom-poms into the containers based on color. You can also challenge them to sort by size or create patterns with the pom-poms.
- **Use tweezers for added difficulty:** For older children, give them tweezers to pick up and sort the pom-poms, adding an extra level of challenge.

Benefits for kids:

- **Improves fine motor skills** as they pick up and sort the pom-poms.
- **Teaches color recognition and sorting**, building early math skills.
- **Encourages focus and concentration**, especially with added challenges.

Benefits for parents:

- **Easy to set up with inexpensive materials**, like pom-poms and containers.
- **Promotes independent play**, keeping children engaged for long periods.
- **Supports early learning concepts**, such as sorting, classification, and color recognition.

108. Obstacle Course in the Living Room

An indoor obstacle course is a great way to get children moving and active when they can't go outside. By creating simple obstacles with household items, children can engage in physical play while developing balance, coordination, and problem-solving skills.

How it works:

- **Set up obstacles:** Use pillows, chairs, and blankets to create a course. For example, they can crawl under a chair, jump over a pillow, or balance on a line of tape on the floor.
- **Give directions:** Guide your child through the course with instructions like "crawl," "jump," or "balance."
- **Add a challenge:** Time your child as they complete the course or give them tasks to complete along the way, like tossing a beanbag into a basket.

Benefits for kids:

- **Improves balance and coordination** through physical challenges.
- **Encourages problem-solving** as they navigate the course.
- **Boosts physical activity**, helping kids stay active indoors.

Benefits for parents:

- **Uses household items**, making it simple and cost-free.
- **Perfect for rainy days** or when outdoor play isn't possible.
- **Great for siblings or friends**, encouraging cooperative play.

109. Paper Plate Weaving

Paper plate weaving is a creative craft that helps children develop fine motor skills and hand-eye coordination. By weaving yarn through slits in a paper plate, children can create beautiful patterns while practicing patience and focus.

How it works:

- **Prepare the plate:** Cut slits around the edges of a paper plate, making sure they're evenly spaced.
- **Start weaving:** Give your child yarn or string, and have them weave the yarn in and out of the slits, creating patterns as they go. They can use multiple colors to make it more vibrant.

- **Add decorations:** Once the weaving is complete, let your child decorate the plate with markers, stickers, or other craft materials.

Benefits for kids:

- **Develops fine motor skills** through the precise motions of weaving.
- **Encourages creativity** by allowing them to design their own patterns.
- **Improves focus and patience**, especially with the repetitive weaving motion.

Benefits for parents:

- **Simple and inexpensive craft**, requiring only paper plates and yarn.
- **Keeps children engaged for longer periods**, promoting quiet, focused play.
- **Great for developing skills needed for tasks like writing and cutting**.

110. Shape Hunt

A shape hunt is an interactive game that helps children learn about shapes while engaging in a fun scavenger hunt. This activity encourages movement and cognitive development by combining learning with active play.

How it works:

- **Choose shapes:** Pick several basic shapes like circles, squares, triangles, and rectangles.
- **Find objects:** Challenge your child to find objects around the house that match each shape. For example, they might find a round plate for a circle or a book for a rectangle.
- **Make it a challenge:** Add a timer or create a list of specific items to find for an added level of difficulty.

Benefits for kids:

- **Teaches shape recognition** by associating shapes with real-world objects.
- **Encourages physical activity**, as they move around the house searching for shapes.
- **Boosts problem-solving skills** by finding objects that fit the shape criteria.

Benefits for parents:

- **No special materials needed**, making it a spontaneous and easy-to-play game.
- **Promotes active learning**, combining movement with cognitive development.
- **Great for younger children**, helping them develop early math skills in a playful way.

111. Egg Carton Caterpillar Craft

Making an egg carton caterpillar is a simple craft that sparks creativity and helps develop fine motor skills. Using recycled materials like egg cartons, children can create their own colorful caterpillars.

How it works:

- **Prepare the carton:** Cut an egg carton into a row of cups to form the caterpillar's body.
- **Decorate the caterpillar:** Let your child paint or color the egg carton, adding googly eyes, pipe cleaners for antennae, and other decorations to bring the caterpillar to life.
- **Add details:** Encourage your child to get creative by adding spots, stripes, or glitter to make the caterpillar unique.

Benefits for kids:

- **Develops fine motor skills** through cutting, painting, and decorating.
- **Encourages creativity** by allowing them to personalize their caterpillar.
- **Teaches recycling and reusing**, using common household materials for crafting.

Benefits for parents:

- **Eco-friendly and cost-effective**, using recycled egg cartons.
- **Provides a fun, mess-free craft** that can be done indoors.
- **Promotes creativity and independent play**, while also being great for bonding.

---

112. DIY Lava Lamp

Creating a DIY lava lamp is a fun science activity that teaches children about density and chemical reactions. It's a mesmerizing experiment that also offers sensory stimulation.

How it works:

- **Fill a jar:** Use a clear jar or bottle and fill it two-thirds with vegetable oil and one-third with water. Add a few drops of food coloring to the water.
- **Add the reaction:** Drop a tablet of Alka-Seltzer or a fizzy antacid into the jar, and watch the bubbles form as the water and oil react.
- **Repeat the process:** Once the bubbles settle, you can add another tablet to watch the process happen again.

Benefits for kids:

- **Encourages scientific curiosity** by teaching them about density and chemical reactions.
- **Provides sensory stimulation** through the colorful, bubbling effect.
- **Promotes hands-on learning**, making science fun and interactive.

Benefits for parents:

- **Easy to set up** with common household items like oil and water.
- **Reusable experiment**, as the reaction can be repeated with more tablets.
- **Great for indoor play**, providing a captivating activity that's also educational.

113. Pipe Cleaner Sculptures

Creating sculptures with pipe cleaners is a creative way to develop fine motor skills and artistic expression. Children can bend and twist pipe cleaners into various shapes, animals, or abstract designs.

How it works:

- **Provide pipe cleaners:** Give your child a variety of colorful pipe cleaners to work with.
- **Create sculptures:** Show them how to twist, bend, and shape the pipe cleaners into figures, such as animals, flowers, or geometric shapes.
- **Encourage creativity:** Let them add beads or other decorations to their sculptures for extra flair.

Benefits for kids:

- **Improves fine motor skills** as they manipulate the flexible pipe cleaners.
- **Encourages creativity** by allowing them to design and build their own sculptures.
- **Boosts concentration and focus**, especially with intricate designs.

Benefits for parents:

- **Affordable craft materials**, easy to find at most stores.
- **Simple to clean up**, with no mess or glue needed.
- **Encourages independent play**, keeping kids engaged for long periods.

114. Dance Freeze with Flashlight

Dance freeze with a flashlight adds an exciting twist to the classic freeze dance game. By dancing in the dark and using a flashlight to signal when to stop, this game combines movement, rhythm, and fun.

How it works:

- **Play music:** Turn off the lights and play your child's favorite music.
- **Use the flashlight:** Shine a flashlight around the room while your child dances. When you turn off the flashlight, they must freeze in place.
- **Add challenges:** Make it more fun by calling out silly poses or asking them to freeze in specific positions, like balancing on one foot.

Benefits for kids:

- **Improves coordination and rhythm** through dancing to the music.
- **Teaches listening and focus,** as they freeze when the light goes out.
- **Encourages self-expression** through movement and creativity.

Benefits for parents:

- **Easy to play indoors,** with minimal setup.
- **Promotes physical activity,** helping kids stay active in a fun way.
- **Engages children in both physical and cognitive play,** improving multiple skills at once.

115. Build a Bird Feeder

Building a bird feeder is a simple nature-focused craft that helps children learn about animals and encourages them to observe birds in their natural habitat. It's a hands-on activity that also teaches responsibility and care for wildlife.

How it works:

- **Use recycled materials:** You can make a bird feeder from a toilet paper roll, pinecone, or a plastic bottle. Coat the roll or pinecone with peanut butter and roll it in birdseed.
- **Hang it outside:** Once the feeder is ready, hang it from a tree branch or place it in a visible spot in the yard.
- **Watch the birds:** Encourage your child to observe the birds that come to visit the feeder and even keep a bird journal to track the different species they see.

Benefits for kids:

- **Teaches responsibility** by caring for wildlife and feeding birds.
- **Promotes outdoor learning** and observation of nature.
- **Develops fine motor skills** through creating the bird feeder.

Benefits for parents:

- **Simple and inexpensive project,** using recycled materials.
- **Encourages outdoor time** and connection with nature.
- **Provides an ongoing activity,** as children can refill the feeder and track bird visits.

116. Create a Moon Phases Chart

Creating a moon phases chart is an educational activity that helps children learn about the lunar cycle. By tracking the moon's phases over time, kids develop an understanding of astronomy and patterns in nature.

How it works:

- **Draw the chart:** On a large piece of paper, create a circle for each day of the lunar cycle.
- **Track the moon:** Each night, have your child observe the moon and color in the corresponding circle to represent the phase (new moon, waxing crescent, full moon, etc.).
- **Discuss the phases:** As the month progresses, talk about the different phases and what they mean.

Benefits for kids:

- **Teaches basic astronomy** by learning about the moon's phases.
- **Promotes observation skills**, encouraging them to watch the night sky.
- **Builds an understanding of cycles and patterns** in nature.

Benefits for parents:

- **Educational and engaging**, introducing children to science in a fun way.
- **Simple to create with paper and markers**, requiring minimal setup.
- **Great for family bonding**, as you observe the moon together each night.

117. DIY Story Cubes

DIY story cubes are a fun way to encourage storytelling and creative thinking. By rolling cubes with different pictures on each side, children can use the images as prompts to create imaginative stories.

How it works:

- **Make the cubes:** Use wooden blocks or small cardboard boxes and draw or glue pictures of various objects, animals, or places on each side.
- **Roll the cubes:** Let your child roll the cubes and use the images that come up to create a story. For example, if they roll a cube with a dog, a tree, and a boat, they might tell a story about a dog who sails a boat under a tree.
- **Take turns:** Make it a collaborative activity by taking turns adding to the story based on the cubes rolled.

Benefits for kids:

- **Boosts creativity and imagination** through storytelling.
- **Improves language and communication skills** as they narrate their stories.
- **Teaches sequencing and narrative structure**, helping them organize their thoughts.

Benefits for parents:

- **Encourages family bonding** through shared storytelling.
- **Simple to make**, using everyday materials like cardboard or wood blocks.
- **Promotes independent play**, as children can create stories on their own.

118. Create a Time Capsule

A time capsule is a fun way for children to document their current interests, favorite items, and memories to be rediscovered in the future. It encourages reflection and excitement about the future.

How it works:

- **Find a container:** Use a small box or tin as the time capsule. Have your child decorate the outside to make it personal.
- **Choose items:** Let your child pick a few special items to include, such as a favorite toy, a drawing, or a letter to their future self.
- **Bury or store the capsule:** Once the time capsule is filled, decide on a date to open it (e.g., in one year or five years), and store it somewhere safe, or bury it in the yard.

Benefits for kids:

- **Encourages reflection and self-awareness** as they choose items that represent their current life.
- **Builds excitement for the future**, giving them something to look forward to.
- **Teaches organization** by carefully selecting and preserving special items.

Benefits for parents:

- **Creates a lasting memory** that the family can enjoy together in the future.
- **Fosters creativity and decision-making**, as children pick meaningful items.
- **Simple and meaningful**, requiring only a container and a few personal items.

---

119. Magnetic Fishing Game

The magnetic fishing game is a fun and interactive way to teach children about magnetism while developing hand-eye coordination. By "fishing" for magnetic objects, kids can practice patience, focus, and coordination.

How it works:

- **Make the fish:** Cut out fish shapes from paper or felt and attach a small magnet to each one.
- **Create a fishing rod:** Use a stick or dowel with a string attached, and tie a magnet to the end of the string to act as the fishing hook.
- **Go fishing:** Scatter the fish on the floor or in a box, and let your child use the rod to "catch" the fish by attracting the magnets.

Benefits for kids:

- **Teaches basic science concepts** like magnetism.

- **Improves hand-eye coordination** as they aim and "catch" the fish.
- **Encourages focus and patience**, especially when fishing takes time.

Benefits for parents:

- **Easy to create** with basic craft materials.
- **Educational and engaging**, combining science with play.
- **Perfect for independent or group play**, keeping children entertained for extended periods.

120. Create a DIY Kaleidoscope

A DIY kaleidoscope is a hands-on craft that teaches children about light and reflection. By making their own kaleidoscope, kids can explore the world of colors and patterns in a fun, interactive way.

How it works:

- **Gather materials:** Use a cardboard tube, small mirrors or reflective paper, and colorful beads or sequins.
- **Assemble the kaleidoscope:** Place the mirrors inside the tube in a triangular shape, and seal one end with a piece of clear plastic or wax paper. Add the colorful beads to the other end.
- **Watch the patterns:** Let your child look through the tube and twist it to see the changing patterns created by the light reflecting off the beads and mirrors.

Benefits for kids:

- **Teaches basic physics concepts** like light reflection and symmetry.
- **Encourages creativity** through designing and assembling the kaleidoscope.
- **Provides sensory stimulation**, especially through the vibrant colors and patterns.

Benefits for parents:

- **Simple to make with household materials**, requiring minimal effort.
- **Educational and visually stimulating**, offering a fun way to learn about light.
- **Engages children in a calming, focused activity**, promoting mindfulness and concentration.

121. DIY Puzzle Cards

DIY puzzle cards are a creative way for children to develop problem-solving skills and fine motor coordination by making and solving their own puzzles. This activity allows kids to combine art and logic.

How it works:

- **Create the puzzle:** Have your child draw or color a picture on a piece of sturdy paper or cardboard.
- **Cut the picture into pieces:** Once the drawing is complete, cut the paper into puzzle-like pieces (simple shapes for younger kids, more complex for older ones).
- **Solve the puzzle:** Mix up the pieces and challenge your child to put their puzzle back together. You can also swap puzzles with siblings or friends for extra fun.

Benefits for kids:

- **Develops problem-solving skills** by figuring out how to fit the pieces together.
- **Encourages creativity** through drawing and puzzle design.
- **Improves fine motor skills** as they handle and manipulate the puzzle pieces.

Benefits for parents:

- **Simple and cost-effective**, using materials like paper and scissors.
- **Promotes independent play**, giving children an engaging task.
- **Reusable activity**, as puzzles can be taken apart and solved again.

---

122. Water Balloon Toss

A water balloon toss is an exciting outdoor game that combines physical activity, hand-eye coordination, and teamwork. It's a fun way to stay cool on hot days while encouraging active play.

How it works:

- **Fill the balloons:** Prepare several water balloons for the game.
- **Start the toss:** Stand across from your child or another player and gently toss the balloon back and forth.
- **Add challenges:** As you play, take a step back after each successful toss to make the game harder. Keep going until the balloon breaks!

Benefits for kids:

- **Improves hand-eye coordination** through catching and tossing.
- **Encourages physical activity**, keeping kids active outdoors.
- **Promotes teamwork** and turn-taking during the game.

Benefits for parents:

- **Simple and inexpensive**, using only water and balloons.
- **Perfect for hot weather**, providing a way to cool off while playing.
- **Encourages family bonding**, with room for friendly competition.

123. Nature Collage

A nature collage is a creative project that encourages children to explore the outdoors and use natural materials to create art. It combines nature discovery with artistic expression.

How it works:

- **Go on a nature walk:** Take your child outside to collect items like leaves, flowers, twigs, and pebbles.
- **Create the collage:** Once you're back home, provide a sheet of paper and glue, and have your child arrange and stick the natural materials onto the paper to create a unique collage.
- **Discuss the materials:** Talk with your child about where each item came from and what makes it special, adding an educational element to the craft.

Benefits for kids:

- **Encourages outdoor exploration**, fostering a connection with nature.
- **Promotes creativity** by allowing them to design their own collage with natural materials.
- **Develops fine motor skills** through arranging and gluing the objects.

Benefits for parents:

- **Inexpensive and eco-friendly**, using natural materials from the outdoors.
- **Combines outdoor play with artistic expression**, keeping kids active and creative.
- **Great for family bonding**, especially during nature walks and crafting together.

---

124. Pasta Jewelry Making

Pasta jewelry making is a fun craft that helps children develop fine motor skills and creativity by stringing colorful pasta shapes into necklaces or bracelets. This activity also introduces pattern-making concepts.

How it works:

- **Prepare the pasta:** Use large pasta shapes like penne or rigatoni. For added fun, dye the pasta different colors with food coloring and vinegar.
- **String the pasta:** Provide yarn or string and let your child thread the pasta onto it to create necklaces or bracelets.
- **Create patterns:** Encourage your child to create patterns with the different colors of pasta.

Benefits for kids:

- **Improves fine motor skills** through threading the pasta onto the string.
- **Teaches pattern recognition** by arranging the pasta in different sequences.
- **Boosts creativity** as they design their own jewelry.

Benefits for parents:

- **Affordable and easy to set up** with simple pasta and string.
- **Encourages independent play**, while still allowing for family participation.
- **Reusable materials**, with pasta and string that can be used again for future crafts.

---

125. Cloud Watching

Cloud watching is a calming, reflective activity that encourages children to use their imagination while observing nature. It's a great way to slow down and appreciate the beauty of the sky.

How it works:

- **Find a spot to lie down:** Take a blanket outside and lie down with your child to look up at the sky.
- **Observe the clouds:** Encourage your child to describe the shapes they see in the clouds, using their imagination to interpret the different formations.
- **Create stories:** As a fun twist, ask your child to make up stories about the clouds they see, turning the activity into a creative storytelling session.

Benefits for kids:

- **Encourages mindfulness** by focusing on the present moment and the natural world.
- **Sparks imagination** as they interpret cloud shapes into different animals, objects, or scenes.
- **Promotes relaxation**, offering a calm, peaceful activity.

Benefits for parents:

- **Simple and stress-free**, requiring only a clear sky and some time outdoors.
- **Fosters connection with nature**, providing a break from screen time.
- **Great for family bonding**, offering a peaceful, reflective moment together.

---

126. Shadow Tracing

Shadow tracing is an outdoor art activity that combines creativity with physical play. By tracing shadows, children can explore shapes, movement, and light while creating fun drawings.

How it works:

- **Find a sunny spot:** Go outside on a sunny day and stand near a surface like a driveway or sidewalk.
- **Trace the shadows:** Use sidewalk chalk to trace the shadows of objects or people onto the ground. Kids can also trace their own shadows or those of their toys.

- **Decorate the shapes:** After tracing, encourage your child to add details or color in the shadows to create characters, animals, or abstract designs.

Benefits for kids:

- **Teaches about light and shadows**, introducing basic science concepts.
- **Encourages creativity** by transforming simple shadows into artwork.
- **Develops fine motor skills** through tracing and decorating.

Benefits for parents:

- **Requires minimal materials**, just chalk and sunlight.
- **Encourages outdoor play**, combining art with physical activity.
- **Great for family collaboration**, making it a fun, shared experience.

127. Mud Kitchen Play

A mud kitchen is an outdoor play activity that encourages imaginative, sensory-rich exploration. Children use mud, water, and other natural materials to "cook" and create in their pretend kitchen.

How it works:

- **Set up a mud kitchen:** Use an old table, pots, pans, and utensils in an outdoor space. Provide buckets of water, soil, and natural materials like leaves, sticks, and rocks.
- **Encourage pretend play:** Let your child mix the mud and natural materials to "cook" pretend meals, bake mud pies, or make potions.
- **Add challenges:** Give them fun prompts, like creating a "recipe" or preparing a pretend meal for the family.

Benefits for kids:

- **Promotes sensory exploration** through tactile play with mud and natural materials.
- **Encourages imaginative play**, allowing them to create their own kitchen scenarios.
- **Improves problem-solving** as they figure out how to mix and "cook" different materials.

Benefits for parents:

- **Simple and eco-friendly**, using natural materials for play.
- **Encourages outdoor time**, offering a healthy, screen-free activity.
- **Promotes independent play**, allowing kids to engage in open-ended, creative play.

128. Create a Leaf Rubbing

Leaf rubbing is a classic outdoor art activity that teaches children about texture while fostering creativity. By placing paper over a leaf and rubbing it with crayons, children create detailed imprints of the leaf's texture.

How it works:

- **Collect leaves:** Go on a nature walk with your child and collect different types of leaves with interesting shapes and textures.
- **Place the leaf under paper:** Back at home, put the leaf under a sheet of paper.
- **Rub with a crayon:** Show your child how to gently rub the side of a crayon over the paper, revealing the leaf's texture and shape.

Benefits for kids:

- **Teaches texture and pattern recognition**, helping them explore the natural world.
- **Encourages creativity** by experimenting with different leaf shapes and colors.
- **Improves fine motor skills** through the rubbing process.

Benefits for parents:

- **Simple setup** with just paper, leaves, and crayons.
- **Great for combining outdoor exploration with art**, making it a well-rounded activity.
- **Encourages nature appreciation**, turning a simple walk into a learning experience.

---

129. Rock Painting

Rock painting is a fun and creative activity that turns ordinary stones into colorful works of art. It's a simple craft that allows children to express their creativity while exploring the outdoors.

How it works:

- **Collect rocks:** Find smooth rocks or stones during a walk or in your yard.
- **Paint the rocks:** Provide paints, markers, and brushes for your child to decorate the rocks with patterns, animals, or faces.
- **Display or hide the rocks:** Once the rocks are dry, your child can use them as decorations, give them as gifts, or hide them in the yard for others to find.

Benefits for kids:

- **Encourages creativity** through painting and designing unique rocks.
- **Improves fine motor skills** as they paint detailed designs.
- **Promotes outdoor exploration**, by collecting rocks and using them as the canvas.

Benefits for parents:

- **Affordable and easy to set up**, with just rocks and paint.

- **Offers a versatile craft** that can be done indoors or outdoors.
- **Encourages family bonding**, especially if done together.

---

130. String Art

String art is a hands-on craft that involves wrapping string around nails or pins to create colorful geometric designs. This activity helps develop fine motor skills, patience, and creativity.

How it works:

- **Set up a board:** Use a piece of cardboard or wood and mark out a simple design (such as a heart, star, or initial).
- **Add nails or pins:** Place small nails or pushpins along the outline of the design.
- **Wrap the string:** Give your child colorful string or yarn and let them wrap it around the nails or pins to create a pattern. They can crisscross the string to fill in the design.

Benefits for kids:

- **Enhances fine motor skills** through careful wrapping and weaving of the string.
- **Teaches patience and focus**, as the activity requires careful attention to detail.
- **Encourages creativity** through designing their own patterns and choosing colors.

Benefits for parents:

- **Simple setup** with nails, string, and a board.
- **Promotes independent play** while also being a relaxing, quiet activity.
- **Great for developing skills needed for writing**, improving hand control and precision.

131. Sensory Balloon Play

Sensory balloons are a fun and tactile activity that engages children's senses by letting them squish, squeeze, and explore the different textures inside the balloons. This activity helps develop fine motor skills and sensory awareness.

How it works:

- **Fill the balloons:** Fill several balloons with different materials like rice, flour, water, sand, or beans. Be sure to tie the balloons tightly to prevent spills.
- **Explore the textures:** Let your child squish and squeeze the balloons, describing how each one feels. Encourage them to guess what's inside based on the texture.
- **Add a challenge:** Create a matching game where your child matches the sensory balloons by feel alone.

Benefits for kids:

- **Promotes sensory exploration** by engaging their sense of touch.
- **Improves fine motor skills** through squeezing and manipulating the balloons.
- **Encourages vocabulary development** as they describe the different textures.

Benefits for parents:

- **Simple to set up** with everyday household materials.
- **Mess-free sensory play**, offering tactile engagement without the cleanup.
- **Great for travel or quiet time**, as the balloons are portable and quiet.

132. Ice Cube Treasure Hunt

The ice cube treasure hunt is a fun science experiment and sensory activity where children free small objects from frozen ice cubes, teaching them about melting and patience.

How it works:

- **Freeze small toys:** Place small plastic toys, coins, or beads in ice cube trays filled with water and freeze them.
- **Start the hunt:** Once the ice cubes are frozen, give your child safe tools like plastic spoons or warm water to melt the ice and rescue the treasures inside.
- **Talk about the science:** Discuss how heat and water help melt the ice, teaching them basic science concepts.

Benefits for kids:

- **Teaches patience and problem-solving** as they figure out how to melt the ice.
- **Encourages sensory exploration** through the cold texture of ice.
- **Introduces basic science concepts**, like states of matter and melting.

Benefits for parents:

- **Inexpensive and easy to prepare**, requiring just water and small objects.
- **Engages children for a long time**, as melting the ice takes effort and focus.
- **Educational and fun**, combining science with play.

133. Create a Rain Gauge

A rain gauge is a simple weather-tracking tool that teaches children about precipitation and helps them engage with nature and science. By measuring rainfall, children can learn more about weather patterns.

How it works:

- **Make the gauge:** Use an empty plastic bottle or jar, and mark measurements on the side to track how much rain falls.

- **Place it outside:** Set the rain gauge in an open area where it can collect rain.
- **Measure the rain:** After it rains, let your child check the rain gauge and record how much water has collected. You can keep a rain journal to track how much rain falls over time.

Benefits for kids:

- **Teaches weather and science** by tracking rainfall.
- **Encourages outdoor exploration,** connecting them with nature.
- **Promotes observation and data collection,** reinforcing early science skills.

Benefits for parents:

- **Easy to create** with a plastic bottle and a marker.
- **Provides an ongoing educational activity,** tracking rain over time.
- **Great for family bonding,** as you can discuss the weather and rainfall together.

134. Marshmallow and Toothpick Building

Marshmallow and toothpick building is a creative and structural activity that challenges children to build 3D shapes and structures using marshmallows and toothpicks. It's a fun way to teach engineering and problem-solving skills.

How it works:

- **Provide materials:** Give your child toothpicks and marshmallows to use as building materials.
- **Build structures:** Encourage them to connect the toothpicks with marshmallows to create towers, bridges, or other shapes. They can experiment with different designs and see which ones are the most stable.
- **Add a challenge:** Ask your child to build a structure that holds weight or reaches a certain height.

Benefits for kids:

- **Encourages creativity and problem-solving** through building and experimentation.
- **Teaches basic engineering principles,** such as balance and stability.
- **Develops fine motor skills** as they connect the marshmallows and toothpicks.

Benefits for parents:

- **Simple, low-cost activity,** using just toothpicks and marshmallows.
- **Promotes independent play,** while also offering opportunities for teamwork.
- **Educational and hands-on,** combining STEM learning with fun.

135. Color Mixing with Water

Color mixing with water is a visually stimulating activity that teaches children about colors and how they combine to create new ones. It's a simple and engaging way to introduce basic science concepts.

How it works:

- **Prepare colored water:** Fill several clear cups with water and add a few drops of different food coloring to each (e.g., red, blue, yellow).
- **Mix the colors:** Let your child pour the colored water from one cup to another, experimenting with how different colors combine. For example, mix blue and yellow to make green.
- **Explore different combinations:** Encourage your child to guess what colors will form when mixing two different colored waters.

Benefits for kids:

- **Teaches color theory** by showing how primary colors mix to form secondary colors.
- **Encourages scientific thinking** through experimentation and observation.
- **Improves fine motor skills** as they pour and mix the water.

Benefits for parents:

- **Simple to set up with minimal materials**, just water and food coloring.
- **Educational and engaging**, introducing science concepts in a hands-on way.
- **Easy to clean up**, as it involves only water and non-toxic food coloring.

136. Sock Basketball

Sock basketball is an indoor game that encourages physical activity and coordination while being safe for indoor play. Using rolled-up socks as a basketball, kids can practice their throwing and aiming skills.

How it works:

- **Make a basket:** Use a laundry basket or box as the hoop.
- **Roll up socks:** Roll up a few pairs of socks to use as "basketballs."
- **Shoot hoops:** Encourage your child to stand at different distances and try to throw the socks into the basket. You can keep score or add challenges like shooting with their non-dominant hand.

Benefits for kids:

- **Improves hand-eye coordination** through aiming and throwing.
- **Encourages physical activity**, even in a small indoor space.
- **Boosts confidence**, especially when they successfully make baskets.

Benefits for parents:

- **Safe for indoor play**, with soft socks that won't damage furniture.
- **Easy to set up** with items you already have at home.
- **Great for burning energy**, keeping kids active indoors.

137. Create a Firework Painting

Firework painting is a fun and creative craft that allows children to make colorful artwork that mimics the look of fireworks. It's a great activity for holidays like the Fourth of July or New Year's.

How it works:

- **Prepare the materials:** Cut a toilet paper roll into fringe-like strips at the bottom to create a "firework stamp."
- **Paint the fireworks:** Dip the fringe end of the roll into paint, and press it onto paper to create a firework-like effect. Use different colors for multiple layers of fireworks.
- **Add details:** Let your child add glitter or use a paintbrush to add extra details, like stars or sparkles.

Benefits for kids:

- **Encourages creativity** by allowing them to design their own fireworks.
- **Develops fine motor skills** through stamping and painting.
- **Teaches color blending** by overlapping different colors of paint.

Benefits for parents:

- **Simple and inexpensive**, using household items like toilet paper rolls.
- **Great for festive occasions**, offering a themed craft for holidays.
- **Keeps kids engaged in artistic play**, while promoting creativity.

138. Create a Suncatcher

A suncatcher is a colorful craft that captures sunlight, creating beautiful patterns and reflections. Children can design their own suncatchers using simple materials and hang them in a window for a bright display.

How it works:

- **Cut out the base:** Use clear contact paper or wax paper as the base of the suncatcher.
- **Decorate the suncatcher:** Let your child stick tissue paper, glitter, or sequins onto the base to create a colorful design. Once they're done, cover the decorations with another layer of contact paper to seal it.
- **Hang it in a window:** Use string or tape to hang the suncatcher in a sunny window, and watch the light shine through.

Benefits for kids:

- **Encourages creativity** by letting them design their own colorful suncatchers.
- **Teaches color and light concepts**, showing how sunlight interacts with transparent materials.
- **Develops fine motor skills** through cutting and sticking the decorations.

Benefits for parents:

- **Simple setup** with affordable materials like contact paper and tissue.
- **Beautiful end result**, providing a decorative craft that brightens your home.
- **Great for holiday or seasonal themes**, adding a festive touch to windows.

139. Create a Nature Journal

A nature journal is a personalized notebook where children can record their observations and discoveries from the natural world. It's a wonderful way to encourage mindfulness, creativity, and an appreciation for nature.

How it works:

- **Get a notebook:** Provide your child with a blank notebook or journal.
- **Go on nature walks:** Take your child outside to observe plants, animals, or weather. Encourage them to draw or write about what they see, hear, or feel.
- **Document findings:** Your child can press flowers, collect leaves, or sketch animals they see, making the journal a creative and educational keepsake.

Benefits for kids:

- **Encourages mindfulness** and observation of the natural world.
- **Promotes creativity** through drawing, writing, and collecting nature items.
- **Enhances knowledge of science and nature**, reinforcing early learning.

Benefits for parents:

- **Great for outdoor bonding**, offering a shared experience in nature.
- **Encourages daily reflection**, helping kids process and understand the world around them.
- **Educational tool**, combining science with art and writing.

140. Obstacle Course for Cars

An obstacle course for toy cars is a fun and creative way for children to use their imagination while practicing fine motor skills. By building a track with obstacles, kids can test their toy cars and experiment with different challenges.

How it works:

- **Create the course:** Use blocks, cardboard, pillows, or books to create ramps, tunnels, and obstacles for the toy cars to navigate.
- **Race the cars:** Let your child push or drive their cars through the obstacle course, seeing how fast they can go or how many obstacles they can conquer.
- **Add challenges:** Set goals, like completing the course without knocking over obstacles or making it through a certain number of tunnels.

Benefits for kids:

- **Encourages problem-solving and engineering** by creating a functional course.
- **Improves fine motor skills** as they push, steer, and navigate the cars.
- **Promotes imaginative play**, allowing them to create and adapt new challenges.

Benefits for parents:

- **Simple and creative indoor play**, using household items for the course.
- **Great for sibling or group play**, encouraging teamwork and competition.
- **Provides a long-lasting activity**, as the course can be rebuilt or changed for new challenges.

---

141. Balloon Rockets

Balloon rockets are a fun, hands-on science experiment that teaches children about propulsion and movement. By creating rockets powered by air from a balloon, kids can learn basic physics while enjoying a playful activity.

How it works:

- **Prepare the materials:** You'll need a long piece of string, a balloon, tape, and a straw.
- **Set up the rocket:** Thread the string through the straw and tie each end of the string to two stationary objects (like chairs) across the room. Blow up the balloon without tying it and tape it to the straw.
- **Launch the rocket:** Let go of the balloon and watch it zoom along the string as the air escapes.

Benefits for kids:

- **Teaches basic physics concepts** like propulsion and motion.
- **Encourages problem-solving** as they experiment with different balloon sizes and air amounts.
- **Develops fine motor skills** through assembling and launching the rocket.

Benefits for parents:

- **Inexpensive and easy to set up**, requiring only common household items.

- **Educational and fun**, combining play with science learning.
- **Keeps kids entertained** as they experiment with different rocket setups.

---

142. Create a Storyboard

A storyboard is a visual way to tell a story by drawing key scenes in sequence. It encourages creativity, storytelling, and planning, helping children develop narrative skills while having fun with art.

How it works:

- **Provide a template:** Draw a series of boxes on a piece of paper or print a storyboard template.
- **Create a story:** Ask your child to come up with a short story or a sequence of events. Encourage them to draw each scene in one of the boxes, showing the progression of the story.
- **Add details:** They can add speech bubbles, captions, or character dialogue to make the story come to life.

Benefits for kids:

- **Develops storytelling and sequencing skills** through visual storytelling.
- **Encourages creativity** as they design characters and scenes.
- **Improves fine motor skills** through drawing and writing.

Benefits for parents:

- **Simple to set up**, using paper and markers.
- **Promotes independent play**, as children can work on their storyboards alone.
- **Great for teaching narrative structure**, helping with language and literacy development.

---

143. Create a DIY Abacus

A DIY abacus is a hands-on math tool that helps children understand counting, addition, and subtraction. By making their own abacus, kids can practice math skills in a visual and tactile way.

How it works:

- **Prepare materials:** Use a small cardboard frame or an old picture frame, string, and beads.
- **Assemble the abacus:** Thread beads onto the strings and tie them across the frame to create rows.
- **Start counting:** Teach your child how to use the abacus to count, add, and subtract by moving the beads across the strings.

Benefits for kids:

- **Teaches basic math skills** like counting, addition, and subtraction.
- **Enhances fine motor skills** as they move the beads along the strings.
- **Promotes hands-on learning**, making abstract math concepts more concrete.

Benefits for parents:

- **Educational and engaging**, turning math practice into a fun activity.
- **Inexpensive and easy to make**, using simple materials like beads and string.
- **Encourages independent play**, allowing children to explore math concepts at their own pace.

---

144. Alphabet Relay Race

An alphabet relay race is a fast-paced, active game that helps children practice letter recognition while improving their physical coordination. It's a great way to combine learning and movement.

How it works:

- **Prepare letter cards:** Write each letter of the alphabet on individual cards and spread them out around the room or yard.
- **Start the race:** Call out a letter, and have your child run to find the corresponding letter card and bring it back to you.
- **Add challenges:** You can increase the difficulty by asking them to find letters in order, spell words, or complete an obstacle course on the way to the letters.

Benefits for kids:

- **Teaches letter recognition** and phonics in a fun, active way.
- **Improves coordination and balance** through running and navigating obstacles.
- **Encourages teamwork**, especially if played in a group.

Benefits for parents:

- **Easy to set up**, using simple letter cards and a space to run.
- **Promotes physical activity**, helping kids burn off energy while learning.
- **Versatile and adaptable**, allowing you to tailor the difficulty to your child's skill level.

---

145. Nature Scavenger Hunt

A nature scavenger hunt is an outdoor exploration game that encourages children to observe and connect with their environment. By searching for natural items, kids learn about the world around them while developing observational skills.

How it works:

- **Create a list:** Write down or print a list of items for your child to find in nature, such as "a leaf," "a smooth rock," or "something yellow."
- **Go exploring:** Take your child outside to a park, backyard, or nature trail, and challenge them to find everything on the list.
- **Collect or document:** Depending on the items, your child can either collect the objects or take photos of them to document their findings.

Benefits for kids:

- **Promotes outdoor exploration**, fostering a connection with nature.
- **Improves observational skills** by encouraging them to look closely at their surroundings.
- **Teaches about the natural world**, including plants, animals, and ecosystems.

Benefits for parents:

- **Encourages physical activity** and outdoor play.
- **Simple to set up** with a list and a nature space.
- **Great for family bonding**, as everyone can participate in the scavenger hunt.

---

146. Create a Paper Mâché Volcano

A paper mâché volcano is a classic science project that teaches children about chemical reactions and geology. By building and erupting their own volcano, kids can enjoy a fun and educational hands-on experience.

How it works:

- **Build the volcano:** Use a plastic bottle as the volcano's core and cover it with layers of paper mâché to create the volcano's shape. Let it dry and then paint it to look like a real volcano.
- **Create the eruption:** Pour baking soda into the bottle, and add a mix of vinegar and red food coloring for the lava. Watch as the volcano erupts!
- **Discuss the science:** Talk with your child about how the baking soda and vinegar react to create carbon dioxide, mimicking a volcanic eruption.

Benefits for kids:

- **Teaches basic chemistry** through the baking soda and vinegar reaction.
- **Encourages creativity** by designing and building their own volcano.
- **Improves fine motor skills** through paper mâché construction and painting.

Benefits for parents:

- **Educational and exciting**, combining science with hands-on fun.
- **Simple to set up**, using everyday household ingredients.
- **Keeps kids engaged**, with both the building process and the eruption being equally fun.

---

147. Cardboard Castle Building

Building a cardboard castle is a creative and imaginative project that allows children to design their own castle using recycled materials. It's an engaging way to encourage problem-solving, creativity, and fine motor skills.

How it works:

- **Gather materials:** Collect cardboard boxes, paper towel rolls, and other recyclable materials.
- **Design the castle:** Help your child sketch out their castle, then cut and assemble the cardboard to bring the design to life. Use glue, tape, or string to hold the pieces together.
- **Decorate the castle:** Let your child paint or decorate the castle with markers, stickers, or fabric scraps.

Benefits for kids:

- **Promotes creativity** by allowing them to design and build their own structure.
- **Develops fine motor skills** through cutting, assembling, and decorating.
- **Encourages problem-solving** as they figure out how to create different castle features.

Benefits for parents:

- **Eco-friendly and low-cost**, using recyclable materials.
- **Encourages independent play**, with kids fully immersed in the building process.
- **Great for collaborative play**, allowing siblings or friends to work together.

---

148. Create a Moon Sand Sensory Bin

Moon sand is a fun, moldable material that feels like wet sand but doesn't dry out. Creating a moon sand sensory bin provides children with a calming, hands-on experience that engages their sense of touch and encourages creativity.

How it works:

- **Make the moon sand:** Mix 8 cups of flour with 1 cup of baby oil or vegetable oil until it has a moldable texture.
- **Set up a sensory bin:** Place the moon sand in a large container and add scoops, cups, and molds for your child to use.
- **Encourage play:** Let your child squish, mold, and shape the moon sand, using their imagination to create castles, animals, or other objects.

Benefits for kids:

- **Promotes sensory exploration** through the tactile experience of molding sand.
- **Improves fine motor skills** as they shape and manipulate the sand.
- **Encourages creative play,** allowing them to invent their own designs and scenarios.

Benefits for parents:

- **Easy to make** with simple ingredients like flour and oil.
- **Provides a mess-free sensory activity,** as moon sand is easy to clean up.
- **Great for indoor play,** offering a calming, quiet activity.

---

149. Finger Painting with a Twist

Finger painting is a classic activity, but adding a twist—like using unusual tools or incorporating sensory elements—can make it even more fun and creative. Children can explore texture, color, and movement in a new way.

How it works:

- **Prepare the paints:** Use washable, non-toxic finger paints. For added texture, you can mix in materials like sand, rice, or glitter.
- **Add a twist:** Let your child paint with not only their fingers but also other objects, like sponges, cotton balls, or toy cars.
- **Create art:** Encourage your child to experiment with different tools and textures to create abstract designs, patterns, or landscapes.

Benefits for kids:

- **Encourages sensory exploration** through tactile play with paint and textures.
- **Develops fine motor skills** through painting and manipulating different tools.
- **Promotes creativity** by allowing them to experiment with colors, shapes, and patterns.

Benefits for parents:

- **Easy setup** with minimal materials required.
- **Promotes free expression,** encouraging children to be creative without restrictions.
- **Great for both indoor and outdoor play,** making it a versatile activity.

150. Sponge Boat Races

Sponge boat races are a simple water-based activity that combines creativity and physical play. Children can build their own sponge boats and race them in a tub, pool, or large bowl of water.

How it works:

- **Make the boats:** Cut sponges into boat shapes and attach a toothpick with a paper sail.
- **Set up the race:** Fill a bathtub, pool, or large bowl with water, and place the sponge boats at the starting line.
- **Race the boats:** Use straws to blow air on the sails and propel the boats across the water. See which boat reaches the other side first.

Benefits for kids:

- **Develops fine motor skills** through building and steering the boats.
- **Teaches basic principles of movement and wind** as they use air to push the boats.
- **Encourages creativity** by allowing them to design their own boats.

Benefits for parents:

- **Inexpensive and easy to set up**, using sponges and household items.
- **Great for group play**, encouraging teamwork and friendly competition.
- **Promotes outdoor play**, especially on hot days when water activities are appealing.

---

151. Create a Salt Dough Map

A salt dough map is an educational and creative way for children to learn about geography while developing their crafting skills. By making a 3D map out of salt dough, kids can explore different landforms and geographical features.

How it works:

- **Make the salt dough:** Combine 2 cups of flour, 1 cup of salt, and 1 cup of water to create a dough.
- **Shape the map:** Roll out the dough and shape it into a map of a region, country, or world. Add mountains, rivers, and valleys by molding the dough.
- **Let it dry:** Once the map is complete, let it air dry or bake it in the oven at a low temperature until it hardens.
- **Paint the map:** Once dry, let your child paint the map to represent different geographical features like forests, water, and mountains.

Benefits for kids:

- **Teaches geography and landforms** through hands-on learning.
- **Encourages creativity** by letting them design and paint their map.

- **Develops fine motor skills** through shaping and molding the dough.

Benefits for parents:

- **Simple to set up** with basic ingredients like flour, salt, and water.
- **Combines education and creativity**, reinforcing geography in a fun way.
- **Keeps kids engaged**, as the process involves multiple steps like sculpting, drying, and painting.

---

152. Sock Puppet Theater

Sock puppet theater is a creative storytelling activity where children use handmade sock puppets to perform their own shows. This activity encourages imagination, language skills, and emotional expression.

How it works:

- **Make the puppets:** Use old socks and decorate them with markers, buttons, yarn, and fabric scraps to create unique characters.
- **Create a stage:** Set up a simple stage using a table or a cardboard box where the puppets can perform.
- **Put on a show:** Encourage your child to come up with a story for the puppets and perform it for family members or friends. They can use different voices and act out scenarios with the puppets.

Benefits for kids:

- **Encourages creative storytelling** through puppet play.
- **Develops language and communication skills** by acting out stories.
- **Boosts emotional expression**, allowing children to explore different characters and feelings.

Benefits for parents:

- **Simple and low-cost**, using materials like socks and fabric scraps.
- **Promotes independent and imaginative play**, while also offering family bonding opportunities.
- **Great for sibling collaboration**, as kids can create and perform shows together.

---

153. Sensory Walk

A sensory walk is an outdoor or indoor activity that encourages children to explore different textures and surfaces with their bare feet. It's a calming, sensory-rich experience that helps children engage with their environment.

How it works:

- **Set up the walk:** Lay down different materials, such as sand, grass, smooth stones, bubble wrap, and fabric, on the ground in a path.
- **Walk barefoot:** Let your child walk across the materials, feeling the different textures with their feet. Encourage them to describe how each surface feels.
- **Add a challenge:** For an added element of fun, you can blindfold your child and ask them to guess the material based on how it feels.

Benefits for kids:

- **Promotes sensory exploration** by engaging their sense of touch.
- **Encourages mindfulness** and focus as they concentrate on each texture.
- **Develops vocabulary**, especially as they describe the different sensations.

Benefits for parents:

- **Simple to set up** with materials you already have at home.
- **Provides a calming activity**, great for children who benefit from sensory input.
- **Perfect for indoor or outdoor play**, making it a versatile option for different settings.

---

154. Create a Story Jar

A story jar is a fun way to inspire creative storytelling by offering random prompts. Children can use the jar to come up with unique stories and stretch their imagination.

How it works:

- **Prepare the jar:** Write or print out various story prompts on small slips of paper (e.g., "a dragon that can swim" or "a lost treasure"). Place them in a jar.
- **Pick a prompt:** Have your child pick one or more prompts from the jar and use them to create a story.
- **Tell or write the story:** Let your child tell the story aloud or write it down. They can also draw illustrations to go along with their story.

Benefits for kids:

- **Boosts imagination and creativity** by providing random story prompts.
- **Improves storytelling and language skills** through narration or writing.
- **Encourages critical thinking**, as they connect the prompts to form a cohesive story.

Benefits for parents:

- **Easy to create**, using a jar and paper.
- **Promotes family bonding**, as you can take turns creating stories together.
- **Reusable**, offering endless storytelling possibilities.

155. Edible Finger Painting

Edible finger painting is a creative, sensory-rich activity that combines art with taste. It's perfect for young children who enjoy hands-on play and offers a safe way to explore painting without worrying about toxic materials.

How it works:

- **Make edible paint:** Mix yogurt or pudding with a few drops of food coloring to create vibrant, safe-to-eat "paint."
- **Set up a painting area:** Lay down wax paper or a large tray for your child to paint on.
- **Paint and taste:** Let your child use their fingers to paint, draw, and explore the textures of the edible paint. They can taste the paint as they go, making it a multi-sensory experience.

Benefits for kids:

- **Encourages sensory exploration**, engaging both touch and taste.
- **Promotes creativity** by letting them experiment with colors and textures.
- **Develops fine motor skills** through finger painting and manipulation.

Benefits for parents:

- **Safe for young children**, using edible ingredients.
- **Mess-free cleanup**, with non-toxic, washable materials.
- **Promotes independent play**, while also offering a fun family activity.

---

156. Create a Dinosaur Dig

A dinosaur dig is an exciting, hands-on activity where children excavate "fossils" from sand or dirt. It teaches patience, attention to detail, and introduces basic paleontology concepts.

How it works:

- **Set up the dig site:** Bury small plastic dinosaur toys or "fossils" (rocks or bones) in a sandbox or container filled with sand or dirt.
- **Excavate the fossils:** Give your child small tools like brushes, spoons, or shovels to carefully dig and uncover the dinosaurs.
- **Document the find:** Encourage your child to pretend they're paleontologists by drawing or labeling their discoveries.

Benefits for kids:

- **Teaches patience and attention to detail** through the careful excavation process.

- **Promotes imaginative play**, as they role-play as paleontologists.
- **Encourages scientific thinking**, introducing them to paleontology and fossils.

Benefits for parents:

- **Inexpensive and easy to set up**, with toys and sand or dirt.
- **Keeps kids engaged** for long periods, as the excavation process takes time.
- **Educational and fun**, combining science with sensory play.

---

157. Create a Chalk Mandala

Creating a chalk mandala is a calming and creative outdoor activity that teaches children about patterns, symmetry, and mindfulness. By drawing intricate designs with sidewalk chalk, kids can practice fine motor skills and focus.

How it works:

- **Draw the center:** Start by drawing a circle in the middle of the sidewalk or driveway.
- **Add patterns:** From the center, encourage your child to create repeating patterns, lines, and shapes that radiate outward, creating a mandala design.
- **Use colors and symmetry:** Teach them about symmetry by encouraging them to keep the design balanced, using the same shapes and colors on all sides of the mandala.

Benefits for kids:

- **Teaches pattern recognition and symmetry**, reinforcing math concepts.
- **Encourages mindfulness**, helping them focus on the process of creating.
- **Develops fine motor skills** through detailed drawing and design work.

Benefits for parents:

- **Simple and inexpensive**, using sidewalk chalk.
- **Promotes outdoor play**, encouraging kids to be creative in nature.
- **Calming and meditative**, offering a quiet, focused activity.

---

158. Glow Stick Ring Toss

Glow stick ring toss is a fun, active game that's perfect for nighttime play. Using glow sticks as both rings and targets, this game encourages hand-eye coordination while adding a magical glow to the activity.

How it works:

- **Create the rings:** Connect glow sticks into circles to make the rings.

- **Set up the target:** Use a glow stick bracelet or place a bottle with a glow stick inside as the target.
- **Play the game:** Let your child stand a few feet away and try to toss the glow stick rings onto the target.

Benefits for kids:

- **Improves hand-eye coordination** through tossing and aiming.
- **Encourages physical activity**, keeping kids moving and engaged.
- **Adds excitement** with the glowing effect, especially in low light.

Benefits for parents:

- **Inexpensive and easy to set up**, with glow sticks and a simple target.
- **Perfect for outdoor evening play**, adding a fun twist to a classic game.
- **Encourages family participation**, making it a great group activity.

---

159. Create a DIY Rainstick

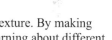

A DIY rainstick is a craft project that teaches children about sound and texture. By making their own rainstick, kids can explore the soothing sound of rain while learning about different materials.

How it works:

- **Gather materials:** Use a cardboard tube (like a paper towel roll), aluminum foil, and rice or small beans.
- **Assemble the rainstick:** Crumple the aluminum foil and insert it into the tube to create obstacles for the rice. Seal one end of the tube with tape or paper, pour the rice inside, and then seal the other end.
- **Shake the rainstick:** Let your child tilt and shake the rainstick to hear the sound of rain as the rice falls through the tube.

Benefits for kids:

- **Teaches about sound and rhythm** by exploring how different materials create different sounds.
- **Develops fine motor skills** through assembling the rainstick.
- **Encourages sensory exploration**, offering a calming, rhythmic activity.

Benefits for parents:

- **Easy to make** with recyclable materials.
- **Educational and creative**, introducing music and sound concepts.
- **Calming and meditative**, offering a soothing sensory experience.

---

160. Build a Straw Maze

Building a straw maze is a creative engineering activity that challenges children to design and construct a functional maze. By building a maze for small objects or marbles, kids can practice problem-solving and design skills.

How it works:

- **Set up the base:** Use a piece of cardboard or a tray as the base for the maze.
- **Build the maze:** Use straws, tape, and scissors to create a maze on the base. Your child can design paths, dead ends, and tunnels for the marble to travel through.
- **Test the maze:** Once the maze is complete, have your child roll a marble or small ball through the maze, making adjustments as needed.

Benefits for kids:

- **Encourages problem-solving and critical thinking** through designing and testing the maze.
- **Teaches engineering concepts** like structure and pathways.
- **Improves fine motor skills** through cutting, taping, and assembling the maze.

Benefits for parents:

- **Inexpensive and easy to set up**, using simple materials like straws and cardboard.
- **Promotes independent play**, allowing kids to experiment and adjust their designs.
- **Educational and engaging**, combining creativity with STEM learning.

---

161. Build a Paper Roller Coaster

Building a paper roller coaster is a fun, creative engineering activity that helps children explore physics and problem-solving skills. Using paper, tape, and marbles, kids can design and build their own roller coaster tracks.

How it works:

- **Create the track:** Use strips of paper to create ramps, loops, and turns. Tape them to a sturdy base like cardboard or a table.
- **Test with a marble:** Let your child roll a marble down the track and see if it makes it through the course.
- **Make adjustments:** Encourage your child to change the track to make it faster, smoother, or add more challenging loops.

Benefits for kids:

- **Teaches physics concepts** like gravity and momentum.
- **Develops problem-solving skills** by experimenting with different track designs.
- **Improves fine motor skills** through cutting, folding, and taping the paper.

Benefits for parents:

- **Inexpensive and simple setup** using paper and tape.
- **Promotes creativity and STEM learning,** combining art and science.
- **Keeps kids engaged,** as they work to improve their designs.

---

162. Create a Bubble Wrap Runway

A bubble wrap runway is a sensory and physical activity that encourages children to move while enjoying the texture and sound of bubble wrap. It's a fun way to get kids active indoors.

How it works:

- **Lay down bubble wrap:** Spread a long piece of bubble wrap on the floor to create a "runway."
- **Walk, hop, or run:** Let your child walk, hop, or run down the bubble wrap, enjoying the popping sounds and sensations.
- **Add challenges:** Turn it into a game by asking them to walk backward, balance on one foot, or hop down the runway.

Benefits for kids:

- **Encourages physical activity** in a fun, engaging way.
- **Provides sensory stimulation** through the tactile feedback of bubble wrap.
- **Improves balance and coordination** by adding different movement challenges.

Benefits for parents:

- **Simple to set up,** using bubble wrap you already have at home.
- **Great for burning off energy indoors,** especially on rainy days.
- **Encourages sensory exploration,** making it ideal for children who enjoy tactile play.

---

163. String Painting

String painting is a creative and artistic activity that allows children to explore textures and patterns using string dipped in paint. This technique produces unique and colorful artwork.

How it works:

- **Prepare the materials:** Dip pieces of string into different colors of paint.
- **Paint with string:** Encourage your child to drag or press the paint-covered string onto paper, creating swirls, lines, and abstract shapes.

- **Experiment with designs:** Let them experiment with different techniques, like pulling the string across the paper to make streaks or dabbing it to create textured patterns.

Benefits for kids:

- **Encourages creativity** by allowing them to experiment with a new painting technique.
- **Improves fine motor skills** through manipulating the string.
- **Promotes sensory exploration**, engaging their sense of touch.

Benefits for parents:

- **Simple and inexpensive**, using string and paint.
- **Great for outdoor or messy play**, encouraging kids to explore art freely.
- **Promotes independent play**, as children can create unique designs on their own.

---

164. DIY Moon Sand Letters

Creating moon sand letters is a fun way for children to practice letter recognition and fine motor skills. By shaping moon sand into letters, kids can learn through hands-on, sensory play.

How it works:

- **Make moon sand:** Mix flour and baby oil or vegetable oil to create moon sand.
- **Shape the letters:** Encourage your child to use cookie cutters, molds, or their hands to form letters out of the moon sand.
- **Spell words:** Once the letters are formed, you can help your child arrange them to spell simple words or their name.

Benefits for kids:

- **Teaches letter recognition** and early literacy skills.
- **Develops fine motor skills** through shaping and molding the sand.
- **Encourages sensory play**, making learning tactile and engaging.

Benefits for parents:

- **Easy to make at home** with flour and oil.
- **Combines learning and play**, making letter recognition fun.
- **Great for sensory seekers**, offering a hands-on approach to literacy.

---

165. Fizzy Ice Experiment

The fizzy ice experiment combines science and sensory play by showing children how baking soda and vinegar react on ice, creating bubbles and fizz.

How it works:

- **Prepare the ice:** Freeze water mixed with baking soda in ice cube trays.
- **Create the reaction:** Give your child a dropper or small spoon to pour vinegar over the ice cubes and watch the reaction as they fizz and bubble.
- **Discuss the science:** Talk about how the baking soda and vinegar create carbon dioxide, causing the fizz.

Benefits for kids:

- **Teaches basic science concepts**, like chemical reactions and states of matter.
- **Promotes sensory exploration**, engaging their sense of touch and sight.
- **Develops fine motor skills** through using droppers or spoons.

Benefits for parents:

- **Easy setup** with common household ingredients like baking soda and vinegar.
- **Educational and fun**, combining play with learning.
- **Great for independent play**, as kids can repeat the experiment themselves.

---

166. Alphabet Soup Sensory Bin

An alphabet soup sensory bin is a playful way for children to practice letter recognition and early literacy skills while enjoying sensory play.

How it works:

- **Create the soup:** Fill a large container with water and add foam or plastic letters, spoons, and bowls.
- **Play with the letters:** Encourage your child to "cook" the soup by stirring the letters with the spoon and scooping them into bowls.
- **Spell words:** As they play, help them identify the letters or arrange them to spell simple words.

Benefits for kids:

- **Teaches letter recognition** in a hands-on, playful way.
- **Promotes sensory exploration**, engaging their sense of touch and sight.
- **Improves fine motor skills** through scooping and stirring.

Benefits for parents:

- **Simple setup** with water and foam letters.
- **Combines sensory play with learning**, reinforcing early literacy.
- **Keeps kids engaged**, allowing for independent play and discovery.

167. Create a Spaghetti Tower

Building a spaghetti tower is a fun engineering challenge that encourages children to problem-solve and think creatively while constructing a tall, stable structure using uncooked spaghetti and marshmallows.

How it works:

- **Provide the materials:** Give your child uncooked spaghetti and marshmallows or clay as connectors.
- **Build the tower:** Encourage them to build the tallest tower possible using only the spaghetti and marshmallows. They can experiment with different designs and shapes for stability.
- **Challenge the design:** Add weight to the top or create a height challenge to see how tall or strong the tower can get.

Benefits for kids:

- **Teaches engineering principles** like balance, stability, and structure.
- **Encourages problem-solving** through trial and error.
- **Develops fine motor skills** as they assemble and adjust the tower.

Benefits for parents:

- **Inexpensive materials**, with spaghetti and marshmallows easily available.
- **Promotes independent play**, as kids can experiment and rebuild on their own.
- **Educational and fun**, combining STEM learning with hands-on play.

---

168. Rainbow Rice Sensory Bottle

A rainbow rice sensory bottle is a calming, visually stimulating tool that helps children explore color and movement. It's perfect for quiet time or as a calming aid.

How it works:

- **Make rainbow rice:** Dye uncooked rice with food coloring and let it dry.
- **Fill the bottle:** Layer the colored rice in a clear plastic bottle, creating a rainbow effect. Seal the cap tightly.
- **Explore the bottle:** Let your child shake, turn, and roll the bottle, watching the rice move and mix together.

Benefits for kids:

- **Provides sensory stimulation** through visual and tactile exploration.
- **Teaches color recognition** as they observe the different layers.

- **Promotes calm and focus**, making it a great tool for managing emotions.

Benefits for parents:

- **Simple and quick to make**, with rice and food coloring.
- **Offers a portable sensory tool**, perfect for travel or quiet time.
- **Encourages independent play**, as kids can explore the bottle on their own.

---

169. Shape Sorting with Playdough

Shape sorting with playdough is a hands-on learning activity that helps children recognize different shapes while enhancing their fine motor skills.

How it works:

- **Make playdough:** Use store-bought or homemade playdough in various colors.
- **Create shapes:** Roll out the playdough and use cookie cutters or molds to make different shapes like circles, squares, and triangles.
- **Sort the shapes:** Ask your child to sort the shapes by type, color, or size. They can also use the shapes to build or create patterns.

Benefits for kids:

- **Teaches shape recognition** and early math concepts.
- **Encourages sensory play**, engaging their sense of touch.
- **Improves fine motor skills** through shaping and sorting.

Benefits for parents:

- **Simple setup** with playdough and cookie cutters.
- **Combines learning with play**, reinforcing math skills in a fun way.
- **Keeps kids engaged**, offering a versatile activity with many possibilities.

---

170. Glow Stick Hide and Seek

Glow stick hide and seek is a fun nighttime twist on the classic game, perfect for outdoor evening play. The glow sticks add an exciting element as kids search for glowing objects in the dark.

How it works:

- **Activate the glow sticks:** Crack several glow sticks to activate them, then hide them around the yard or house.
- **Start the game:** Let your child search for the hidden glow sticks, collecting them as they go.

- **Add a challenge:** For older kids, add rules like only using flashlights or timing how fast they can find all the glow sticks.

Benefits for kids:

- **Encourages physical activity** and movement, especially in a group.
- **Adds excitement** with the glowing effect in the dark.
- **Teaches observation skills** through searching for hidden objects.

Benefits for parents:

- **Inexpensive and easy to set up**, using glow sticks and a dark space.
- **Perfect for evening play**, keeping kids entertained after dark.
- **Great for group play**, encouraging teamwork and friendly competition.

---

171. Water Balloon Painting

Water balloon painting is a messy, exciting art activity that combines creativity with physical play. By tossing water balloons filled with paint onto a canvas or paper, kids can create splatter art.

How it works:

- **Fill the balloons:** Fill small water balloons with water and washable, non-toxic paint.
- **Set up the canvas:** Place a large sheet of paper or canvas on the ground outdoors.
- **Toss the balloons:** Let your child throw the balloons onto the canvas, watching as the paint splatters and creates colorful patterns.

Benefits for kids:

- **Encourages creativity and free expression** through splatter painting.
- **Promotes physical activity** as they toss and aim the balloons.
- **Teaches color mixing** as the paint splatters combine on the canvas.

Benefits for parents:

- **Great for outdoor play**, with easy cleanup.
- **Exciting and engaging**, keeping kids active and creative.
- **Inexpensive setup**, using balloons, water, and paint.

---

172. Create a Leaf Maze

A leaf maze is a nature-based activity where children use leaves to design and navigate a maze. It's a creative way to explore outdoor play while engaging problem-solving skills.

How it works:

- **Gather leaves:** Collect a pile of fallen leaves in your yard or a park.
- **Build the maze:** Help your child create paths and walls using the leaves to design a maze on the ground.
- **Navigate the maze:** Once the maze is complete, let your child (or a sibling or friend) walk through it, trying to find their way to the exit.

Benefits for kids:

- **Encourages outdoor exploration** and physical activity.
- **Teaches problem-solving** by navigating and building the maze.
- **Promotes creativity**, allowing them to design their own course.

Benefits for parents:

- **Inexpensive and eco-friendly**, using natural materials.
- **Great for fall play**, when leaves are abundant.
- **Encourages family bonding**, as you can work together to build and navigate the maze.

---

173. Create a Yarn Balloon

A yarn balloon is a creative craft that involves wrapping yarn around a balloon to create a decorative hanging ball. It's a fun way for children to develop fine motor skills while making their own art.

How it works:

- **Inflate the balloon:** Blow up a small balloon to your desired size.
- **Wrap the yarn:** Dip pieces of yarn in a glue-water mixture and wrap them around the balloon. Let it dry completely.
- **Pop the balloon:** Once the yarn is dry and hard, pop the balloon and carefully remove it, leaving a hollow yarn ball.

Benefits for kids:

- **Teaches patience and concentration**, as they carefully wrap the yarn.
- **Improves fine motor skills** through wrapping and dipping the yarn.
- **Encourages creativity** by letting them choose colors and designs.

Benefits for parents:

- **Simple and inexpensive**, using yarn, glue, and a balloon.
- **Promotes artistic expression**, offering a creative craft for kids.
- **Great for decoration**, as the finished yarn balloons can be hung in a room.

---

174. Clothespin Drop Game

The clothespin drop game is a simple coordination activity that challenges children to drop a clothespin into a bottle or jar from a standing position. It's a fun, competitive game that improves hand-eye coordination.

How it works:

- **Set up the target:** Place a bottle or jar on the ground.
- **Drop the clothespins:** Have your child stand over the bottle and try to drop a clothespin into the opening from a height.
- **Add challenges:** You can increase the difficulty by having them stand farther away or using smaller bottles as targets.

Benefits for kids:

- **Improves hand-eye coordination** through aiming and dropping.
- **Encourages concentration** and focus.
- **Promotes friendly competition**, especially in a group setting.

Benefits for parents:

- **Inexpensive and easy to set up**, using clothespins and bottles.
- **Perfect for indoor play**, providing a quiet and focused activity.
- **Adaptable for different skill levels**, by adjusting the size of the target.

---

175. Windy Day Kite Making

Making a kite and flying it on a windy day is a classic outdoor activity that combines creativity with physical play. Children can design their own kites and experience the joy of flying them in the wind.

How it works:

- **Create the kite:** Use paper or lightweight plastic for the kite, attaching string and lightweight sticks for support.
- **Decorate the kite:** Let your child decorate their kite with markers, stickers, or streamers.
- **Fly the kite:** On a windy day, take the kite outside and let your child experience the thrill of flying their own creation.

Benefits for kids:

- **Teaches about wind and physics**, introducing basic science concepts.
- **Encourages creativity** by letting them design and decorate their own kite.
- **Promotes physical activity** as they run and fly the kite outdoors.

Benefits for parents:

- **Inexpensive and easy to create**, using simple materials like paper and string.
- **Great for outdoor play**, encouraging movement and exploration.
- **Fosters family bonding**, as everyone can participate in kite-making and flying.

---

176. Create a Button Collage

A button collage is a creative craft that encourages children to use different sizes, shapes, and colors of buttons to make unique art pieces. This activity helps develop fine motor skills and promotes creativity.

How it works:

- **Gather buttons:** Collect buttons in various sizes and colors, along with a piece of cardboard or thick paper as the base.
- **Create the collage:** Let your child arrange the buttons into a design or pattern on the cardboard, then glue them in place.
- **Add details:** They can add extra elements like fabric scraps, paper, or paint to enhance their collage.

Benefits for kids:

- **Develops fine motor skills** through arranging and gluing the buttons.
- **Encourages creativity** by letting them design their own unique artwork.
- **Teaches color and size differentiation** through working with various buttons.

Benefits for parents:

- **Inexpensive craft**, using buttons you already have or from old clothing.
- **Promotes independent play**, as children can create their designs alone.
- **Great for quiet time**, offering a focused, calming activity.

---

177. DIY Nature Paintbrushes

Making nature paintbrushes is a creative way for children to explore textures and experiment with art using natural materials. By creating their own brushes, kids can explore new painting techniques.

How it works:

- **Collect natural materials:** Go outside and gather materials like leaves, pine needles, grass, or small branches.
- **Make the brushes:** Attach the natural materials to sticks using rubber bands or string, creating paintbrushes with different textures.
- **Start painting:** Let your child dip the brushes into paint and experiment with how each brush creates different strokes and textures on the paper.

Benefits for kids:

- **Encourages outdoor exploration**, fostering a connection with nature.
- **Teaches about texture** through hands-on experimentation with different materials.
- **Promotes creativity** as they create their own art using unique tools.

Benefits for parents:

- **Inexpensive and eco-friendly**, using natural materials from outdoors.
- **Encourages outdoor play**, combining art with nature exploration.
- **Great for sensory exploration**, making it a calming and creative activity.

---

178. Balloon Volleyball

Balloon volleyball is a fun, safe indoor game that encourages physical activity while improving hand-eye coordination. It's a simple game that can be played with just a balloon and some space.

How it works:

- **Set up a net:** Use a piece of string or tape stretched across a room to create a "net."
- **Play the game:** Use a balloon as the volleyball and take turns hitting it over the net. The goal is to keep the balloon from touching the ground.
- **Add challenges:** For added difficulty, you can limit how many hits the balloon can take before it goes over the net or increase the distance between players.

Benefits for kids:

- **Improves hand-eye coordination** through hitting and aiming for the balloon.
- **Encourages physical activity**, even in small indoor spaces.
- **Teaches teamwork and cooperation**, especially in group play.

Benefits for parents:

- **Inexpensive and safe**, using a soft balloon instead of a ball.
- **Great for indoor play**, especially on rainy days.
- **Promotes family bonding**, as it's a fun game for all ages.

---

179. Sandpaper Art

Sandpaper art is a unique way for children to explore texture and create colorful designs by drawing on sandpaper with crayons. When transferred to fabric, the designs take on a whole new texture and appearance.

How it works:

- **Provide sandpaper and crayons:** Let your child draw on the rough side of sandpaper using crayons, creating colorful patterns or pictures.
- **Transfer the design:** Once the drawing is complete, place the sandpaper face down on a piece of fabric (like a t-shirt or pillowcase) and iron it to transfer the design.
- **Admire the art:** The wax from the crayons will melt onto the fabric, leaving behind a vibrant, textured design.

Benefits for kids:

- **Teaches about texture** and how different surfaces affect art.
- **Encourages creativity** through designing their own patterns and pictures.
- **Develops fine motor skills** through drawing on the rough sandpaper.

Benefits for parents:

- **Inexpensive and easy to set up**, using crayons and sandpaper.
- **Creates a lasting piece of art**, as the design can be transferred to fabric.
- **Promotes independent play**, allowing children to create at their own pace.

---

180. Nature Color Hunt

A nature color hunt is an outdoor scavenger hunt where children search for items in nature that match specific colors. It's a great way to combine physical activity with learning about the natural world.

How it works:

- **Make a color list:** Write down or create a chart of different colors for your child to find in nature (e.g., green leaf, yellow flower, brown rock).
- **Go on a nature walk:** Take your child outside to a park or backyard and encourage them to find items that match each color on the list.
- **Collect or document:** Your child can either collect the items (if allowed) or take pictures of them as they find each color.

Benefits for kids:

- **Encourages outdoor exploration**, helping them connect with nature.
- **Teaches color recognition** in a hands-on, engaging way.
- **Promotes physical activity**, as they walk and search for items.

Benefits for parents:

- **Simple setup**, requiring only a color list and outdoor space.
- **Great for family bonding**, as everyone can participate in the hunt.
- **Educational and fun**, combining learning with outdoor play.

---

181. Lego Challenge Cards

Lego challenge cards are a fun and creative way to encourage children to build with purpose. By drawing a card with a specific challenge, they can test their building skills and imagination.

How it works:

- **Create the challenge cards:** Write or print out different building challenges on cards (e.g., "build a bridge," "create a spaceship," or "design a zoo").
- **Draw a card:** Let your child choose a challenge card and use their Lego bricks to build the structure or scene.
- **Complete the challenge:** Once they've completed the challenge, they can share their creation or try another card.

Benefits for kids:

- **Encourages creativity and problem-solving** through open-ended building.
- **Improves fine motor skills** as they construct with small pieces.
- **Teaches goal-setting,** as they work toward completing each challenge.

Benefits for parents:

- **Promotes independent play,** allowing children to complete challenges on their own.
- **Easy to set up,** with only Lego bricks and challenge cards needed.
- **Reusable and adaptable,** as new challenges can be added for endless play.

---

182. DIY Birdwatching Binoculars

Making DIY binoculars from toilet paper rolls is a fun craft that sparks children's interest in nature and birdwatching. It's a simple project that combines creativity with outdoor exploration.

How it works:

- **Make the binoculars:** Tape two toilet paper rolls together and let your child decorate them with paint, stickers, or markers.
- **Add a strap:** Attach string or yarn to the sides of the rolls to create a strap they can wear around their neck.
- **Go birdwatching:** Take your child outside to look for birds, encouraging them to use their binoculars to spot different species.

Benefits for kids:

- **Encourages outdoor exploration** and observation of wildlife.
- **Promotes creativity** through decorating their own binoculars.
- **Teaches focus and patience,** especially when birdwatching.

Benefits for parents:

- **Inexpensive craft**, using materials like toilet paper rolls and string.
- **Promotes outdoor play**, helping kids engage with nature.
- **Great for family bonding**, especially when exploring nature together.

---

183. Puzzle Piece Art

Puzzle piece art is a creative way to repurpose old or incomplete puzzles by turning the pieces into colorful artwork. Children can paint, arrange, and glue the pieces to create unique designs.

How it works:

- **Gather puzzle pieces:** Use old puzzle pieces and provide paint, glue, and paper or canvas for the project.
- **Create the art:** Let your child paint the puzzle pieces and arrange them into a design, such as an animal, flower, or abstract shape. Glue the pieces onto the paper or canvas.
- **Display the artwork:** Once dry, you can display the puzzle art in your home or give it as a gift.

Benefits for kids:

- **Encourages creativity** by turning old puzzle pieces into new art.
- **Develops fine motor skills** through painting and gluing the small pieces.
- **Teaches problem-solving** as they arrange the pieces into a cohesive design.

Benefits for parents:

- **Eco-friendly craft**, reusing old puzzle pieces.
- **Easy to set up**, with simple materials like paint and glue.
- **Promotes independent play**, allowing children to create their own designs.

---

184. Pom-Pom Catapult

Building a pom-pom catapult is a fun STEM activity that teaches children about physics and engineering. By constructing a simple catapult, kids can explore how force and motion work.

How it works:

- **Build the catapult:** Use craft sticks, rubber bands, and a plastic spoon to create a small catapult. Stack and secure the craft sticks with rubber bands, attaching the spoon as the launching mechanism.
- **Launch the pom-poms:** Let your child place small pom-poms in the spoon and press down to launch them across the room.

- **Experiment with distance:** Encourage your child to adjust the angle or force to see how far they can launch the pom-poms.

Benefits for kids:

- **Teaches basic physics concepts** like force and motion.
- **Encourages problem-solving** by experimenting with different setups.
- **Improves fine motor skills** through building and launching.

Benefits for parents:

- **Simple and inexpensive,** using craft sticks, rubber bands, and a spoon.
- **Combines learning with fun,** offering a hands-on STEM activity.
- **Promotes independent play,** as kids can experiment with their catapult.

---

185. DIY Playdough Stamps

Creating playdough stamps is a fun way for children to explore shapes, textures, and patterns while playing with playdough. It's a creative and tactile activity that engages their imagination.

How it works:

- **Make or use playdough:** Provide your child with playdough (homemade or store-bought).
- **Create the stamps:** Use items like cookie cutters, bottle caps, or small toys to create impressions in the playdough. They can also design their own stamps by carving shapes into potato halves.
- **Stamp the playdough:** Let your child press the stamps into the playdough to create shapes and patterns.

Benefits for kids:

- **Encourages sensory play,** engaging their sense of touch and creativity.
- **Teaches shape and pattern recognition** through stamping.
- **Develops fine motor skills** by manipulating the stamps and playdough.

Benefits for parents:

- **Inexpensive and easy setup,** using common household items.
- **Great for independent or group play,** keeping kids entertained for hours.
- **Promotes creativity and learning,** combining art with early math concepts.

---

186. Balloon Hovercraft

A balloon hovercraft is a fun and educational activity that teaches children about air pressure and motion. By creating a simple hovercraft, kids can explore how air can lift and move objects.

How it works:

- **Create the hovercraft base:** Use a CD and attach a pop-top cap from a water bottle to the center of the CD with glue.
- **Add the balloon:** Blow up a balloon and twist the neck to keep the air inside. Attach the balloon to the pop-top cap on the CD.
- **Launch the hovercraft:** Release the twist on the balloon, allowing air to escape and lift the CD, causing it to glide across a smooth surface.

Benefits for kids:

- **Teaches basic science concepts** like air pressure and motion.
- **Encourages problem-solving** as they experiment with how far the hovercraft moves.
- **Develops fine motor skills** through assembling and launching the hovercraft.

Benefits for parents:

- **Simple and educational**, using household materials like a CD and balloon.
- **Promotes independent play**, as kids can experiment with different surfaces and balloons.
- **Combines fun with STEM learning**, making science engaging and interactive.

---

187. Nature Mobile Craft

A nature mobile is a creative outdoor craft that lets children collect natural materials and turn them into a beautiful hanging decoration. This activity combines art with nature exploration.

How it works:

- **Collect natural items:** Take your child on a nature walk to gather items like leaves, flowers, pinecones, and sticks.
- **Create the mobile:** Tie the natural materials to a sturdy stick or piece of driftwood using string. Arrange them to hang at different lengths.
- **Hang the mobile:** Once complete, hang the mobile outside or in a window where it can move in the breeze.

Benefits for kids:

- **Encourages outdoor exploration** and appreciation for nature.
- **Promotes creativity** through designing and arranging the mobile.
- **Develops fine motor skills** by tying and arranging the materials.

Benefits for parents:

- **Inexpensive and eco-friendly**, using natural materials from nature.
- **Great for family bonding**, especially during nature walks.
- **Encourages creativity**, offering a unique craft that combines art and nature.

---

188. Rock Balancing

Rock balancing is a simple yet challenging outdoor activity that encourages children to experiment with balance and structure. It's a calming, focused activity that also promotes creativity.

How it works:

- **Find rocks:** Gather rocks of different sizes and shapes, either from your yard, a park, or a nature walk.
- **Start stacking:** Encourage your child to experiment with balancing the rocks on top of one another, finding ways to stack them as high as possible.
- **Challenge the balance:** Add a challenge by asking your child to balance rocks of varying sizes or stack the rocks on uneven surfaces.

Benefits for kids:

- **Teaches patience and focus** through the slow, careful process of balancing rocks.
- **Encourages problem-solving** as they figure out how to balance different shapes.
- **Promotes creativity** by experimenting with rock arrangements.

Benefits for parents:

- **Simple and free**, using natural materials from the outdoors.
- **Promotes mindfulness**, offering a calming, meditative activity.
- **Great for outdoor play**, encouraging physical and mental engagement.

---

189. Create a Sensory Path

A sensory path is an interactive path made from different textures and materials that encourages children to walk, hop, or crawl through different sensory experiences. It's great for both outdoor and indoor play.

How it works:

- **Set up the path:** Use different materials like carpet, bubble wrap, foam mats, and sandpaper to create a series of textures for your child to walk on.
- **Walk the path:** Let your child explore the path by walking, hopping, or crawling across the different textures, describing how each one feels.
- **Add challenges:** For extra fun, blindfold your child and ask them to guess which material they're walking on.

Benefits for kids:

- **Promotes sensory exploration** through engaging different textures.
- **Encourages mindfulness** and focus as they feel and describe the materials.
- **Improves gross motor skills** through walking, hopping, or crawling.

Benefits for parents:

- **Simple setup,** using materials you already have at home.
- **Great for sensory play,** especially for children who benefit from tactile experiences.
- **Perfect for both indoor and outdoor play,** offering a versatile activity.

---

190. Water Xylophone

A water xylophone is a fun musical activity that teaches children about sound, pitch, and music by using water-filled glasses or bottles to create different tones.

How it works:

- **Set up the glasses:** Fill several glasses or bottles with different amounts of water, creating a range of pitches.
- **Play the xylophone:** Let your child tap the glasses with a spoon or small mallet to create different sounds. They can experiment with playing simple tunes or creating their own melodies.
- **Discuss the science:** Talk about how the amount of water in each glass affects the pitch, introducing basic sound concepts.

Benefits for kids:

- **Teaches music and sound concepts,** like pitch and rhythm.
- **Encourages experimentation** with creating different tones.
- **Develops fine motor skills** through tapping and playing the xylophone.

Benefits for parents:

- **Inexpensive and educational,** using just water and glasses.
- **Promotes creativity,** allowing children to create their own music.
- **Great for family participation,** as everyone can join in making music.

---

191. Create a Shoebox Diorama

A shoebox diorama is a fun and creative craft where children can build miniature scenes inside a shoebox, using paper, clay, or small toys to bring their imagination to life.

How it works:

- **Gather a shoebox and materials:** Use an old shoebox as the base, along with construction paper, small toys, or clay to create the scene.
- **Create the diorama:** Let your child choose a theme (e.g., jungle, city, underwater) and design the inside of the shoebox to match the theme. They can create backgrounds, characters, and objects.
- **Add details:** Encourage them to add details like trees, buildings, or animals to bring the scene to life.

Benefits for kids:

- **Encourages creativity and storytelling**, allowing them to design their own world.
- **Develops fine motor skills** through cutting, gluing, and arranging small objects.
- **Teaches planning and design**, as they organize their ideas into a 3D scene.

Benefits for parents:

- **Uses recycled materials**, making it an eco-friendly project.
- **Easy to set up with common household items** like shoeboxes and paper.
- **Keeps kids engaged for long periods**, allowing them to build their diorama at their own pace.

---

192. Baking Soda Volcano

A baking soda volcano is a classic science experiment that teaches children about chemical reactions while providing a fun and exciting visual experience.

How it works:

- **Create the volcano:** Shape a small volcano out of clay, playdough, or paper mâché, with a small container at the top for the "eruption."
- **Add baking soda:** Fill the container with baking soda.
- **Start the eruption:** Pour vinegar and a few drops of food coloring into the container, and watch the "lava" bubble and overflow as the baking soda and vinegar react.

Benefits for kids:

- **Teaches basic chemistry concepts**, like chemical reactions.
- **Encourages scientific thinking**, making it a fun, hands-on experiment.
- **Promotes sensory exploration** through the visual and tactile elements of the eruption.

Benefits for parents:

- **Simple to set up** with baking soda, vinegar, and household items.
- **Educational and exciting**, combining science with play.
- **Engages kids in a long-lasting activity**, as they can repeat the experiment.

193. Create a Water Wall

A water wall is an outdoor activity that encourages children to explore water flow and movement by creating a water system using recycled materials like bottles and tubes.

How it works:

- **Set up the water wall:** Attach bottles, funnels, and tubes to a fence or board, creating different pathways for water to flow through.
- **Pour water:** Let your child pour water into the top funnel and watch it travel down through the system.
- **Experiment with flow:** Encourage them to adjust the bottles and tubes to see how they can change the flow of the water.

Benefits for kids:

- **Teaches basic engineering concepts** like gravity and water flow.
- **Encourages problem-solving**, as they adjust the water system to achieve different results.
- **Promotes sensory play**, making it a tactile and visually engaging activity.

Benefits for parents:

- **Uses recycled materials**, making it an eco-friendly project.
- **Perfect for outdoor play**, especially on warm days.
- **Encourages independent exploration**, as children can modify the water system on their own.

---

194. DIY Pom-Pom Shooter

A DIY pom-pom shooter is a simple craft that lets children build their own launcher using household materials. It combines creativity with physical play, as they shoot soft pom-poms across the room.

How it works:

- **Create the shooter:** Cut the bottom off a plastic cup and attach a balloon to the open end. Tie the balloon's end closed, leaving the rest open.
- **Load and launch:** Let your child place a pom-pom inside the cup and pull back on the balloon. When they release, the pom-pom will shoot out.
- **Experiment with distance:** Encourage them to experiment with launching different sizes of pom-poms and seeing how far they can go.

Benefits for kids:

- **Teaches basic physics concepts**, like force and motion.
- **Improves hand-eye coordination** through aiming and launching.
- **Encourages problem-solving**, as they test different pom-poms and distances.

Benefits for parents:

- **Inexpensive and easy to make**, using common household items.
- **Great for indoor play**, as the soft pom-poms won't damage anything.
- **Keeps kids active**, promoting movement and physical play.

---

195. Create a Sensory Tray

A sensory tray is a hands-on, calming activity that allows children to explore different textures and objects. It's great for tactile development and can be tailored to different themes or seasons.

How it works:

- **Set up the tray:** Fill a shallow tray with materials like rice, sand, beads, or water beads. Add small toys, spoons, or scoops for exploration.
- **Encourage exploration:** Let your child use their hands or tools to sift, pour, and play with the materials, discovering different textures and objects hidden inside.
- **Change themes:** You can change the materials in the tray to match different seasons or holidays, keeping the activity fresh and exciting.

Benefits for kids:

- **Promotes sensory exploration**, engaging their sense of touch.
- **Improves fine motor skills** through pouring, scooping, and sifting.
- **Encourages independent play**, allowing them to explore at their own pace.

Benefits for parents:

- **Easy to set up** with inexpensive materials like rice or beads.
- **Customizable to different themes**, keeping it fresh and engaging.
- **Great for quiet time**, providing a calming, focused activity.

---

196. Ice Cream in a Bag

Making ice cream in a bag is a fun, hands-on cooking activity that teaches children about freezing and science while creating a delicious treat.

How it works:

- **Prepare the ingredients:** In a small ziplock bag, mix half-and-half, sugar, and vanilla. Seal the bag tightly.
- **Create the ice bath:** In a larger ziplock bag, fill it with ice and salt. Place the smaller bag inside the larger one and seal it.

- **Shake it up:** Let your child shake the bags for about 5-10 minutes until the mixture hardens into ice cream. Open the bag and enjoy!

Benefits for kids:

- **Teaches basic science concepts** like freezing and states of matter.
- **Encourages hands-on cooking skills**, making them part of the process.
- **Promotes sensory exploration**, as they shake the ice and feel the cold.

Benefits for parents:

- **Simple and educational**, using basic ingredients.
- **No special equipment needed**, just ziplock bags and household items.
- **Fun and tasty**, offering a rewarding treat at the end of the activity.

---

197. Cardboard Car Racing

Cardboard car racing is a fun, creative activity where children can design and build their own cardboard cars and race them down a ramp. It encourages imaginative play and problem-solving.

How it works:

- **Make the cars:** Provide your child with small cardboard boxes or tubes to use as the base of the cars. Let them decorate their cars with markers, stickers, and small wheels (or bottle caps).
- **Build a ramp:** Use a piece of cardboard or wood as a ramp for the cars.
- **Race the cars:** Let your child race their cars down the ramp and see which one goes the farthest or the fastest.

Benefits for kids:

- **Encourages creativity** through designing and building their own cars.
- **Teaches basic engineering concepts** like friction and speed.
- **Promotes physical play**, as they race and test their cars.

Benefits for parents:

- **Uses recycled materials**, making it an eco-friendly project.
- **Promotes teamwork**, especially when siblings or friends race together.
- **Great for indoor or outdoor play**, offering flexibility in setup.

---

198. DIY Story Stones

Story stones are a creative way for children to use pictures and imagination to tell stories. By painting small rocks with different characters, objects, or scenes, they can use them as prompts for storytelling.

How it works:

- **Collect and paint stones:** Gather small, smooth rocks and let your child paint pictures on each one, such as animals, trees, or houses.
- **Tell a story:** Once the stones are dry, encourage your child to pick a few stones and use them to create a story, connecting the pictures into a narrative.
- **Expand the collection:** As they come up with new ideas, they can keep adding more story stones to their collection.

Benefits for kids:

- **Encourages creativity and imagination** through storytelling.
- **Improves language and communication skills** as they narrate their stories.
- **Teaches sequencing**, helping them organize their thoughts and stories.

Benefits for parents:

- **Simple and inexpensive**, using rocks and paint.
- **Reusable**, as story stones can be used repeatedly for different stories.
- **Promotes family bonding**, as everyone can join in on the storytelling.

---

199. Make Your Own Kaleidoscope

Making a kaleidoscope is a hands-on craft that teaches children about light and reflection while creating a fun visual toy. It's a great way to introduce basic science concepts while making something colorful and interactive.

How it works:

- **Create the kaleidoscope:** Use a cardboard tube as the base. Cut small pieces of reflective paper or plastic and arrange them in a triangular shape inside the tube.
- **Add colorful beads:** Place small, colorful beads or sequins at one end of the tube, covering it with a piece of clear plastic or wax paper.
- **Look through the kaleidoscope:** Encourage your child to rotate the tube and watch the changing patterns as the light reflects off the beads.

Benefits for kids:

- **Teaches about light and reflection**, introducing basic physics concepts.
- **Encourages creativity** by designing their own colorful patterns.
- **Promotes sensory exploration**, offering a visual and interactive experience.

Benefits for parents:

- **Simple to make** with common household materials like cardboard and beads.
- **Educational and fun**, combining science with art.
- **Great for independent play**, as children can explore the kaleidoscope on their own.

---

200. Egg Carton Flower Garden

An egg carton flower garden is a simple, eco-friendly craft that lets children create colorful flowers using recycled egg cartons. It's a great way to introduce sustainability while encouraging creativity.

How it works:

- **Cut the egg carton:** Cut out individual cups from the egg carton to serve as the base for each flower.
- **Paint and decorate:** Let your child paint the egg cups in bright colors and add details like petals or leaves using construction paper or pipe cleaners.
- **Assemble the garden:** Arrange the flowers in a small box or on a sheet of cardboard to create a garden scene.

Benefits for kids:

- **Encourages creativity** through designing and painting their flowers.
- **Teaches recycling and sustainability**, using egg cartons in a new way.
- **Improves fine motor skills** through cutting, painting, and assembling.

Benefits for parents:

- **Eco-friendly craft**, reusing materials from around the house.
- **Inexpensive and simple setup**, with egg cartons and paint.
- **Promotes independent play**, as kids can create their own garden at their own pace.

---

201. Shadow Drawing

Shadow drawing is an outdoor activity that combines art and science by using the shadows of objects to create drawings. It's a creative way for children to explore light and shadow while making art.

How it works:

- **Set up the objects:** On a sunny day, place toys or objects with interesting shapes on a piece of paper outdoors.
- **Trace the shadows:** Let your child use a pencil to trace the shadows cast by the objects onto the paper.
- **Color in the drawings:** Once the shadows are traced, they can color or paint the shapes to turn them into creative characters or scenes.

Benefits for kids:

- **Teaches about light and shadow**, introducing basic science concepts.
- **Encourages creativity** through tracing and decorating the shadows.
- **Improves fine motor skills** through tracing and coloring.

Benefits for parents:

- **Easy outdoor setup**, using toys and paper.
- **Combines science with art**, making it both educational and fun.
- **Great for group play**, allowing siblings or friends to trace each other's objects.

---

202. Building a Stick Fort

Building a stick fort is a classic outdoor activity that allows children to use natural materials to create their own hideaway. It encourages teamwork, problem-solving, and physical play.

How it works:

- **Gather sticks:** Help your child collect sturdy sticks, branches, and leaves from the yard or a park.
- **Build the structure:** Let them arrange the sticks to form a frame for the fort. They can lean the sticks against a tree or create a free-standing structure.
- **Decorate the fort:** Encourage your child to use leaves, rocks, or flowers to decorate the inside of their fort.

Benefits for kids:

- **Teaches engineering concepts** like structure and stability.
- **Encourages problem-solving** as they figure out how to balance and arrange the sticks.
- **Promotes physical activity** through building and collecting materials.

Benefits for parents:

- **Free and eco-friendly**, using natural materials.
- **Encourages outdoor play**, helping kids stay active.
- **Great for teamwork**, especially when siblings or friends build the fort together.

---

203. Ice Cube Painting

Ice cube painting is a sensory art activity that allows children to paint using frozen, colored ice cubes. It's a fun, cooling activity that encourages creativity and exploration of texture and color.

How it works:

- **Prepare the ice cubes:** Mix water with a few drops of food coloring and freeze it in an ice cube tray with popsicle sticks or toothpicks as handles.
- **Start painting:** Let your child use the colored ice cubes to paint on paper. As the ice melts, it will leave vibrant colors behind.
- **Experiment with designs:** Encourage your child to experiment with different techniques, like swirling or dragging the ice cubes across the paper.

Benefits for kids:

- **Engages their sense of touch**, creating a cool, tactile painting experience.
- **Teaches color mixing**, as the melting ice blends together.
- **Encourages creativity** through exploring new painting techniques.

Benefits for parents:

- **Inexpensive and simple**, using water, food coloring, and paper.
- **Mess-free**, as the activity is water-based and easy to clean up.
- **Perfect for hot days**, offering a cooling outdoor activity.

---

204. Scavenger Hunt Bingo

Scavenger Hunt Bingo is a fun, active game that combines the excitement of a scavenger hunt with the format of a bingo game. Children search for items on their bingo cards, promoting exploration and problem-solving.

How it works:

- **Create bingo cards:** Make bingo cards with different items for your child to find, such as "rock," "flower," "bird," or "cloud."
- **Start the hunt:** Take your child outdoors and encourage them to find the items on their bingo card.
- **Call out 'Bingo!':** When they find enough items to complete a row or column, they can call out "Bingo!" and win the game.

Benefits for kids:

- **Encourages outdoor exploration** and observational skills.
- **Teaches problem-solving** as they look for specific items.
- **Promotes physical activity**, keeping them moving and engaged.

Benefits for parents:

- **Simple and adaptable**, with customizable bingo cards for any environment.
- **Perfect for group play**, encouraging teamwork and competition.
- **Combines learning and fun**, making it both educational and exciting.

205. Paper Bag Puppets

Paper bag puppets are a creative way for children to use simple materials to create their own puppet characters. This activity encourages imaginative play and storytelling.

How it works:

- **Create the puppets:** Use paper bags as the base and let your child decorate them with markers, googly eyes, fabric scraps, and yarn to create faces and features.
- **Put on a show:** Once the puppets are complete, encourage your child to use them to perform a puppet show with a story of their creation.
- **Add props:** You can also create props and a stage using boxes or other materials to enhance the puppet show.

Benefits for kids:

- **Encourages creativity and storytelling** through puppet creation and performance.
- **Improves fine motor skills** through cutting, gluing, and decorating the puppets.
- **Promotes language development** as they narrate and perform their stories.

Benefits for parents:

- **Simple and low-cost**, using paper bags and craft materials.
- **Great for quiet play**, offering an activity that can be done independently or with family.
- **Encourages family bonding**, especially when everyone gets involved in the puppet show.

206. Paper Airplane Contest

A paper airplane contest is a fun and competitive activity that encourages children to experiment with design, aerodynamics, and problem-solving as they build and fly paper airplanes.

How it works:

- **Create the airplanes:** Let your child experiment with folding different designs of paper airplanes.
- **Test the planes:** Have them fly the planes to see which design goes the farthest or flies the best.
- **Add challenges:** You can create targets or set distance goals to make the contest more exciting.

Benefits for kids:

- **Teaches basic principles of aerodynamics** like lift and drag.
- **Encourages problem-solving** as they test and adjust their designs.
- **Improves fine motor skills** through folding and constructing the airplanes.

Benefits for parents:

- **Inexpensive and easy to set up**, using just paper.
- **Great for both indoor and outdoor play**, offering flexibility.
- **Encourages friendly competition**, perfect for siblings or group play.

---

207. Nature Painting with Leaves

Nature painting with leaves is a creative and eco-friendly way to use natural materials for artwork. By using leaves as brushes or stamps, children can create beautiful and unique designs.

How it works:

- **Collect leaves:** Take your child outside to collect different types of leaves in various shapes and sizes.
- **Paint with leaves:** Dip the leaves in paint and press them onto paper, or use them as brushes to create different textures and patterns.
- **Experiment with color and shape:** Encourage your child to experiment with different leaves and paint colors to make a nature-inspired masterpiece.

Benefits for kids:

- **Teaches texture and pattern recognition** through hands-on art.
- **Encourages creativity** by using natural materials in a new way.
- **Promotes outdoor exploration**, combining art with nature.

Benefits for parents:

- **Inexpensive and eco-friendly**, using leaves and simple art supplies.
- **Encourages outdoor play**, fostering a connection with nature.
- **Easy setup and cleanup**, making it a simple art activity.

---

208. Obstacle Course with Pillows

An indoor pillow obstacle course is a simple and fun way for children to burn off energy and improve their coordination by navigating through a series of soft obstacles.

How it works:

- **Set up the course:** Arrange pillows, cushions, and other soft objects around a room to create a path with obstacles like "jump over the pillow" or "crawl under the blanket."
- **Navigate the course:** Encourage your child to jump, crawl, and balance through the course without touching the floor in certain areas.
- **Add challenges:** You can add new rules, like walking backward or balancing an object while going through the course.

Benefits for kids:

- **Improves balance and coordination** through navigating obstacles.
- **Encourages physical activity**, even indoors.
- **Promotes problem-solving**, as they figure out how to complete the course.

Benefits for parents:

- **Inexpensive and easy setup**, using household items.
- **Perfect for rainy days**, keeping kids active indoors.
- **Can be adapted for different skill levels**, making it fun for various ages.

---

209. Pom-Pom Sorting Game

The pom-pom sorting game is a simple yet educational activity where children sort colorful pom-poms into containers based on size or color, developing their fine motor skills and early math concepts.

How it works:

- **Provide pom-poms and containers:** Use small, colorful pom-poms and set out cups or bowls for sorting.
- **Sort by color or size:** Ask your child to sort the pom-poms into containers by color or size.
- **Add a challenge:** You can introduce tweezers or tongs to make it more challenging and help improve their fine motor skills.

Benefits for kids:

- **Teaches color and size recognition**, reinforcing early math skills.
- **Develops fine motor skills** through sorting and manipulating small objects.
- **Encourages focus and concentration**, making it a calming activity.

Benefits for parents:

- **Inexpensive and easy to set up**, with pom-poms and containers.
- **Promotes independent play**, keeping children engaged.
- **Great for quiet time**, offering a peaceful, focused activity.

---

210. Make a Dreamcatcher

Making a dreamcatcher is a creative and cultural craft that allows children to design their own dreamcatchers using string, beads, and feathers. It's a calming, hands-on project that also introduces them to Native American traditions.

How it works:

- **Create the base:** Use a hoop or bendable wire to form the frame of the dreamcatcher.
- **Weave the web:** Let your child use string or yarn to weave a web inside the frame.
- **Decorate the dreamcatcher:** Add beads, feathers, and other decorations to personalize it.
- **Hang it up:** Once complete, hang the dreamcatcher in their room.

Benefits for kids:

- **Teaches fine motor skills** through weaving and threading.
- **Encourages creativity** by letting them design their own dreamcatcher.
- **Promotes mindfulness and focus**, especially with the intricate weaving.

Benefits for parents:

- **Inexpensive and easy to set up**, with basic craft materials.
- **Teaches cultural appreciation**, introducing them to the tradition of dreamcatchers.
- **Calming and meditative**, making it a great project for quiet time.

---

211. Marble Painting

Marble painting is a fun and colorful way for children to create abstract art by rolling marbles through paint on paper. It encourages creativity and experimentation with movement and color.

How it works:

- **Set up the tray:** Place a piece of paper inside a shallow box or tray.
- **Dip marbles in paint:** Let your child dip marbles into different colors of paint and then place them in the tray.
- **Roll the marbles:** Have your child tilt the tray to roll the marbles across the paper, creating colorful, abstract designs.

Benefits for kids:

- **Encourages creativity** through abstract painting with movement.
- **Teaches cause and effect** as they see how the marbles create different patterns.
- **Develops fine motor skills** by tilting the tray to guide the marbles.

Benefits for parents:

- **Simple and inexpensive**, using marbles, paint, and paper.
- **Great for messy play**, offering a fun sensory experience.
- **Promotes independent play**, allowing kids to explore the art process on their own.

---

212. Paper Plate Marble Maze

A paper plate marble maze is a simple, DIY game that challenges children to navigate a marble through a maze built on a paper plate. It encourages problem-solving and fine motor skills.

How it works:

- **Create the maze:** Use straws, pipe cleaners, or string to create a maze on a paper plate. Glue the materials down to create walls for the maze.
- **Add the marble:** Give your child a marble and have them tilt the plate to navigate the marble through the maze.
- **Add difficulty:** Make the maze more complex by adding obstacles or narrowing the paths.

Benefits for kids:

- **Develops problem-solving skills** through navigating the marble.
- **Teaches fine motor control** by carefully tilting the plate.
- **Encourages focus and concentration**, especially with more challenging mazes.

Benefits for parents:

- **Inexpensive and simple to make**, using paper plates and household items.
- **Great for independent play**, keeping kids engaged.
- **Portable and easy to clean**, making it a great activity for travel or quiet time.

---

213. Sponge Relay Race

A sponge relay race is an exciting outdoor water activity that combines physical play with problem-solving. Children race to transfer water using sponges, helping improve their coordination and teamwork.

How it works:

- **Set up buckets:** Place two buckets at each end of the yard—one filled with water and one empty.
- **Race with sponges:** Give your child a sponge and have them dip it in the water bucket, race to the other bucket, and squeeze the water out. The goal is to transfer as much water as possible in a set time.
- **Add competition:** For added fun, you can compete against them or have them race against a sibling or friend.

Benefits for kids:

- **Encourages physical activity** through running and racing.
- **Teaches teamwork** if played with others.
- **Promotes coordination and problem-solving**, as they figure out how to transfer water quickly.

Benefits for parents:

- **Inexpensive and fun**, using simple items like sponges and buckets.
- **Perfect for outdoor play**, especially on hot days.
- **Great for group play**, encouraging friendly competition.

---

214. Moon Phase Chart

Creating a moon phase chart helps children learn about the lunar cycle in a hands-on, educational way. It encourages them to observe and document the different phases of the moon.

How it works:

- **Set up the chart:** Provide your child with a large piece of paper and draw circles to represent each day of the month.
- **Observe the moon:** Each night, have your child look outside to observe the moon and draw or color the corresponding phase on the chart.
- **Learn about the phases:** Discuss the different moon phases, such as new moon, waxing crescent, and full moon, as you fill in the chart.

Benefits for kids:

- **Teaches astronomy concepts** like the lunar cycle and moon phases.
- **Encourages observation skills**, helping them notice changes in nature.
- **Develops patience and focus**, as the chart is filled in over time.

Benefits for parents:

- **Educational and fun**, combining learning with hands-on play.
- **Encourages daily routines**, promoting discipline and consistency.
- **Great for family bonding**, as you can observe the moon together each night.

---

215. Balloon Rockets

Balloon rockets are a fun, hands-on science experiment that teaches children about propulsion and movement. By creating rockets powered by air from a balloon, kids can learn basic physics while enjoying a playful activity.

How it works:

- **Prepare the materials:** You'll need a long piece of string, a balloon, tape, and a straw.
- **Set up the rocket:** Thread the string through the straw and tie each end of the string to two stationary objects (like chairs) across the room. Blow up the balloon without tying it and tape it to the straw.
- **Launch the rocket:** Let go of the balloon and watch it zoom along the string as the air escapes.

Benefits for kids:

- **Teaches basic physics concepts** like propulsion and motion.
- **Encourages problem-solving** as they experiment with different balloon sizes and air amounts.
- **Develops fine motor skills** through assembling and launching the rocket.

Benefits for parents:

- **Inexpensive and easy to set up,** requiring only common household items.
- **Educational and fun,** combining play with science learning.
- **Keeps kids entertained** as they experiment with different rocket setups.

---

216. Button Sorting by Color

Sorting buttons by color is a simple, hands-on activity that helps young children develop color recognition and fine motor skills. It's a calming, focused activity that reinforces early learning concepts.

How it works:

- **Provide a variety of buttons:** Use buttons in different colors and sizes, along with small containers or bowls for sorting.
- **Sort by color:** Ask your child to sort the buttons into the containers based on their color.
- **Add challenges:** For older children, you can introduce sorting by size or shape, or create patterns with the buttons.

Benefits for kids:

- **Teaches color recognition** and early math concepts like sorting and classification.
- **Develops fine motor skills** through picking up and sorting small objects.
- **Encourages focus and concentration,** making it a great quiet-time activity.

Benefits for parents:

- **Inexpensive and easy to set up,** using buttons and containers.
- **Promotes independent play,** allowing children to explore on their own.

- **Supports early learning**, combining play with educational concepts.

---

217. Ice Excavation

Ice excavation is a fun, sensory-rich activity where children use tools to "excavate" small toys or objects frozen in ice. It teaches patience, problem-solving, and basic science concepts.

How it works:

- **Freeze small toys:** Place small plastic toys, beads, or coins in ice cube trays or a large container, fill with water, and freeze.
- **Excavate the treasures:** Once frozen, give your child tools like spoons or plastic knives to chip away at the ice and retrieve the hidden objects.
- **Experiment with melting:** You can also provide warm water or salt to help melt the ice faster, teaching them about the effects of temperature.

Benefits for kids:

- **Encourages problem-solving and patience** as they work to free the objects.
- **Teaches basic science concepts** like melting and states of matter.
- **Promotes sensory exploration**, especially with the cold temperature of the ice.

Benefits for parents:

- **Simple to set up**, using water and small toys.
- **Great for outdoor or messy play**, offering an exciting sensory experience.
- **Educational and fun**, combining science with play.

---

218. Cloud Dough Play

Cloud dough is a soft, moldable substance that's easy to make at home and provides a fun, tactile experience for children. It's perfect for sensory play and encourages creativity.

How it works:

- **Make the cloud dough:** Mix 8 cups of flour with 1 cup of baby oil or vegetable oil to create a soft, moldable dough.
- **Encourage play:** Let your child mold the dough into shapes, use cookie cutters, or build structures.
- **Add sensory elements:** You can add glitter, food coloring, or essential oils to make the dough more visually and sensorially engaging.

Benefits for kids:

- **Promotes sensory exploration** through touch and molding.

- **Encourages creativity** by allowing them to build and shape the dough.
- **Develops fine motor skills** through squishing, shaping, and cutting.

Benefits for parents:

- **Inexpensive and easy to make** with flour and oil.
- **Mess-free sensory play**, as cloud dough is easy to clean up.
- **Perfect for independent play**, keeping kids engaged for long periods.

---

219. Scavenger Hunt in Nature

A scavenger hunt in nature is an engaging outdoor activity that encourages children to explore and learn about their environment by searching for specific items.

How it works:

- **Create a list of items:** Write down or draw pictures of items for your child to find, such as a leaf, a flower, a rock, or something yellow.
- **Start the hunt:** Take your child outside to a park, backyard, or nature trail, and challenge them to find everything on the list.
- **Collect or photograph:** Depending on the items, your child can collect the objects or take pictures to document their findings.

Benefits for kids:

- **Encourages outdoor exploration**, helping them connect with nature.
- **Teaches observation skills**, as they search for specific items.
- **Promotes physical activity**, keeping them moving and engaged.

Benefits for parents:

- **Easy to set up**, requiring only a list and outdoor space.
- **Perfect for family bonding**, as everyone can participate in the hunt.
- **Educational and fun**, combining learning with outdoor play.

---

220. Glow-in-the-Dark Bowling

Glow-in-the-dark bowling is a fun nighttime activity that combines physical play with an exciting twist. By using glow sticks and water bottles, children can enjoy a glowing version of the classic bowling game.

How it works:

- **Create the pins:** Place glow sticks inside empty water bottles to make glowing bowling pins.

- **Set up the lane:** Arrange the bottles in a triangle formation at one end of a room or yard.
- **Start bowling:** Use a soft ball or glow-in-the-dark ball to knock over the glowing pins.

Benefits for kids:

- **Encourages physical activity**, especially after dark.
- **Improves hand-eye coordination** through aiming and rolling the ball.
- **Adds excitement** with the glowing effect, making it more engaging.

Benefits for parents:

- **Inexpensive and easy to set up**, using water bottles and glow sticks.
- **Perfect for nighttime outdoor play**, offering a fun twist on bowling.
- **Great for family or group play**, encouraging friendly competition.

---

221. Build a Paper Towel Roll Castle

Building a castle out of paper towel rolls is a creative activity that encourages children to use recycled materials to construct their own medieval fortress. It promotes problem-solving, creativity, and fine motor skills.

How it works:

- **Collect materials:** Use empty paper towel rolls, toilet paper rolls, and cardboard as the building blocks for the castle.
- **Construct the castle:** Let your child stack, glue, or tape the rolls together to create towers, walls, and turrets. They can cut windows and doors into the cardboard.
- **Decorate the castle:** Encourage them to paint or color the castle and add details like flags or drawbridges.

Benefits for kids:

- **Encourages creativity** and imaginative play by designing their own structure.
- **Teaches basic engineering** as they figure out how to balance and connect the rolls.
- **Develops fine motor skills** through cutting, gluing, and decorating.

Benefits for parents:

- **Inexpensive and eco-friendly**, using recycled materials.
- **Promotes independent play**, allowing kids to explore their creativity.
- **Easy to clean up**, with simple materials like cardboard and glue.

---

222. Sensory Rice Bin

A sensory rice bin is a hands-on sensory play activity where children explore different textures and objects hidden in a bin of colored rice. It's great for tactile development and fine motor skills.

How it works:

- **Prepare the rice:** Dye uncooked rice with food coloring and let it dry.
- **Fill the bin:** Fill a large container with the colored rice and add small toys, spoons, cups, or scoops for your child to explore.
- **Encourage sensory exploration:** Let your child dig, pour, and sift through the rice, discovering hidden objects along the way.

Benefits for kids:

- **Encourages sensory exploration** through tactile play with rice and objects.
- **Improves fine motor skills** through scooping, pouring, and grasping.
- **Promotes focus and concentration**, making it a calming activity.

Benefits for parents:

- **Simple setup with household materials**, like rice and small toys.
- **Great for independent play**, keeping kids engaged for long periods.
- **Easy to clean up**, as the rice can be reused for future play.

---

223. Shadow Puppet Theater

Shadow puppets are a fun, creative way for children to tell stories using light and shadow. This activity encourages imagination, storytelling, and problem-solving as they design their own shadow characters.

How it works:

- **Create shadow puppets:** Help your child cut out simple shapes or characters from paper or cardboard and attach them to sticks or straws.
- **Set up a light source:** Use a flashlight or lamp to cast a light against a blank wall or sheet.
- **Put on a show:** Encourage your child to perform a shadow puppet show, using the light to cast shadows of the puppets onto the wall.

Benefits for kids:

- **Encourages creativity and storytelling** through creating and performing with puppets.
- **Teaches problem-solving**, as they figure out how to move the puppets to create shadows.
- **Improves fine motor skills** through cutting and manipulating the puppets.

Benefits for parents:

- **Inexpensive and simple to set up**, using paper and a light source.
- **Promotes independent play**, as kids can perform their own shows.
- **Great for family bonding**, as everyone can get involved in the puppet theater.

---

224. Frozen Dinosaur Eggs

Frozen dinosaur eggs are a fun, science-based sensory activity where children "excavate" toy dinosaurs frozen inside ice eggs. It teaches patience, problem-solving, and basic science concepts like melting.

How it works:

- **Make the eggs:** Fill small balloons with water and place a small toy dinosaur inside. Freeze the balloons overnight.
- **Excavate the dinosaurs:** Remove the balloon, leaving a frozen egg. Give your child tools like spoons, warm water, or salt to melt the ice and free the dinosaur.
- **Experiment with melting:** Talk with your child about how the ice melts faster with warm water or salt, introducing basic science concepts.

Benefits for kids:

- **Teaches problem-solving and patience** through the excavation process.
- **Introduces science concepts** like melting and states of matter.
- **Provides sensory play**, engaging their sense of touch and temperature.

Benefits for parents:

- **Easy to set up**, using water, balloons, and small toys.
- **Engaging and educational**, combining science with play.
- **Great for hot days**, offering a cool and fun activity.

---

225. Color Match Game

The color match game is a simple educational activity where children match objects or cards by color. It's a fun way to reinforce color recognition and fine motor skills.

How it works:

- **Create color cards or use objects:** Use colored paper, cards, or household items in various colors.
- **Start matching:** Encourage your child to sort and match the items by color.
- **Add challenges:** For older children, you can add challenges like timing the sorting or mixing in shades to make it more difficult.

Benefits for kids:

- **Teaches color recognition** and classification.
- **Develops fine motor skills** through sorting and handling small objects.
- **Improves focus and concentration**, as they match the colors.

Benefits for parents:

- **Inexpensive and easy to set up**, using household items.
- **Great for independent play**, promoting self-directed learning.
- **Educational and fun**, reinforcing early learning concepts.

---

226. Pom-Pom Launchers

Pom-pom launchers are a fun, hands-on activity where children use simple materials to build their own launcher and shoot soft pom-poms across the room. It encourages problem-solving, creativity, and coordination.

How it works:

- **Build the launcher:** Use a plastic cup or toilet paper roll, cut a small hole in the bottom, and attach a balloon to the open end.
- **Launch the pom-poms:** Let your child place pom-poms inside the launcher and pull back on the balloon to launch them across the room.
- **Experiment with distance:** Encourage them to test different sizes of pom-poms and see how far they can launch them.

Benefits for kids:

- **Teaches basic physics concepts**, like force and motion.
- **Improves hand-eye coordination** through aiming and launching.
- **Encourages creativity and problem-solving**, as they experiment with their launcher.

Benefits for parents:

- **Simple and inexpensive**, using common household materials.
- **Great for indoor play**, with soft pom-poms that won't damage anything.
- **Keeps kids active**, promoting physical play and experimentation.

---

227. Outdoor Chalk Maze

An outdoor chalk maze is a fun and active way for children to enjoy fresh air while using problem-solving skills to navigate through a maze. It combines creativity, physical activity, and critical thinking.

How it works:

- **Draw the maze:** Use sidewalk chalk to draw a large maze on the driveway, sidewalk, or playground.
- **Navigate the maze:** Challenge your child to find their way through the maze, either walking or using a toy car or ball.
- **Add challenges:** You can make the maze more difficult by adding dead ends or creating a time limit for completing it.

Benefits for kids:

- **Encourages problem-solving and critical thinking** through navigating the maze.
- **Promotes physical activity**, keeping them active outdoors.
- **Develops creativity**, as they can also design their own maze.

Benefits for parents:

- **Inexpensive and simple to set up**, using just sidewalk chalk.
- **Perfect for outdoor play**, encouraging movement and fresh air.
- **Great for siblings or group play**, encouraging teamwork and competition.

---

228. DIY Snow Globe

Making a DIY snow globe is a fun and creative craft that allows children to design their own miniature snow globe using household materials. It encourages imagination and fine motor skills.

How it works:

- **Prepare the jar:** Use a small, clear plastic or glass jar as the base for the snow globe.
- **Create the scene:** Let your child glue a small toy, figurine, or decoration to the inside of the jar's lid.
- **Add the snow:** Fill the jar with water, a few drops of glycerin (to make the snow fall slowly), and glitter. Screw the lid on tightly and shake to watch the "snow" fall.

Benefits for kids:

- **Encourages creativity and imagination** through designing their own snow globe.
- **Develops fine motor skills** through gluing, filling, and assembling the snow globe.
- **Provides sensory stimulation**, especially through watching the glitter swirl.

Benefits for parents:

- **Simple and inexpensive**, using materials like jars and glitter.
- **Promotes creativity**, allowing children to personalize their snow globe.
- **Great for holiday or seasonal crafts**, making it a versatile activity.

229. Sensory Pasta Play

Sensory pasta play is a hands-on, tactile activity where children explore colored or textured pasta with their hands, scoops, and toys. It encourages sensory exploration and fine motor development.

How it works:

- **Prepare the pasta:** Dye uncooked pasta with food coloring or use textured pasta shapes like shells or spirals.
- **Set up the sensory bin:** Fill a large container with the pasta and add scoops, bowls, or small toys for your child to explore.
- **Encourage sensory play:** Let your child dig, pour, and sort the pasta, engaging with different textures and colors.

Benefits for kids:

- **Promotes sensory exploration** through touch, sight, and texture.
- **Improves fine motor skills** through scooping, grasping, and pouring.
- **Encourages creativity** as they use the pasta for pretend play.

Benefits for parents:

- **Simple and inexpensive**, using pasta and food coloring.
- **Mess-free and easy to clean**, as dried pasta is easy to contain and reuse.
- **Great for quiet, independent play**, offering a calming sensory experience.

---

230. Outdoor Bug Hunt

An outdoor bug hunt is a fun and educational way for children to explore nature and learn about different insects. It encourages outdoor exploration, observation, and critical thinking.

How it works:

- **Prepare a checklist:** Make a list of common bugs for your child to find, like ants, butterflies, beetles, or ladybugs.
- **Go on a hunt:** Take your child outside to a garden, park, or backyard to search for the bugs on their checklist.
- **Observe the bugs:** Encourage them to observe the insects up close, using a magnifying glass if you have one, and talk about each bug's characteristics.

Benefits for kids:

- **Encourages outdoor exploration**, fostering a connection with nature.
- **Teaches observational skills**, as they search for and study the bugs.
- **Introduces basic biology concepts**, helping them learn about different species.

Benefits for parents:

- **Simple setup**, requiring only a checklist and outdoor space.
- **Promotes outdoor play**, keeping kids active and curious.
- **Educational and engaging**, combining science with fun.

---

231. Cardboard Boat Race

A cardboard boat race is a creative and competitive activity where children design and build small boats out of cardboard and race them in water. It encourages problem-solving and fine motor skills.

How it works:

- **Build the boats:** Use small pieces of cardboard, straws, and tape to create simple boat designs.
- **Set up the race:** Fill a bathtub, kiddie pool, or large container with water and race the boats by blowing on them or using a small fan.
- **Experiment with designs:** Encourage your child to test different boat shapes and sizes to see which one moves the fastest.

Benefits for kids:

- **Teaches basic engineering concepts** like buoyancy and design.
- **Encourages problem-solving** as they experiment with different boat designs.
- **Improves fine motor skills** through building and racing the boats.

Benefits for parents:

- **Inexpensive and eco-friendly**, using recycled cardboard.
- **Perfect for outdoor or indoor play**, offering flexibility.
- **Encourages teamwork and friendly competition**, making it great for group play.

---

232. Homemade Bubble Solution

Making homemade bubble solution is a simple and fun way for children to explore outdoor play. By creating their own bubbles, they learn about the science of surface tension and have fun experimenting with different bubble shapes and sizes.

How it works:

- **Make the bubble solution:** Mix 6 cups of water, 1 cup of dish soap, and 1 tablespoon of glycerin or corn syrup in a large container.
- **Blow bubbles:** Use bubble wands or homemade tools like straws or pipe cleaners to blow bubbles of different sizes.
- **Experiment with shapes:** Encourage your child to try making bubbles with different shapes or tools and see how they behave.

Benefits for kids:

- **Teaches basic science concepts**, like surface tension and air pressure.
- **Encourages outdoor play**, keeping kids active and engaged.
- **Promotes creativity**, as they experiment with different bubble tools and shapes.

Benefits for parents:

- **Simple and inexpensive**, using water, soap, and household items.
- **Great for outdoor play**, especially on warm days.
- **Easy to set up and clean up**, making it a hassle-free activity.

---

233. Leaf Rubbing Art

Leaf rubbing art is a simple and creative way for children to explore nature and texture while creating beautiful artwork. By rubbing crayons over leaves, they can capture the intricate details of different leaf shapes.

How it works:

- **Collect leaves:** Take your child on a nature walk to collect leaves of different shapes and sizes.
- **Place the leaves under paper:** Back at home, place the leaves under a piece of thin paper.
- **Rub with crayons:** Let your child rub the side of a crayon over the paper, revealing the texture and shape of the leaf underneath.

Benefits for kids:

- **Teaches texture and pattern recognition** through leaf rubbings.
- **Encourages outdoor exploration**, fostering a connection with nature.
- **Develops fine motor skills** through rubbing and coloring.

Benefits for parents:

- **Simple and eco-friendly**, using natural materials and crayons.
- **Combines outdoor exploration with art**, making it a well-rounded activity.
- **Promotes creativity**, allowing kids to experiment with different leaves and colors.

---

234. Sensory Bottle with Glitter

A sensory glitter bottle is a calming, visually stimulating tool that helps children relax and focus. By watching glitter swirl and settle in a bottle of water, kids can use it as a mindfulness or calming tool.

How it works:

- **Fill the bottle:** Fill a clear plastic bottle with water, glitter, and a few drops of glycerin or clear glue to make the glitter fall slowly.
- **Seal the bottle:** Tightly seal the bottle with glue or tape to prevent spills.
- **Shake and watch:** Let your child shake the bottle and watch as the glitter swirls around and slowly settles at the bottom.

Benefits for kids:

- **Encourages sensory exploration**, engaging their sense of sight and touch.
- **Promotes mindfulness and focus**, offering a calming, soothing experience.
- **Develops fine motor skills** through shaking and handling the bottle.

Benefits for parents:

- **Easy to make**, using water, glitter, and household items.
- **Great for calming down**, offering a quiet, focused activity.
- **Perfect for travel or quiet time**, providing a portable sensory tool.

---

235. Toothpick Tower Challenge

The toothpick tower challenge is a creative engineering activity where children build tall structures using toothpicks and marshmallows. It encourages problem-solving, creativity, and fine motor skills.

How it works:

- **Build the tower:** Let your child use toothpicks and marshmallows to build a tower as tall as possible.
- **Add stability:** Encourage them to experiment with different shapes and structures to make their tower more stable.
- **Test the strength:** See how much weight the tower can hold by placing small objects on top.

Benefits for kids:

- **Teaches engineering and physics concepts** like stability and balance.
- **Encourages problem-solving** through experimenting with different designs.
- **Develops fine motor skills** through building and balancing the tower.

Benefits for parents:

- **Inexpensive and simple to set up**, using toothpicks and marshmallows.
- **Promotes independent play**, as kids can work on their tower alone.
- **Great for STEM learning**, combining creativity with basic engineering.

---

236. DIY Wind Chime

Making a DIY wind chime is a creative and musical activity that allows children to design their own wind chime using household materials. It encourages creativity, fine motor skills, and an appreciation for sound.

How it works:

- **Gather materials:** Use items like string, beads, small bells, shells, or metal objects to create the chime.
- **Assemble the wind chime:** Let your child tie the objects to a sturdy stick or hoop, spacing them out so they can make noise when the wind blows.
- **Hang the wind chime:** Once complete, hang the wind chime outside and listen to the sounds it makes.

Benefits for kids:

- **Encourages creativity** through designing and assembling the chime.
- **Teaches about sound and wind**, introducing basic science concepts.
- **Develops fine motor skills** through threading and tying the materials.

Benefits for parents:

- **Simple and inexpensive**, using household items like string and small objects.
- **Great for outdoor play**, as the wind chime can be enjoyed outside.
- **Promotes sensory exploration**, especially through sound and texture.

---

237. Rainbow Fish Collage

A rainbow fish collage is a creative craft that allows children to design their own colorful fish using paper, glitter, and sequins. It encourages artistic expression and fine motor skills.

How it works:

- **Cut out a fish shape:** Let your child cut out a large fish shape from construction paper.
- **Decorate the fish:** Provide materials like colored paper, glitter, sequins, and glue for them to decorate the fish with bright, shiny scales.
- **Display the fish:** Once complete, you can hang the fish on the wall or use it as a decoration.

Benefits for kids:

- **Encourages creativity and artistic expression** through designing their own fish.
- **Develops fine motor skills** through cutting, gluing, and decorating.
- **Teaches color recognition**, especially through using different colored scales.

Benefits for parents:

- **Simple and inexpensive**, using craft materials like paper and glue.
- **Promotes independent play**, as children can decorate their fish at their own pace.
- **Great for themed crafts**, especially for ocean or sea-themed lessons.

---

238. Shaving Cream Sensory Play

Shaving cream sensory play is a fun and messy activity that engages children's sense of touch while encouraging creativity. It's great for sensory exploration and fine motor development.

How it works:

- **Set up the shaving cream:** Spray shaving cream onto a large tray or surface and let your child play with it, creating shapes, letters, or drawings.
- **Add color:** You can add drops of food coloring to make the shaving cream more visually stimulating.
- **Encourage sensory exploration:** Let your child squish, swirl, and spread the shaving cream, enjoying the texture and coolness.

Benefits for kids:

- **Promotes sensory exploration** through touch and sight.
- **Encourages creativity**, as they can draw and shape the shaving cream.
- **Develops fine motor skills** through squeezing and spreading the cream.

Benefits for parents:

- **Inexpensive and simple to set up**, using shaving cream and a tray.
- **Easy to clean up**, as shaving cream is water-soluble and wipes away easily.
- **Great for messy play**, offering a fun and engaging sensory experience.

---

239. Nature Scavenger Hunt Bingo

Nature Scavenger Hunt Bingo is a fun outdoor game where children explore nature while searching for items that match pictures or words on a bingo card. It promotes outdoor exploration and observational skills.

How it works:

- **Create bingo cards:** Draw or print bingo cards with pictures or names of natural items like "leaf," "rock," or "butterfly."
- **Go on a hunt:** Take your child outside and have them search for the items on their bingo card.
- **Call out Bingo:** When they find all the items in a row or column, they can call out "Bingo!" to win the game.

Benefits for kids:

- **Encourages outdoor exploration**, helping them connect with nature.
- **Teaches observational skills**, as they search for specific items.
- **Promotes physical activity**, keeping them moving and engaged.

Benefits for parents:

- **Simple to set up**, requiring only bingo cards and outdoor space.
- **Perfect for group play**, encouraging teamwork and friendly competition.
- **Combines learning and fun**, making it both educational and exciting.

240. DIY Paper Spinner

A DIY paper spinner is a simple, fun craft that lets children create their own colorful spinning toy. It encourages creativity, problem-solving, and fine motor skills.

How it works:

- **Create the spinner:** Let your child draw or color a circle on paper and cut it out. Pierce the center with a toothpick or small stick, creating a spinning mechanism.
- **Decorate the spinner:** They can add colors, patterns, or designs to make the spinner more visually exciting when it spins.
- **Start spinning:** Encourage your child to spin the toy and watch the patterns blur together.

Benefits for kids:

- **Teaches physics concepts** like motion and spinning.
- **Encourages creativity** through designing their own spinner.
- **Develops fine motor skills** through cutting, drawing, and spinning.

Benefits for parents:

- **Simple and inexpensive**, using paper and household items.
- **Promotes independent play**, as children can design and spin their toy alone.
- **Great for quiet play**, offering a calming, focused activity.

241. Foil Boat Challenge

The foil boat challenge is a hands-on engineering activity where children design and build boats out of aluminum foil and test how many objects they can hold before sinking. It encourages problem-solving, creativity, and basic engineering concepts.

How it works:

- **Build the boats:** Let your child mold a boat shape out of aluminum foil.
- **Test the boats:** Fill a container with water and have your child float their boat. Gradually add small objects (like coins or pebbles) to see how much weight the boat can hold before sinking.
- **Experiment with designs:** Encourage them to try different boat shapes and sizes to see which design holds the most weight.

Benefits for kids:

- **Teaches engineering and physics concepts** like buoyancy and weight distribution.
- **Encourages problem-solving** through experimenting with different boat designs.
- **Promotes creativity**, as they design their own boats.

Benefits for parents:

- **Inexpensive and easy to set up**, using aluminum foil and household items.
- **Perfect for indoor or outdoor play**, offering flexibility.
- **Educational and fun**, combining STEM learning with hands-on play.

---

242. Create a Paper Mâché Planet

Making a paper mâché planet is a fun, artistic activity that allows children to create their own model of a planet. It's a great way to combine art with science and space exploration.

How it works:

- **Create the base:** Inflate a small balloon to serve as the base of the planet.
- **Apply the paper mâché:** Dip strips of newspaper in a glue-water mixture and cover the balloon with layers of paper mâché. Let it dry.
- **Paint the planet:** Once the paper mâché is dry, let your child paint the planet, adding details like craters, oceans, or rings.

Benefits for kids:

- **Teaches science concepts** like planets and space.
- **Encourages creativity** through designing and painting the planet.
- **Develops fine motor skills** through applying the paper mâché and painting.

Benefits for parents:

- **Simple and inexpensive**, using materials like balloons, newspaper, and paint.
- **Educational and fun**, combining art with science learning.
- **Great for space-themed lessons**, making it a versatile craft.

---

243. Sensory Walk with Textures

A sensory walk with textures is a fun activity that allows children to explore different textures by walking barefoot over various surfaces. It helps develop sensory awareness and encourages mindfulness.

How it works:

- **Set up the path:** Use materials like grass, sand, bubble wrap, fabric, and smooth stones to create a series of different textures on the ground.
- **Walk barefoot:** Let your child walk slowly over the different surfaces, encouraging them to feel each texture with their feet.
- **Describe the sensations:** Talk about how each texture feels—soft, rough, smooth, or bumpy.

Benefits for kids:

- **Encourages sensory exploration**, engaging their sense of touch.
- **Promotes mindfulness** and focus, as they experience each texture.
- **Improves balance and coordination**, especially with varied surfaces.

Benefits for parents:

- **Easy to set up**, using household or outdoor materials.
- **Great for sensory development**, especially for children who enjoy tactile play.
- **Perfect for indoor or outdoor play**, depending on the materials used.

---

244. Rainbow Sensory Bottles

Rainbow sensory bottles are colorful, calming tools that help children explore colors and textures while providing a soothing, visual sensory experience. They're great for quiet time or as calming tools.

How it works:

- **Fill the bottle:** Layer different colors of rice, water beads, or small colored objects inside a clear plastic bottle.
- **Seal the bottle:** Secure the cap tightly to prevent spills, using glue if necessary.
- **Shake and explore:** Let your child shake, roll, or turn the bottle, watching the colors mix and settle.

Benefits for kids:

- **Teaches color recognition** in a fun, hands-on way.
- **Encourages sensory exploration**, engaging their sight and touch.
- **Promotes calm and focus**, offering a soothing, visual experience.

Benefits for parents:

- **Easy to make**, using household items like rice or beads.

- **Portable and quiet**, making it perfect for travel or quiet time.
- **Mess-free sensory play**, with the materials contained inside the bottle.

---

245. Salt Dough Ornaments

Salt dough ornaments are a creative craft that allows children to make their own personalized ornaments or decorations using a simple salt dough recipe. It encourages creativity and fine motor skills.

How it works:

- **Make the dough:** Mix 2 cups of flour, 1 cup of salt, and 1 cup of water to create the dough.
- **Shape the ornaments:** Let your child shape the dough into different forms, using cookie cutters or their hands to create stars, hearts, or other designs.
- **Bake and decorate:** Bake the ornaments in the oven at a low temperature until hard, then paint or decorate them with markers, glitter, or stickers.

Benefits for kids:

- **Encourages creativity**, allowing them to design and decorate their own ornaments.
- **Teaches basic crafting skills** like rolling, cutting, and decorating.
- **Improves fine motor skills** through shaping and painting the dough.

Benefits for parents:

- **Inexpensive and easy to make**, using common kitchen ingredients.
- **Great for seasonal crafts**, especially around holidays.
- **Keeps kids engaged for a long time**, with multiple steps in the process.

---

246. Ice Block Painting

Ice block painting is a fun and sensory-rich activity where children paint on large blocks of ice, watching the colors melt and blend together. It's a cooling, creative outdoor activity perfect for warm days.

How it works:

- **Prepare the ice block:** Freeze water in a large container to create a big block of ice.
- **Paint on the ice:** Let your child use washable paints or food coloring to paint directly onto the ice block.
- **Watch the colors mix:** As the ice melts, the colors will blend, creating a unique piece of art.

Benefits for kids:

- **Encourages sensory exploration**, engaging touch and sight.
- **Teaches color mixing** as the paints blend together on the melting ice.
- **Provides a cooling sensory experience**, especially on hot days.

Benefits for parents:

- **Simple setup**, using water and paint.
- **Perfect for outdoor play**, keeping the mess outside.
- **Engaging and educational**, combining sensory play with art.

---

247. DIY Rain Cloud in a Jar

The rain cloud in a jar experiment is a fun and educational activity that teaches children about weather and how rain forms in clouds. It's a simple science experiment that also provides visual sensory stimulation.

How it works:

- **Prepare the jar:** Fill a clear jar with water, leaving space at the top.
- **Create the cloud:** Add shaving cream on top of the water to represent the cloud.
- **Make it rain:** Drop blue food coloring onto the shaving cream, and watch as it filters through the "cloud" and into the water like rain.

Benefits for kids:

- **Teaches basic science concepts** like weather and precipitation.
- **Encourages curiosity** and scientific thinking through observation.
- **Promotes sensory exploration**, engaging sight and touch.

Benefits for parents:

- **Inexpensive and easy to set up**, using water, shaving cream, and food coloring.
- **Combines science with play**, making it both educational and fun.
- **Great for quiet time**, offering a calming, focused activity.

---

248. DIY Sock Puppets

Sock puppets are a classic, creative craft that allows children to design their own characters using old socks, fabric, and craft supplies. It encourages imaginative play, storytelling, and fine motor skills.

How it works:

- **Make the puppet:** Use an old sock as the base, and let your child decorate it with googly eyes, yarn for hair, and fabric scraps for clothing.

- **Create a puppet show:** Once the puppet is complete, encourage your child to put on a show, using different voices and personalities for their puppet.
- **Add props:** You can create a simple puppet theater using a cardboard box and let your child perform their show for the family.

Benefits for kids:

- **Encourages creativity and storytelling**, allowing them to create their own characters.
- **Improves fine motor skills** through decorating and handling the puppets.
- **Promotes emotional expression**, as they act out different roles and scenarios.

Benefits for parents:

- **Inexpensive and eco-friendly**, using old socks and simple craft materials.
- **Promotes family bonding**, especially when putting on a puppet show together.
- **Great for quiet play**, encouraging imaginative and independent play.

---

249. DIY Magnetic Fishing Game

A magnetic fishing game is a fun, homemade game that helps children practice fine motor skills and hand-eye coordination by "fishing" for magnetic objects. It also introduces basic physics concepts like magnetism.

How it works:

- **Create the fish:** Cut out fish shapes from paper or cardboard and attach a small metal paperclip to each fish.
- **Make the fishing rod:** Tie a string to a stick or dowel, and attach a magnet to the end of the string.
- **Go fishing:** Place the fish in a shallow container or on the floor, and let your child use the magnetic fishing rod to "catch" the fish.

Benefits for kids:

- **Teaches basic physics concepts** like magnetism.
- **Improves hand-eye coordination** through aiming and catching the fish.
- **Encourages creativity**, especially if they decorate the fish themselves.

Benefits for parents:

- **Inexpensive and simple to make**, using household materials like paper and magnets.
- **Great for indoor play**, offering a quiet, focused activity.
- **Perfect for group play**, encouraging friendly competition.

---

250. DIY Lava Lamp

A homemade lava lamp is a fun and visually stimulating activity that teaches children about liquid density and chemical reactions. It's a great way to combine art and science.

How it works:

- **Prepare the lamp:** Fill a clear plastic bottle with water, vegetable oil, and a few drops of food coloring.
- **Create the reaction:** Drop an antacid tablet into the bottle and watch as the colored water moves up and down through the oil like a lava lamp.
- **Experiment with different colors:** Let your child try different food coloring combinations to create new effects.

Benefits for kids:

- **Teaches science concepts** like density and chemical reactions.
- **Encourages sensory exploration**, engaging sight and movement.
- **Promotes curiosity and experimentation**, allowing them to test different colors.

Benefits for parents:

- **Inexpensive and easy to make**, using common household ingredients.
- **Great for science-themed play**, combining fun with learning.
- **Engaging and calming**, offering a soothing visual experience.

---

251. Flower Pressing

Flower pressing is a timeless craft that teaches children about nature and preservation. By pressing flowers, they can create beautiful art while learning about different plants and flowers.

How it works:

- **Collect flowers:** Take your child on a nature walk to collect small flowers or leaves.
- **Press the flowers:** Place the flowers between sheets of paper inside a heavy book. Let them sit for a few days to flatten and dry.
- **Create art:** Once the flowers are dry, let your child glue them onto paper or use them to create bookmarks or cards.

Benefits for kids:

- **Teaches about nature and plant life**, introducing basic botany.
- **Encourages creativity**, as they design art with the pressed flowers.
- **Promotes patience**, as they wait for the flowers to dry.

Benefits for parents:

- **Simple and eco-friendly**, using natural materials from outdoors.
- **Great for quiet play**, providing a focused, creative activity.
- **Educational and fun**, combining nature exploration with art.

---

252. DIY Kaleidoscope

Making a kaleidoscope is a hands-on craft that teaches children about light and reflection while creating a fun visual toy. It's a great way to introduce basic science concepts while making something colorful and interactive.

How it works:

- **Create the kaleidoscope:** Use a cardboard tube as the base. Cut small pieces of reflective paper or plastic and arrange them in a triangular shape inside the tube.
- **Add colorful beads:** Place small, colorful beads or sequins at one end of the tube, covering it with a piece of clear plastic or wax paper.
- **Look through the kaleidoscope:** Encourage your child to rotate the tube and watch the changing patterns as the light reflects off the beads.

Benefits for kids:

- **Teaches about light and reflection**, introducing basic physics concepts.
- **Encourages creativity** by designing their own colorful patterns.
- **Promotes sensory exploration**, offering a visual and interactive experience.

Benefits for parents:

- **Simple to make** with common household materials like cardboard and beads.
- **Educational and fun**, combining science with art.
- **Great for independent play**, as children can explore the kaleidoscope on their own.

---

253. String Art for Kids

String art is a creative, hands-on activity that allows children to create designs using string and nails or pins on a board. It helps develop fine motor skills, creativity, and patience.

How it works:

- **Set up the board:** Provide a piece of cardboard or wood and let your child hammer small nails or pushpins in the shape of a simple design, like a heart or star.
- **Create the string art:** Let your child wrap colorful string around the nails to form the design, crisscrossing the string to fill in the shape.
- **Experiment with colors and patterns:** Encourage them to use different colors of string to create a vibrant, layered effect.

Benefits for kids:

- **Teaches patience and fine motor skills** through string wrapping and nail placement.
- **Encourages creativity**, as they design and create their own art.
- **Develops problem-solving skills**, especially in deciding how to wrap the string for the best effect.

Benefits for parents:

- **Inexpensive and simple**, using string, cardboard, and nails or pins.
- **Great for independent or group play**, allowing for collaboration.
- **Promotes artistic expression**, making it a versatile craft.

---

254. Paper Airplane Landing Game

A paper airplane landing game is a fun, active way for children to experiment with paper airplane designs while practicing their aim and coordination. It combines creativity, problem-solving, and physical play.

How it works:

- **Make the airplanes:** Let your child fold and decorate paper airplanes.
- **Create landing zones:** Set up landing zones using hoops, baskets, or pieces of paper on the floor, assigning different point values to each zone.
- **Start flying:** Have your child aim their airplane at the landing zones and see how many points they can score.

Benefits for kids:

- **Encourages creativity**, as they experiment with different airplane designs.
- **Improves hand-eye coordination** through aiming and flying.
- **Promotes problem-solving**, as they adjust their designs for better flight.

Benefits for parents:

- **Inexpensive and simple to set up**, using paper and household items.
- **Great for indoor or outdoor play**, offering flexibility.
- **Encourages friendly competition**, perfect for siblings or friends.

---

255. Sock Bowling

Sock bowling is a fun, indoor activity that turns rolled-up socks into bowling balls and plastic cups or bottles into pins. It's a simple, active game that promotes coordination and physical play.

How it works:

- **Set up the pins:** Use plastic cups or empty water bottles as the bowling pins, arranging them in a triangle formation.
- **Roll the socks:** Roll up a pair of socks into a ball and let your child "bowl" by rolling the sock ball toward the pins.
- **Score the game:** You can keep score, awarding points for each pin knocked down, just like a traditional bowling game.

Benefits for kids:

- **Improves hand-eye coordination** through aiming and rolling.
- **Encourages physical activity**, especially for indoor play.
- **Teaches basic math skills**, like counting and keeping score.

Benefits for parents:

- **Inexpensive and easy to set up**, using socks and household items.
- **Perfect for indoor play**, keeping kids active and entertained.
- **Encourages family bonding**, especially if everyone participates.

---

256. Glow Stick Tic-Tac-Toe

Glow stick tic-tac-toe is a simple nighttime version of the classic game, where children use glowing sticks to create the grid and play the game with different colors. It's a fun twist on tic-tac-toe that also encourages outdoor play after dark.

How it works:

- **Create the grid:** Use glow sticks to form a large tic-tac-toe grid on the ground or table.
- **Play the game:** Use two different colors of glow sticks for Xs and Os, and take turns placing the glow sticks on the grid.
- **Enjoy the glow:** Play the game in low light or darkness to enjoy the glowing effect.

Benefits for kids:

- **Encourages problem-solving** and strategic thinking through playing tic-tac-toe.
- **Adds excitement** with the glowing effect, making it more engaging.
- **Promotes outdoor play**, especially after dark.

Benefits for parents:

- **Inexpensive and easy to set up**, using glow sticks.
- **Perfect for nighttime play**, adding a fun twist to a classic game.
- **Great for group play**, encouraging teamwork and competition.

---

257. Musical Water Jars

Musical water jars is an easy, hands-on activity where children experiment with sound by filling jars with different levels of water and tapping them to create music. It's a simple introduction to musical concepts and sound exploration.

How it works:

- **Set up the jars:** Fill several glass jars with different levels of water, creating a range of pitches.
- **Make music:** Let your child tap the jars with a spoon or small mallet, experimenting with different sounds and rhythms.
- **Discuss the science:** Talk about how the amount of water in each jar changes the pitch of the sound.

Benefits for kids:

- **Teaches basic musical concepts** like pitch and rhythm.
- **Encourages creativity**, as they experiment with making different sounds.
- **Promotes sensory exploration**, especially through sound and sight.

Benefits for parents:

- **Inexpensive and simple to set up**, using water and jars.
- **Educational and fun**, combining music with science learning.
- **Perfect for quiet play**, as the sounds are soft and calming.

---

258. DIY Scratch Art

DIY scratch art is a creative craft where children make their own scratch-off designs by covering a colored surface with black paint and scratching off designs to reveal the colors underneath. It encourages artistic expression and fine motor skills.

How it works:

- **Create the base:** Let your child color a piece of paper with bright crayons, covering the entire surface.
- **Paint over the colors:** Paint over the crayon with black acrylic paint or a mixture of dish soap and black paint.
- **Scratch the design:** Once dry, let your child use a toothpick or other tool to scratch designs into the paint, revealing the colors underneath.

Benefits for kids:

- **Encourages creativity** through designing their own artwork.
- **Teaches fine motor skills**, especially in controlling the scratching tool.
- **Provides a sensory art experience**, combining texture and color.

Benefits for parents:

- **Inexpensive and easy to make**, using crayons, paint, and paper.
- **Great for independent play**, allowing children to explore their creativity.
- **Mess-free once dry**, making it easy to clean up after play.

---

259. Miniature Garden

Creating a miniature garden is a fun, hands-on project where children design their own tiny garden using small plants, pebbles, and miniature decorations. It encourages creativity, responsibility, and an appreciation for nature.

How it works:

- **Set up the garden:** Use a shallow container or planter as the base. Let your child arrange small plants, soil, and pebbles to create a miniature landscape.
- **Add decorations:** They can add small toys, fairy houses, or other miniature items to personalize their garden.
- **Care for the garden:** Teach your child how to water and care for their plants, introducing them to gardening basics.

Benefits for kids:

- **Encourages responsibility**, especially in caring for the plants.
- **Teaches basic gardening skills** like planting and watering.
- **Promotes creativity**, as they design their own miniature landscape.

Benefits for parents:

- **Eco-friendly and educational**, teaching kids about nature and plants.
- **Great for outdoor play**, encouraging time in the garden.
- **Promotes family bonding**, especially when designing the garden together.

---

260. Obstacle Course for Toy Cars

An obstacle course for toy cars is a fun and creative way for children to use their imagination while practicing fine motor skills. By building a track with obstacles, kids can test their toy cars and experiment with different challenges.

How it works:

- **Create the course:** Use blocks, cardboard, pillows, or books to create ramps, tunnels, and obstacles for the toy cars to navigate.
- **Test the cars:** Let your child push their cars through the course, experimenting with different paths and obstacles.

- **Add challenges:** You can add time limits or new obstacles to make the course more difficult.

Benefits for kids:

- **Encourages problem-solving** as they navigate the toy cars through obstacles.
- **Promotes creativity** in designing and building the course.
- **Develops fine motor skills** through handling and pushing the cars.

Benefits for parents:

- **Inexpensive and simple to set up**, using household items.
- **Great for independent play**, allowing children to experiment with their course.
- **Encourages physical activity**, as kids move around the room to complete the course.

---

261. DIY Nature Paintbrushes

Making nature paintbrushes is a creative way for children to explore textures and experiment with art using natural materials. By creating their own brushes, kids can explore new painting techniques.

How it works:

- **Collect natural materials:** Go outside and gather materials like leaves, pine needles, grass, or small branches.
- **Make the brushes:** Attach the natural materials to sticks using rubber bands or string, creating paintbrushes with different textures.
- **Start painting:** Let your child dip the brushes into paint and experiment with how each brush creates different strokes and textures on the paper.

Benefits for kids:

- **Encourages outdoor exploration**, fostering a connection with nature.
- **Teaches about texture** through hands-on experimentation with different materials.
- **Promotes creativity** as they create their own art using unique tools.

Benefits for parents:

- **Inexpensive and eco-friendly**, using natural materials from outdoors.
- **Encourages outdoor play**, combining art with nature exploration.
- **Great for sensory exploration**, making it a calming and creative activity.

---

262. Pom-Pom Drop Game

The pom-pom drop game is a simple yet engaging activity where children drop pom-poms into tubes or containers, practicing hand-eye coordination and fine motor skills.

How it works:

- **Set up the tubes:** Attach cardboard tubes (toilet paper rolls or paper towel rolls) vertically to a wall or a large piece of cardboard.
- **Drop the pom-poms:** Let your child drop small pom-poms into the top of the tubes and watch them come out the bottom.
- **Add a challenge:** For older children, you can make it more challenging by labeling the tubes with different point values or by timing how fast they can drop all the pom-poms.

Benefits for kids:

- **Improves hand-eye coordination** as they aim and drop the pom-poms.
- **Develops fine motor skills** through grasping and dropping.
- **Encourages focus and patience**, especially when adding challenges.

Benefits for parents:

- **Inexpensive and simple to set up**, using cardboard tubes and pom-poms.
- **Perfect for quiet, independent play**, offering a calming activity.
- **Promotes creativity**, as kids can also decorate the tubes or arrange them in patterns.

---

263. DIY Bubble Wands

Creating DIY bubble wands is a creative, hands-on activity where children design their own wands to blow bubbles, encouraging fine motor skills and creativity.

How it works:

- **Create the wands:** Use pipe cleaners or wire to shape bubble wands into different forms like circles, hearts, or stars.
- **Mix bubble solution:** Make homemade bubble solution using 6 cups of water, 1 cup of dish soap, and 1 tablespoon of glycerin or corn syrup.
- **Blow bubbles:** Let your child dip their custom-made wands into the solution and blow bubbles of different sizes and shapes.

Benefits for kids:

- **Encourages creativity** as they design and shape their wands.
- **Improves fine motor skills** through twisting wire and blowing bubbles.
- **Promotes outdoor play**, especially on warm days.

Benefits for parents:

- **Inexpensive and easy to make**, using household items like pipe cleaners.

- **Mess-free and fun**, making bubbles is easy to clean up.
- **Great for group play**, as kids can share their wands and bubble-making techniques.

---

264. DIY Pinwheel

Making a DIY pinwheel is a fun and simple craft that introduces children to wind and movement. It's a great hands-on project that combines art and science.

How it works:

- **Create the pinwheel:** Let your child color or decorate a square piece of paper. Cut slits from each corner toward the center and fold the edges inward to form the pinwheel.
- **Attach to a stick:** Use a pushpin to attach the center of the pinwheel to a stick or pencil, allowing it to spin freely.
- **Watch it spin:** Take the pinwheel outside on a windy day or blow on it to see it spin.

Benefits for kids:

- **Teaches basic physics concepts** like wind and motion.
- **Encourages creativity** through decorating their own pinwheel.
- **Develops fine motor skills** through cutting, folding, and attaching.

Benefits for parents:

- **Simple and inexpensive**, using paper and household items.
- **Great for outdoor play**, encouraging movement and exploration.
- **Promotes STEM learning**, combining art with basic science.

---

265. Sticky Note Matching Game

The sticky note matching game is a simple educational activity that helps children practice memory skills, color recognition, and matching while having fun.

How it works:

- **Set up the game:** Write numbers, letters, or draw pictures on sticky notes and place them face-down on a flat surface.
- **Start matching:** Let your child turn over two sticky notes at a time, trying to find a matching pair.
- **Add a challenge:** For older kids, you can increase the number of notes or use sight words to add a literacy component.

Benefits for kids:

- **Teaches memory and matching skills**, reinforcing cognitive development.
- **Encourages focus and concentration** through the matching process.
- **Reinforces literacy and math skills**, depending on the content on the notes.

Benefits for parents:

- **Inexpensive and easy to set up**, using sticky notes and simple drawings or words.
- **Great for quiet play**, helping children develop memory skills in a fun way.
- **Perfect for siblings or group play**, encouraging friendly competition.

---

266. Jelly Bean Sorting Game

The jelly bean sorting game is a fun, hands-on activity that teaches children about colors, counting, and fine motor skills. It's also a tasty way to engage kids in learning.

How it works:

- **Provide the jelly beans:** Give your child a small bowl of jelly beans in various colors.
- **Sort by color:** Ask them to sort the jelly beans by color into different containers.
- **Count the beans:** For older children, you can also have them count how many of each color they have, teaching them basic math skills.

Benefits for kids:

- **Teaches color recognition** and counting in a hands-on way.
- **Develops fine motor skills** through picking up and sorting the jelly beans.
- **Promotes focus and concentration**, especially when sorting and counting.

Benefits for parents:

- **Simple and inexpensive**, using jelly beans or other small candies.
- **Great for reinforcing math and color concepts**, making learning fun.
- **A sweet reward at the end**, as kids can enjoy their jelly beans after sorting.

---

267. Alphabet Treasure Hunt

The alphabet treasure hunt is an exciting, interactive way for children to practice letter recognition while engaging in a physical activity. It encourages movement and early literacy skills.

How it works:

- **Set up the treasure hunt:** Hide alphabet cards or objects that start with each letter of the alphabet around the house or yard.

- **Start the hunt:** Give your child clues or a list of letters they need to find and send them on a treasure hunt.
- **Identify the letters:** As they find each item, have them identify the letter or sound that goes with it.

Benefits for kids:

- **Teaches letter recognition** and early literacy skills in a fun, interactive way.
- **Encourages physical activity**, combining learning with movement.
- **Promotes problem-solving** as they figure out where the treasures are hidden.

Benefits for parents:

- **Inexpensive and simple to set up**, using alphabet cards or toys.
- **Perfect for indoor or outdoor play**, offering flexibility in location.
- **Great for family bonding**, especially when siblings or parents join in the hunt.

---

268. Tissue Paper Collage

A tissue paper collage is a creative art project where children use colorful tissue paper to make layered designs. It encourages fine motor development, creativity, and sensory exploration.

How it works:

- **Set up the materials:** Provide your child with colorful tissue paper, glue, and a large piece of paper or cardboard as the base.
- **Tear and arrange the tissue paper:** Let your child tear or cut the tissue paper into pieces and arrange them on the base to create patterns or pictures.
- **Glue it down:** Once they're happy with the design, they can glue the tissue paper pieces in place.

Benefits for kids:

- **Encourages creativity** through designing their own collage.
- **Develops fine motor skills** through tearing, cutting, and gluing.
- **Provides sensory exploration**, especially with the texture of tissue paper.

Benefits for parents:

- **Simple and inexpensive**, using tissue paper and basic art supplies.
- **Great for independent play**, allowing children to explore their creativity at their own pace.
- **Promotes creativity**, with endless design possibilities.

---

269. Sock Matching Game

The sock matching game is a fun and practical activity that helps children practice matching skills while also assisting with chores. It's a great way to combine play with responsibility.

How it works:

- **Gather the socks:** Provide your child with a pile of clean, unmatched socks.
- **Start matching:** Ask them to find the matching pairs and fold them together.
- **Add a challenge:** For older children, you can time them to see how quickly they can match all the socks.

Benefits for kids:

- **Teaches matching and sorting skills**, which are early math concepts.
- **Develops fine motor skills** through folding and handling the socks.
- **Encourages responsibility**, as they help with household chores.

Benefits for parents:

- **No special materials needed**, just clean socks.
- **Promotes family involvement**, making chores more fun.
- **Great for independent or group play**, especially with siblings.

---

270. Shape Scavenger Hunt

A shape scavenger hunt is a fun way for children to practice shape recognition while exploring their environment. It encourages movement, problem-solving, and early math skills.

How it works:

- **Create a shape list:** Write or draw pictures of shapes (circle, square, triangle, etc.) on a piece of paper.
- **Start the hunt:** Ask your child to find objects around the house or yard that match each shape on the list.
- **Identify and discuss:** As they find each shape, talk about where they found it and how it fits the shape category.

Benefits for kids:

- **Teaches shape recognition**, reinforcing early math skills.
- **Encourages problem-solving** as they search for the correct shapes.
- **Promotes physical activity**, combining learning with movement.

Benefits for parents:

- **Inexpensive and simple to set up**, using a list and household objects.

- **Perfect for indoor or outdoor play**, offering flexibility.
- **Great for family bonding**, as everyone can join in the search.

---

271. DIY Binoculars

Making DIY binoculars is a creative craft that sparks children's interest in nature and exploration. It's a simple project that combines creativity with outdoor play.

How it works:

- **Make the binoculars:** Use two toilet paper rolls or cut a paper towel roll in half. Tape or glue the two rolls together to create binoculars.
- **Decorate the binoculars:** Let your child decorate their binoculars with paint, markers, or stickers.
- **Go exploring:** Take the binoculars outside for a nature walk, encouraging your child to look for birds, bugs, or other interesting sights.

Benefits for kids:

- **Encourages outdoor exploration** and observation skills.
- **Promotes creativity** through designing their own binoculars.
- **Teaches focus and patience**, especially when observing nature.

Benefits for parents:

- **Inexpensive craft**, using toilet paper rolls and simple art supplies.
- **Perfect for outdoor play**, encouraging movement and exploration.
- **Great for family bonding**, especially during nature walks.

---

272. Animal Yoga

Animal yoga is a fun, active way for children to stretch, move, and pretend to be different animals while practicing basic yoga poses. It promotes physical activity, mindfulness, and creativity.

How it works:

- **Teach the poses:** Show your child different yoga poses that mimic animal shapes, such as downward dog (dog), cobra (snake), and butterfly.
- **Pretend to be the animals:** As they move into each pose, encourage them to act like the animal by making sounds or movements that match.
- **Create a yoga story:** You can also create a story where they travel through the jungle or zoo, meeting different animals and doing yoga poses along the way.

Benefits for kids:

- **Promotes physical activity and flexibility** through yoga poses.
- **Encourages creativity** through imaginative play and pretending to be animals.
- **Teaches mindfulness and focus**, helping them concentrate on their movements and breathing.

Benefits for parents:

- **No special equipment needed**, just a mat or comfortable space to move.
- **Great for indoor play**, offering a fun way to stay active indoors.
- **Promotes family bonding**, especially if parents join in the yoga fun.

---

273. Sensory Sand Tray

A sensory sand tray is a tactile activity where children can explore writing, drawing, or playing with small toys in a shallow tray of sand. It promotes sensory development and fine motor skills.

How it works:

- **Prepare the tray:** Fill a shallow tray with clean, dry sand. You can also use colored sand for added fun.
- **Encourage exploration:** Let your child use their fingers or small tools to draw, write letters, or create patterns in the sand.
- **Add toys:** Provide small cars, animals, or objects to make the play even more engaging.

Benefits for kids:

- **Encourages sensory exploration**, engaging their sense of touch.
- **Improves fine motor skills** through drawing, writing, and manipulating objects.
- **Promotes creativity and calm**, offering a focused, relaxing activity.

Benefits for parents:

- **Easy to set up**, using sand and a shallow tray.
- **Great for independent play**, allowing children to explore at their own pace.
- **Perfect for sensory development**, especially for children who enjoy tactile play.

---

274. Cardboard Box City

Building a cardboard box city is a creative and imaginative activity that encourages children to design and construct a cityscape using cardboard boxes. It promotes creativity, fine motor skills, and problem-solving.

How it works:

- **Collect boxes:** Gather small to medium cardboard boxes of various sizes.
- **Design the city:** Let your child decorate the boxes with markers, paint, or stickers to represent buildings, roads, and parks.
- **Assemble the city:** Arrange the decorated boxes to create a city, adding toy cars, figurines, or trees made from craft materials.

Benefits for kids:

- **Encourages creativity** through designing and building a miniature city.
- **Develops problem-solving skills**, especially in deciding how to arrange the buildings.
- **Improves fine motor skills** through cutting, coloring, and assembling.

Benefits for parents:

- **Uses recyclable materials**, making it an eco-friendly project.
- **Great for group play**, encouraging teamwork and collaboration.
- **Perfect for independent or family play**, providing hours of creative fun.

---

275. Paper Plate Dream Catcher

A paper plate dream catcher is a fun craft that allows children to create their own dream catcher using a paper plate, yarn, and decorations. It introduces them to cultural traditions while fostering creativity.

How it works:

- **Prepare the plate:** Cut out the center of a paper plate to form a ring.
- **Weave the web:** Let your child weave yarn across the opening, attaching it to the edges of the plate to create the "web."
- **Decorate the catcher:** Add beads, feathers, or ribbons to the bottom of the dream catcher for decoration.
- **Hang it up:** Once complete, hang the dream catcher in their room.

Benefits for kids:

- **Teaches about cultural traditions** in a hands-on way.
- **Develops fine motor skills** through weaving and decorating.
- **Encourages creativity**, as they design their own dream catcher.

Benefits for parents:

- **Simple and inexpensive**, using common craft materials.
- **Great for quiet, focused play**, helping kids develop patience and concentration.
- **Provides a lasting decoration**, making it a memorable craft project.

276. Nature Bracelet

A nature bracelet is a fun outdoor craft that encourages children to explore nature while creating a wearable piece of art. It combines creativity with outdoor exploration.

How it works:

- **Prepare the bracelet:** Wrap a piece of wide masking tape (sticky side out) around your child's wrist to form a bracelet.
- **Go on a nature walk:** Take your child outside to collect small leaves, flowers, and other natural materials to stick to the bracelet.
- **Create the bracelet:** Let your child stick the natural objects onto the tape, creating a nature-inspired design.

Benefits for kids:

- **Encourages outdoor exploration**, helping them connect with nature.
- **Promotes creativity**, as they design their own bracelet.
- **Develops fine motor skills**, especially in handling small objects like leaves and flowers.

Benefits for parents:

- **Inexpensive and simple to set up**, using tape and natural materials.
- **Perfect for outdoor play**, combining art with nature.
- **Great for group play**, encouraging collaboration and sharing ideas.

---

277. Clothespin Animals

Clothespin animals are a fun, hands-on craft where children create animal figures using clothespins, paint, and craft materials. It encourages creativity, fine motor skills, and imaginative play.

How it works:

- **Paint the clothespins:** Let your child paint wooden clothespins in the colors of their favorite animals.
- **Add details:** Use googly eyes, felt, pipe cleaners, and markers to add features like ears, tails, and legs.
- **Create a zoo:** Once the animals are complete, your child can create a mini zoo or animal parade with their new creations.

Benefits for kids:

- **Encourages creativity** through designing and decorating their own animals.

- **Develops fine motor skills** through painting and assembling.
- **Promotes imaginative play**, allowing them to use the animals in creative scenarios.

Benefits for parents:

- **Inexpensive and easy to set up**, using clothespins and craft supplies.
- **Great for independent play**, offering a quiet and focused activity.
- **Perfect for themed learning**, such as animal or zoo-related lessons.

---

278. Outdoor Water Painting

Outdoor water painting is a fun, mess-free activity that allows children to "paint" using water on sidewalks or driveways. It's a creative way to stay cool while engaging in outdoor play.

How it works:

- **Provide water and tools:** Give your child a bucket of water and paintbrushes, sponges, or rollers.
- **Paint on the pavement:** Let your child use the water to "paint" pictures on the sidewalk, watching how the water creates dark marks on the surface.
- **Experiment with patterns:** Encourage them to experiment with different shapes, patterns, and brushstrokes.

Benefits for kids:

- **Encourages creativity**, allowing them to paint without permanent marks.
- **Promotes physical activity**, keeping them engaged and moving outdoors.
- **Provides a cooling sensory experience**, especially on hot days.

Benefits for parents:

- **Mess-free and easy to set up**, requiring only water and brushes.
- **Perfect for outdoor play**, with no cleanup needed.
- **Encourages independent or group play**, keeping kids engaged and active.

---

279. Cardboard Tube Animals

Creating cardboard tube animals is a simple and eco-friendly craft that allows children to turn toilet paper or paper towel rolls into animal figures. It promotes creativity, problem-solving, and fine motor skills.

How it works:

- **Prepare the tubes:** Provide your child with empty cardboard tubes and craft supplies like paint, markers, googly eyes, and paper.

- **Create the animals:** Let your child paint and decorate the tubes to resemble different animals. They can add ears, tails, wings, or fins with paper or felt.
- **Make a zoo or jungle:** Once the animals are complete, they can arrange them in a zoo, jungle, or farm scene.

Benefits for kids:

- **Encourages creativity** through designing their own animals.
- **Teaches problem-solving**, especially in figuring out how to add features like legs or wings.
- **Develops fine motor skills** through cutting, gluing, and decorating.

Benefits for parents:

- **Eco-friendly and inexpensive**, using recycled materials.
- **Great for independent play**, keeping kids engaged in creative activities.
- **Perfect for themed learning**, like animal, farm, or jungle lessons.

---

280. Rainbow Bubble Snakes

Rainbow bubble snakes are a fun and colorful outdoor activity where children blow long bubbles through a homemade bubble blower. It combines sensory play, science, and creativity.

How it works:

- **Create the bubble blower:** Cut the bottom off a plastic bottle and cover it with an old sock or piece of fabric. Secure the fabric with a rubber band.
- **Make the bubble solution:** Mix water, dish soap, and a few drops of food coloring in a shallow dish.
- **Blow bubbles:** Dip the fabric-covered end of the bottle into the solution and blow through the bottle's mouth to create long, colorful "bubble snakes."

Benefits for kids:

- **Teaches basic science concepts**, like air pressure and surface tension.
- **Encourages sensory exploration** through the texture and sight of bubbles.
- **Promotes outdoor play**, keeping them active and engaged.

Benefits for parents:

- **Inexpensive and easy to make**, using household items.
- **Perfect for outdoor play**, offering a mess-free activity.
- **Great for group play**, encouraging friendly competition in bubble-making.

---

281. Miniature Volcano Experiment

The miniature volcano experiment is a fun and educational activity where children create their own "erupting" volcano using baking soda and vinegar. It teaches basic chemistry while being visually exciting.

How it works:

- **Build the volcano:** Use clay or a mound of dirt to form a volcano shape around a small container.
- **Add the ingredients:** Pour baking soda into the container inside the volcano.
- **Create the eruption:** Pour vinegar and red food coloring (optional) into the container, and watch the volcano "erupt."

Benefits for kids:

- **Teaches basic chemistry concepts**, like chemical reactions.
- **Encourages curiosity and scientific thinking**, through hands-on experimentation.
- **Promotes sensory exploration**, engaging their sense of sight and touch.

Benefits for parents:

- **Simple and educational**, using common household ingredients.
- **Combines science with play**, making learning fun.
- **Great for outdoor or messy play**, keeping the mess contained outside.

---

282. Ice Cream Stick Puzzles

Ice cream stick puzzles are a creative and simple craft where children make their own puzzles using craft sticks. It promotes problem-solving, fine motor skills, and creativity.

How it works:

- **Create the puzzle:** Line up several ice cream sticks side by side and tape them together on the back.
- **Draw a picture:** Let your child draw or paint a picture on the sticks.
- **Break apart the puzzle:** Once the picture is dry, remove the tape and mix up the sticks. Your child can then try to reassemble the puzzle by aligning the pieces correctly.

Benefits for kids:

- **Encourages problem-solving** as they figure out how to put the puzzle together.
- **Develops fine motor skills** through drawing and assembling the sticks.
- **Promotes creativity**, allowing them to design their own puzzles.

Benefits for parents:

- **Inexpensive and easy to set up**, using craft sticks and art supplies.
- **Perfect for independent play**, keeping kids engaged.
- **Great for reinforcing problem-solving skills**, especially for younger children.

---

283. Balloon Tennis

Balloon tennis is an active, indoor game that encourages physical activity and coordination using balloons and homemade rackets. It's a safe, fun way to keep kids moving.

How it works:

- **Make the rackets:** Attach a paper plate to a wooden spoon or stick to create a simple tennis racket.
- **Blow up the balloon:** Inflate a balloon to use as the ball.
- **Start playing:** Let your child hit the balloon back and forth using their racket. The goal is to keep the balloon off the ground for as long as possible.

Benefits for kids:

- **Improves hand-eye coordination** through aiming and hitting the balloon.
- **Encourages physical activity**, especially indoors.
- **Promotes teamwork** when played with others, reinforcing cooperation.

Benefits for parents:

- **Inexpensive and easy to make**, using household items like paper plates and balloons.
- **Safe for indoor play**, as the balloon is soft and won't damage anything.
- **Perfect for rainy days**, keeping kids active and entertained inside.

---

284. Flower Petal Suncatchers

Flower petal suncatchers are a beautiful and eco-friendly craft where children use pressed flower petals to create colorful window decorations. It combines nature exploration with art.

How it works:

- **Collect flower petals:** Take your child on a nature walk to collect small flowers or petals.
- **Create the suncatcher:** Arrange the petals between two pieces of contact paper or wax paper, sealing the edges with tape.
- **Hang in the window:** Once complete, hang the suncatcher in a sunny window to admire the colors and patterns as the light shines through.

Benefits for kids:

- **Encourages outdoor exploration**, helping them connect with nature.
- **Promotes creativity**, as they design their own suncatcher.
- **Teaches about light and color**, especially as they observe the suncatcher in sunlight.

Benefits for parents:

- **Simple and eco-friendly**, using natural materials like flowers.
- **Perfect for seasonal crafts**, such as spring or summer projects.
- **Provides a lasting decoration**, making it a memorable craft.

---

285. Bubble Wrap Stomp Painting

Bubble wrap stomp painting is a fun, messy outdoor activity where children create colorful artwork by stomping on paint-covered bubble wrap. It encourages sensory exploration and physical activity.

How it works:

- **Prepare the bubble wrap:** Lay large sheets of bubble wrap on the ground and cover them with washable paint in various colors.
- **Stomp and paint:** Let your child stomp or walk across the bubble wrap, transferring the paint onto large sheets of paper underneath.
- **Create colorful patterns:** As they stomp, the paint will create unique, abstract patterns on the paper.

Benefits for kids:

- **Encourages sensory exploration** through touch and movement.
- **Promotes physical activity**, keeping kids engaged and moving.
- **Develops creativity**, as they explore different ways to make patterns.

Benefits for parents:

- **Inexpensive and easy to set up**, using bubble wrap and paint.
- **Perfect for outdoor play**, minimizing mess inside.
- **Great for group play**, encouraging collaboration and fun.

---

286. Nature Crown Craft

Nature crowns are a fun and creative way for children to explore the outdoors while making a crown using natural materials like leaves, flowers, and twigs. This activity encourages outdoor play and creativity.

How it works:

- **Prepare the base:** Cut a strip of construction paper or cardboard long enough to fit around your child's head and staple or tape the ends together to form a crown.
- **Collect materials:** Go on a nature walk to gather leaves, flowers, twigs, and other natural items.
- **Decorate the crown:** Let your child glue or tape the natural materials onto the crown, creating their own nature-inspired design.

Benefits for kids:

- **Encourages outdoor exploration,** fostering a connection with nature.
- **Promotes creativity,** as they design their own unique crown.
- **Develops fine motor skills** through gluing and arranging natural materials.

Benefits for parents:

- **Inexpensive and eco-friendly,** using natural materials from outdoors.
- **Great for outdoor play,** combining crafting with nature exploration.
- **Promotes family bonding,** especially if parents join in the crown-making process.

---

287. Puffy Paint Art

Puffy paint art is a fun and tactile craft where children use homemade puffy paint to create textured, colorful artwork. It's a great way to introduce a new medium of art while promoting sensory exploration.

How it works:

- **Make the puffy paint:** Mix equal parts of shaving cream, white glue, and food coloring in separate bowls.
- **Start painting:** Let your child use a paintbrush or their fingers to apply the puffy paint onto paper, creating textured designs.
- **Watch it dry:** As the puffy paint dries, it will retain its raised, fluffy texture, adding a unique dimension to their artwork.

Benefits for kids:

- **Encourages sensory exploration,** engaging their sense of touch and sight.
- **Promotes creativity,** allowing them to explore a new art medium.
- **Develops fine motor skills,** especially through applying the paint.

Benefits for parents:

- **Inexpensive and easy to make,** using shaving cream and glue.
- **Great for independent play,** as kids can explore the texture and colors.
- **Perfect for sensory development,** providing a fun and tactile experience.

---

288. DIY Sensory Bottles

Sensory bottles are calming, visually stimulating tools that help children explore colors, textures, and movement while providing a soothing sensory experience.

How it works:

- **Fill the bottle:** Use a clear plastic bottle and fill it with water, glitter, beads, or other small objects. You can add food coloring for extra visual interest.
- **Seal the bottle:** Secure the lid tightly with glue to prevent spills.
- **Shake and explore:** Let your child shake, roll, or turn the bottle, watching how the objects move inside.

Benefits for kids:

- **Encourages sensory exploration**, engaging sight and touch.
- **Promotes calm and focus**, offering a soothing, visual experience.
- **Teaches about cause and effect**, as they watch how the objects move.

Benefits for parents:

- **Simple and inexpensive**, using household items like bottles and beads.
- **Perfect for calming down**, providing a quiet, focused activity.
- **Great for travel**, offering a portable sensory tool for quiet time.

---

289. Toy Car Painting

Toy car painting is a creative and active art project where children use toy cars as paintbrushes to create colorful tracks and designs on paper. It combines movement, art, and sensory exploration.

How it works:

- **Prepare the paint:** Pour washable paint onto plates or shallow containers.
- **Use the toy cars:** Let your child dip the wheels of toy cars into the paint and drive them across large sheets of paper, creating colorful tracks.
- **Experiment with patterns:** Encourage them to use different cars or combine colors for unique patterns and designs.

Benefits for kids:

- **Encourages creativity**, allowing them to paint in a new and fun way.
- **Promotes sensory exploration**, as they interact with textures and colors.
- **Improves fine motor skills**, especially through handling and moving the cars.

Benefits for parents:

- **Inexpensive and simple to set up**, using toy cars and paint.

- **Perfect for outdoor or messy play**, minimizing cleanup inside.
- **Encourages active play**, keeping kids engaged and moving while creating art.

---

290. DIY Stepping Stones

Making DIY stepping stones is a creative outdoor activity where children design their own garden stones using cement, paint, and decorations like pebbles or shells. It promotes creativity and fine motor skills while creating lasting outdoor decor.

How it works:

- **Prepare the cement:** Mix quick-setting cement according to the instructions and pour it into shallow molds or trays.
- **Decorate the stones:** Let your child press pebbles, shells, beads, or handprints into the wet cement to create their own designs.
- **Let it dry:** Once the cement dries, your child can paint their stone for added decoration and place it in the garden.

Benefits for kids:

- **Encourages creativity**, allowing them to design their own stepping stones.
- **Teaches patience and responsibility**, as they wait for the cement to dry.
- **Develops fine motor skills**, especially through pressing and decorating the stones.

Benefits for parents:

- **Inexpensive and long-lasting**, using cement and simple decorations.
- **Great for outdoor play**, providing an outdoor art project.
- **Promotes family bonding**, as everyone can make their own personalized stepping stone.

---

291. Pom-Pom Caterpillars

Pom-pom caterpillars are a fun, easy craft where children create colorful caterpillars using pom-poms and craft supplies. It promotes creativity, fine motor skills, and imaginative play.

How it works:

- **Create the caterpillar:** Let your child glue a row of pom-poms together to form a caterpillar body.
- **Add details:** Use googly eyes, pipe cleaners for antennae, and markers to decorate the caterpillar.
- **Make a habitat:** Your child can use paper, leaves, and other craft materials to create a habitat for their caterpillar.

Benefits for kids:

- **Encourages creativity**, allowing them to design their own caterpillar.
- **Develops fine motor skills** through gluing and decorating.
- **Promotes imaginative play**, especially when creating a habitat.

Benefits for parents:

- **Inexpensive and simple**, using basic craft materials like pom-poms.
- **Great for independent play**, keeping kids engaged.
- **Perfect for themed learning**, such as insect or nature-related lessons.

---

292. Rock Painting

Rock painting is a creative and simple activity where children paint designs, animals, or patterns onto rocks. It encourages creativity, fine motor skills, and outdoor play.

How it works:

- **Collect the rocks:** Take your child outside to collect smooth rocks of different shapes and sizes.
- **Paint the rocks:** Let them use acrylic paint or paint pens to decorate the rocks with colorful patterns, animals, or messages.
- **Hide or display the rocks:** Your child can hide the painted rocks around the yard or display them in a special garden spot.

Benefits for kids:

- **Encourages creativity**, allowing them to design and paint unique patterns.
- **Develops fine motor skills** through painting on small, uneven surfaces.
- **Promotes outdoor exploration**, especially when collecting or hiding the rocks.

Benefits for parents:

- **Simple and inexpensive**, using rocks and paint.
- **Perfect for outdoor play**, combining art with nature.
- **Great for family bonding**, especially during rock hunts or garden displays.

---

293. Pasta Necklaces

Making pasta necklaces is a simple craft that helps children develop fine motor skills while creating wearable art using colored pasta. It's a fun and creative way to explore patterns and colors.

How it works:

- **Dye the pasta:** Use food coloring to dye uncooked pasta in different colors.
- **Thread the pasta:** Let your child thread the pasta onto a piece of string or yarn, creating patterns or designs with the different colors.
- **Wear the necklace:** Once the necklace is complete, they can wear their creation or give it as a gift.

Benefits for kids:

- **Teaches patterns and color recognition**, especially through stringing different colored pasta.
- **Develops fine motor skills** through threading the pasta onto the string.
- **Encourages creativity**, allowing them to design their own wearable art.

Benefits for parents:

- **Inexpensive and easy to set up**, using uncooked pasta and string.
- **Great for independent play**, as kids can explore their creativity at their own pace.
- **Perfect for family bonding**, as parents can help with threading and design.

---

294. Fizzy Color Mixing Experiment

The fizzy color mixing experiment is a fun and educational activity where children mix baking soda, vinegar, and food coloring to explore chemical reactions and color blending.

How it works:

- **Set up the experiment:** Spread baking soda on a tray and prepare cups of vinegar mixed with different food coloring.
- **Create the reaction:** Let your child use a dropper or spoon to drop the colored vinegar onto the baking soda, watching as it fizzes and reacts.
- **Experiment with colors:** Encourage them to mix the different colored vinegar to see how new colors are formed.

Benefits for kids:

- **Teaches basic science concepts**, like chemical reactions and color mixing.
- **Encourages sensory exploration**, engaging sight and sound through the fizzing reaction.
- **Promotes curiosity and experimentation**, allowing them to test different color combinations.

Benefits for parents:

- **Inexpensive and easy to set up**, using baking soda and vinegar.
- **Educational and fun**, combining science with hands-on play.
- **Perfect for group play**, as multiple children can explore the reactions together.

295. Paper Plate Frisbee

Making a paper plate frisbee is a fun and active craft where children design their own frisbees using paper plates and paint. It combines creativity with physical play.

How it works:

- **Create the frisbee:** Let your child decorate two paper plates with paint, markers, or stickers.
- **Assemble the frisbee:** Staple or glue the two plates together, with the decorated sides facing outward, to create a lightweight frisbee.
- **Start playing:** Take the frisbee outside and encourage your child to throw and catch it, experimenting with how far it can fly.

Benefits for kids:

- **Encourages creativity**, allowing them to design their own frisbee.
- **Promotes physical activity**, especially through throwing and catching.
- **Develops hand-eye coordination**, especially in aiming and catching the frisbee.

Benefits for parents:

- **Inexpensive and easy to make**, using paper plates and simple craft materials.
- **Perfect for outdoor play**, keeping kids active and engaged.
- **Great for group play**, encouraging friendly competition or teamwork.

---

296. Homemade Slime

Homemade slime is a fun, tactile activity where children create stretchy, squishy slime using simple ingredients. It's a sensory-rich experience that promotes creativity and fine motor skills.

How it works:

- **Make the slime:** Mix 1 cup of glue with 1 tablespoon of baking soda, then slowly add contact lens solution until the mixture becomes stretchy and holds together.
- **Customize the slime:** Let your child add food coloring, glitter, or small beads to personalize their slime.
- **Play and explore:** Encourage them to stretch, squish, and mold the slime, experimenting with its texture and movement.

Benefits for kids:

- **Encourages sensory exploration**, especially through touch.
- **Promotes creativity**, as they customize their slime with colors and textures.
- **Develops fine motor skills**, especially through stretching and molding the slime.

Benefits for parents:

- **Simple and inexpensive**, using household ingredients like glue and baking soda.
- **Perfect for independent play**, providing hours of sensory exploration.
- **Great for quiet play**, offering a calming, focused activity.

---

297. Leaf Threading

Leaf threading is a calming, nature-inspired activity that encourages children to explore the outdoors and practice their fine motor skills by threading leaves onto string or yarn. It's a fun way to combine outdoor play with crafting.

How it works:

- **Collect leaves:** Take your child outside to collect leaves of various shapes and sizes.
- **Thread the leaves:** Let your child use a blunt needle or punch holes in the leaves with a hole punch and thread the leaves onto a piece of yarn or string.
- **Create a garland or necklace:** Once they've threaded enough leaves, they can wear their creation as a necklace or use it to decorate their room.

Benefits for kids:

- **Promotes fine motor skills**, especially through threading and handling delicate leaves.
- **Encourages outdoor exploration**, connecting with nature.
- **Fosters creativity**, as they design their own garland or necklace.

Benefits for parents:

- **Inexpensive and eco-friendly**, using natural materials.
- **Great for outdoor play**, combining nature with art.
- **Perfect for calming, focused play**, encouraging mindfulness.

---

298. Egg Carton Creatures

Egg carton creatures are a simple craft where children turn old egg cartons into cute, creative animals or insects. It promotes creativity, fine motor skills, and imaginative play.

How it works:

- **Cut the egg carton:** Cut individual sections of the egg carton to form the body of each creature.
- **Decorate the creatures:** Let your child paint and decorate the egg carton sections with googly eyes, pipe cleaners for legs, or wings made from paper.
- **Create a collection:** Encourage your child to make a whole collection of creatures, such as bugs, caterpillars, or animals.

Benefits for kids:

- **Encourages creativity**, allowing them to design their own creatures.
- **Develops fine motor skills** through cutting, painting, and assembling.
- **Promotes imaginative play**, as they create stories for their creatures.

Benefits for parents:

- **Eco-friendly and inexpensive**, using recycled egg cartons.
- **Perfect for independent play**, keeping kids engaged.
- **Great for themed lessons**, such as animal or insect studies.

---

299. Ice Cube Melting Race

The ice cube melting race is a simple science-based activity where children race to melt ice cubes using different methods, such as salt, warm water, or friction. It encourages experimentation and scientific thinking.

How it works:

- **Prepare the ice cubes:** Freeze several small ice cubes in advance.
- **Start the race:** Give your child various tools or materials (e.g., salt, warm water, their hands) and have them race to see which method melts the ice fastest.
- **Discuss the science:** Talk about how each method affects the ice and why some work faster than others.

Benefits for kids:

- **Teaches basic science concepts** like states of matter and melting points.
- **Encourages problem-solving and experimentation**, as they test different methods.
- **Promotes sensory exploration**, engaging their sense of touch and temperature.

Benefits for parents:

- **Simple and inexpensive**, using ice and household materials.
- **Great for outdoor or messy play**, offering an easy-to-clean activity.
- **Educational and fun**, combining science with hands-on play.

---

300. Chalk Obstacle Course

A chalk obstacle course is a creative and active outdoor activity where children design their own obstacle course using sidewalk chalk. It combines physical play with creativity and problem-solving.

How it works:

- **Create the course:** Let your child use sidewalk chalk to draw different challenges, such as hopscotch, zigzag lines to follow, or places to jump.
- **Add instructions:** Encourage them to include instructions like "jump," "spin," or "run," as part of the course.
- **Complete the course:** Once the obstacle course is drawn, they can race through it, or challenge a friend or sibling to complete it as fast as possible.

Benefits for kids:

- **Promotes physical activity**, keeping them engaged and active.
- **Encourages creativity**, as they design their own course.
- **Develops problem-solving skills**, especially in figuring out how to complete the course.

Benefits for parents:

- **Inexpensive and simple to set up**, using sidewalk chalk.
- **Great for outdoor play**, offering an active and fun way to enjoy the outdoors.
- **Perfect for group play**, encouraging teamwork or friendly competition.

---

301. Moon Sand Play

Moon sand is a moldable, crumbly sand-like material that children can make at home for sensory play. It's soft, easy to mold, and provides endless opportunities for creative play.

How it works:

- **Make the moon sand:** Mix 8 cups of flour with 1 cup of vegetable oil to create moon sand. You can add food coloring for fun variations.
- **Start molding:** Let your child mold the sand into shapes, castles, or anything else they can imagine using cookie cutters or their hands.
- **Explore textures:** Encourage them to explore the texture by squeezing, pressing, and shaping the sand.

Benefits for kids:

- **Promotes sensory exploration**, engaging their sense of touch.
- **Encourages creativity**, as they mold and shape the sand.
- **Develops fine motor skills** through handling and shaping the sand.

Benefits for parents:

- **Inexpensive and easy to make**, using flour and oil.
- **Great for quiet, independent play**, offering a calming sensory experience.
- **Mess-free**, as moon sand is easy to clean up.

---

302. DIY Bird Feeder

Creating a DIY bird feeder is a hands-on craft that introduces children to the concept of caring for nature. It promotes outdoor exploration, responsibility, and creativity.

How it works:

- **Prepare the base:** Use a toilet paper roll, pinecone, or small plastic container as the base for the bird feeder.
- **Add the birdseed:** Spread peanut butter (or a peanut butter alternative) on the base and roll it in birdseed.
- **Hang it outside:** Let your child hang the bird feeder in the yard or garden, and watch as birds come to visit.

Benefits for kids:

- **Encourages outdoor exploration**, connecting them with nature.
- **Teaches responsibility**, as they care for the birds by providing food.
- **Promotes creativity**, allowing them to personalize their feeder.

Benefits for parents:

- **Inexpensive and eco-friendly**, using recycled materials.
- **Perfect for outdoor play**, encouraging environmental awareness.
- **Great for family bonding**, especially while watching birds together.

---

303. Balloon Rocket Race

A balloon rocket race is a fun, hands-on science activity where children race balloons along strings, exploring the principles of air pressure and motion.

How it works:

- **Set up the race track:** Attach a long piece of string between two stationary objects (like chairs) and thread a straw onto the string.
- **Prepare the balloon:** Blow up a balloon without tying it and tape it to the straw.
- **Launch the rocket:** Let go of the balloon and watch as it zips along the string, propelled by the escaping air.

Benefits for kids:

- **Teaches basic physics concepts**, like air pressure and motion.
- **Encourages problem-solving**, as they experiment with different balloon sizes and air amounts.
- **Develops fine motor skills** through assembling and launching the rocket.

Benefits for parents:

- **Inexpensive and easy to set up**, using string, balloons, and household items.
- **Perfect for group play**, encouraging friendly competition.
- **Educational and fun**, combining science with play.

---

304. Salt Painting

Salt painting is a creative and sensory-rich activity where children create textured, colorful artwork using glue, salt, and watercolors. It's a fun way to combine art with a sensory experience.

How it works:

- **Draw with glue:** Let your child use glue to draw a picture or pattern on a piece of paper.
- **Add salt:** Sprinkle salt over the glue, covering the design, then shake off the excess salt.
- **Paint with watercolors:** Using a paintbrush, let your child gently dab watercolors onto the salt, watching as the colors spread and blend.

Benefits for kids:

- **Encourages creativity**, allowing them to design their own artwork.
- **Promotes sensory exploration**, especially through the texture of salt.
- **Teaches color mixing**, as the watercolors blend on the salt.

Benefits for parents:

- **Inexpensive and simple to set up**, using household materials.
- **Great for independent play**, keeping kids engaged.
- **Perfect for sensory development**, offering a calming, focused activity.

---

305. Sensory Balloon Faces

Sensory balloon faces are a fun and tactile activity where children create squishy balloons filled with different materials, drawing faces on them to explore different textures.

How it works:

- **Prepare the balloons:** Fill balloons with materials like rice, beans, sand, or flour to create different textures.
- **Draw faces:** Let your child draw faces on the balloons using markers, adding expressions like happy, sad, or surprised.
- **Explore the textures:** Encourage your child to squish and feel the balloons, noticing the differences between the fillings.

Benefits for kids:

- **Encourages sensory exploration**, engaging their sense of touch.
- **Promotes creativity**, as they design different facial expressions.
- **Develops fine motor skills**, especially through squeezing and handling the balloons.

Benefits for parents:

- **Inexpensive and easy to make**, using balloons and household materials.
- **Great for quiet, independent play**, providing a calming sensory experience.
- **Perfect for sensory development**, especially for kids who enjoy tactile activities.

---

306. Felt Pizza Craft

The felt pizza craft is a fun, hands-on activity where children create their own "pizza" using felt pieces for the crust, sauce, and toppings. It promotes creativity, fine motor skills, and imaginative play.

How it works:

- **Create the pizza base:** Cut a large circle from brown felt for the pizza crust, and a smaller red circle for the sauce.
- **Make the toppings:** Let your child cut out toppings from different colored felt, such as green for peppers, yellow for cheese, or black for olives.
- **Assemble the pizza:** Your child can assemble and reassemble their pizza, experimenting with different topping combinations.

Benefits for kids:

- **Encourages creativity**, allowing them to design their own pizza.
- **Develops fine motor skills**, especially through cutting and arranging the felt pieces.
- **Promotes imaginative play**, as they "cook" and serve their pizza.

Benefits for parents:

- **Simple and reusable**, providing hours of creative play.
- **Perfect for themed play**, especially around food or cooking lessons.
- **Great for group play**, encouraging sharing and collaboration.

---

307. Cotton Ball Snowman

The cotton ball snowman is a winter-themed craft where children create their own fluffy snowman using cotton balls, glue, and decorations. It promotes creativity and fine motor skills.

How it works:

- **Create the snowman base:** Let your child glue cotton balls onto a piece of paper in the shape of a snowman.
- **Add details:** They can decorate the snowman with googly eyes, a paper hat, buttons, and a carrot nose made from colored paper.
- **Display the snowman:** Once complete, they can hang their snowman as a winter decoration.

Benefits for kids:

- **Encourages creativity,** allowing them to design their own snowman.
- **Develops fine motor skills,** especially through gluing and arranging the cotton balls.
- **Promotes seasonal play,** especially during the winter months.

Benefits for parents:

- **Simple and inexpensive,** using cotton balls and craft supplies.
- **Perfect for holiday crafts,** making it a fun seasonal activity.
- **Great for independent play,** keeping kids engaged and focused.

---

308. Nature Weaving

Nature weaving is an eco-friendly craft that encourages children to collect natural materials like leaves, flowers, and twigs, and weave them into a simple loom made from cardboard or sticks. It promotes creativity, fine motor skills, and outdoor exploration.

How it works:

- **Create the loom:** Make a simple loom using a piece of cardboard or sticks tied together with string.
- **Collect materials:** Go on a nature walk to gather leaves, flowers, grass, or twigs for weaving.
- **Weave the materials:** Let your child weave the natural materials through the strings of the loom to create a beautiful, nature-inspired design.

Benefits for kids:

- **Encourages outdoor exploration,** helping them connect with nature.
- **Develops fine motor skills,** especially through weaving.
- **Promotes creativity,** as they design their own nature weavings.

Benefits for parents:

- **Inexpensive and eco-friendly,** using natural materials.
- **Perfect for outdoor play,** combining art with nature exploration.
- **Great for calming, focused play,** offering a relaxing, mindful activity.

309. Paper Plate Shakers

Paper plate shakers are a fun and simple musical craft where children create their own musical instruments using paper plates and dried beans or rice. It encourages creativity, sensory play, and musical exploration.

How it works:

- **Prepare the plates:** Let your child decorate two paper plates with markers, paint, or stickers.
- **Add the filling:** Place dried beans, rice, or small beads between the two plates.
- **Seal the shaker:** Staple or glue the plates together and let your child shake their new instrument to create music.

Benefits for kids:

- **Encourages creativity**, allowing them to design their own instrument.
- **Promotes sensory exploration**, especially through sound and movement.
- **Teaches basic musical concepts** like rhythm and sound.

Benefits for parents:

- **Inexpensive and easy to make**, using household materials.
- **Perfect for group play**, encouraging musical collaboration.
- **Great for quiet or active play**, offering a range of musical exploration.

310. Homemade Playdough

Homemade playdough is a soft, moldable substance that children can make at home and use for sensory play and creative sculpting. It's a hands-on activity that fosters creativity and fine motor development.

How it works:

- **Make the playdough:** Mix 2 cups of flour, 1 cup of salt, 1 tablespoon of vegetable oil, and 1 cup of water in a bowl. Add food coloring for different colors.
- **Start molding:** Let your child use cookie cutters, plastic tools, or their hands to mold and shape the playdough into different creations.
- **Store it:** After playtime, store the playdough in an airtight container to keep it soft for future use.

Benefits for kids:

- **Encourages creativity**, allowing them to mold and shape the dough into various forms.
- **Develops fine motor skills** through squeezing, rolling, and cutting.
- **Promotes sensory exploration**, engaging their sense of touch.

Benefits for parents:

- **Inexpensive and easy to make**, using common kitchen ingredients.
- **Reusable**, providing long-lasting play with proper storage.
- **Perfect for quiet, independent play**, offering a calming activity.

---

311. Shadow Drawing

Shadow drawing is an outdoor art activity that combines nature and creativity by using the shadows of objects to create drawings. Children learn about light and shadow while making unique artwork.

How it works:

- **Set up the objects:** Place toys, plants, or interesting-shaped objects on a piece of paper outdoors where the sun casts strong shadows.
- **Trace the shadows:** Encourage your child to trace the shadows onto the paper with a pencil or marker.
- **Color the drawings:** Once the shadows are traced, they can color or paint the shapes to create fun characters or designs.

Benefits for kids:

- **Teaches basic science concepts**, like light and shadow.
- **Encourages creativity**, allowing them to turn shadows into art.
- **Promotes fine motor skills** through tracing and coloring.

Benefits for parents:

- **Inexpensive and simple to set up**, using outdoor objects and paper.
- **Great for outdoor play**, combining nature and art.
- **Perfect for group play**, encouraging collaboration and creativity.

---

312. Popsicle Stick Catapults

Popsicle stick catapults are a fun engineering project where children build small catapults using popsicle sticks and rubber bands, launching small objects like pom-poms or cotton balls. It's a great introduction to physics and engineering.

How it works:

- **Build the catapult:** Stack popsicle sticks and secure them with rubber bands to create a lever. Attach a spoon or small container to the end as a launching platform.
- **Test the launch:** Let your child place a pom-pom or cotton ball on the spoon and launch it by pressing down on the opposite end.
- **Experiment with distance:** Encourage them to adjust the catapult design to see how far they can launch the object.

Benefits for kids:

- **Teaches basic physics concepts**, like force and motion.
- **Encourages problem-solving**, as they experiment with different designs.
- **Develops fine motor skills** through assembling the catapult.

Benefits for parents:

- **Inexpensive and easy to make**, using popsicle sticks and rubber bands.
- **Perfect for STEM learning**, combining science with hands-on play.
- **Great for group play**, encouraging friendly competition or collaboration.

---

313. Nature Collage

A nature collage is a creative art project where children use natural materials like leaves, flowers, and twigs to create beautiful collages. It encourages outdoor exploration and creativity.

How it works:

- **Collect natural materials:** Take your child on a nature walk to gather leaves, flowers, twigs, and other items.
- **Create the collage:** Let them glue the natural materials onto a piece of paper or cardboard, arranging them to form patterns, animals, or abstract designs.
- **Decorate the collage:** They can add paint, glitter, or markers to enhance the collage and make it more colorful.

Benefits for kids:

- **Encourages outdoor exploration**, helping them connect with nature.
- **Promotes creativity**, allowing them to design their own art using natural materials.
- **Develops fine motor skills** through handling and arranging small items.

Benefits for parents:

- **Inexpensive and eco-friendly**, using natural materials from outdoors.
- **Great for quiet, independent play**, fostering mindfulness and focus.
- **Perfect for seasonal crafts**, like autumn leaf collages or spring flower art.

---

314. DIY Paper Airplane Launcher

A DIY paper airplane launcher is a simple engineering project where children create a launcher to send paper airplanes flying. It's a great way to combine creativity, problem-solving, and STEM learning.

How it works:

- **Build the launcher:** Attach a rubber band to a sturdy frame (such as a cardboard box) and let your child hook a paper airplane to the rubber band.
- **Launch the airplane:** Let your child pull back on the rubber band and release to send the paper airplane flying.
- **Experiment with designs:** Encourage them to try different paper airplane designs to see which one flies the farthest.

Benefits for kids:

- **Teaches basic physics concepts**, like tension and flight.
- **Encourages problem-solving**, as they test different airplane designs.
- **Promotes creativity**, allowing them to experiment with their launcher.

Benefits for parents:

- **Inexpensive and simple to set up**, using household materials.
- **Great for outdoor play**, encouraging physical activity.
- **Perfect for STEM learning**, combining engineering with creativity.

---

315. Sponge Boats

Sponge boats are a creative and simple water activity where children build their own floating boats using sponges and straws or paper sails. It promotes creativity, problem-solving, and outdoor play.

How it works:

- **Create the boats:** Let your child cut sponges into boat shapes and attach a straw with a paper sail.
- **Test the boats:** Take the boats outside to a pool, pond, or bathtub, and see how well they float and sail.
- **Experiment with designs:** Encourage them to try different sponge shapes or sail sizes to see which design sails the fastest or floats the longest.

Benefits for kids:

- **Teaches basic science concepts**, like buoyancy and wind power.
- **Encourages problem-solving**, as they experiment with boat designs.
- **Promotes outdoor play**, especially on warm, sunny days.

Benefits for parents:

- **Inexpensive and eco-friendly**, using household materials like sponges.
- **Perfect for outdoor water play**, encouraging movement and exploration.
- **Great for independent play**, as kids can experiment with different designs on their own.

---

316. Button Sorting Game

The button sorting game is a fun, hands-on activity that teaches young children about colors, shapes, and early math concepts like sorting and categorization. It encourages focus, concentration, and fine motor development.

How it works:

- **Provide buttons and containers:** Give your child a variety of colorful buttons and small containers or bowls.
- **Sort by color or shape:** Ask your child to sort the buttons into different containers based on color, size, or shape.
- **Add a challenge:** For older children, you can add a time limit or create patterns to match with the buttons.

Benefits for kids:

- **Teaches sorting and classification**, reinforcing early math skills.
- **Improves fine motor skills**, especially through handling small objects.
- **Encourages focus and concentration**, making it a calming activity.

Benefits for parents:

- **Inexpensive and easy to set up**, using buttons and household containers.
- **Great for independent play**, keeping kids engaged.
- **Perfect for quiet time**, offering a focused, calming activity.

---

317. Rainbow Milk Experiment

The rainbow milk experiment is a simple science experiment where children explore how soap interacts with fat molecules in milk to create swirling colors. It's a fun and educational introduction to chemistry.

How it works:

- **Set up the experiment:** Pour a thin layer of milk onto a plate or shallow dish. Add a few drops of different food coloring around the milk.

- **Add the soap:** Dip a cotton swab in dish soap and touch it to the surface of the milk. Watch as the colors swirl and spread across the dish.
- **Experiment with different patterns:** Encourage your child to move the soap around and create different swirling patterns.

Benefits for kids:

- **Teaches basic chemistry concepts**, like the interaction of soap and fat molecules.
- **Encourages curiosity and scientific thinking**, as they observe the reaction.
- **Promotes sensory exploration**, especially through sight and touch.

Benefits for parents:

- **Inexpensive and easy to set up**, using milk, food coloring, and soap.
- **Perfect for quick, engaging science lessons**, combining education with fun.
- **Great for group play**, encouraging kids to experiment together.

---

318. DIY Windmill Craft

Making a DIY windmill is a creative, hands-on craft that introduces children to the concept of wind energy. It promotes creativity, problem-solving, and fine motor skills.

How it works:

- **Create the windmill:** Cut out a windmill shape from paper or cardstock, with four blades. Attach it to a pencil or straw using a pushpin.
- **Test the windmill:** Take the windmill outside and watch it spin in the wind. You can also blow on it to see how it moves.
- **Experiment with designs:** Encourage your child to experiment with different windmill shapes or sizes to see which one spins the fastest.

Benefits for kids:

- **Teaches basic physics concepts**, like wind energy and motion.
- **Encourages creativity**, allowing them to design their own windmill.
- **Develops fine motor skills** through cutting, assembling, and testing the windmill.

Benefits for parents:

- **Inexpensive and easy to make**, using paper and household materials.
- **Perfect for outdoor play**, combining creativity with science.
- **Great for STEM learning**, introducing basic engineering concepts.

---

319. Tinfoil River Adventure

Tinfoil river adventures are a fun and creative outdoor water play activity where children create a miniature river using tinfoil, adding boats, rocks, and other natural elements to explore.

How it works:

- **Build the river:** Lay out a long piece of tinfoil in a slight dip or slope in your yard to create the riverbed.
- **Add water and obstacles:** Let your child pour water down the tinfoil river and place small rocks, twigs, and leaves along the way to create obstacles or dams.
- **Float boats:** Create small boats from leaves, corks, or paper, and float them down the river.

Benefits for kids:

- **Encourages outdoor exploration**, connecting with nature through play.
- **Teaches basic physics concepts**, like water flow and buoyancy.
- **Promotes problem-solving**, as they build obstacles and adjust the river's flow.

Benefits for parents:

- **Inexpensive and eco-friendly**, using tinfoil and natural materials.
- **Perfect for outdoor water play**, encouraging movement and creativity.
- **Great for family bonding**, as parents can join in the river-building fun.

---

320. Felt Animal Finger Puppets

Felt animal finger puppets are a fun and creative craft where children make their own animal puppets using felt, glue, and decorations. It promotes creativity, fine motor skills, and imaginative play.

How it works:

- **Cut out the shapes:** Help your child cut out simple animal shapes from felt, such as cats, dogs, or birds.
- **Assemble the puppets:** Glue or sew the felt pieces together, leaving room for your child's fingers to fit inside as the puppet's "legs."
- **Add details:** Let your child decorate their puppets with googly eyes, fabric scraps for ears, or markers for additional details.
- **Put on a show:** Once the puppets are complete, encourage your child to use them in an imaginative puppet show.

Benefits for kids:

- **Encourages creativity and storytelling**, allowing them to create their own characters.
- **Develops fine motor skills** through cutting, gluing, and assembling the puppets.
- **Promotes imaginative play**, especially when using the puppets for storytelling.

Benefits for parents:

- **Inexpensive and easy to make**, using felt and simple craft materials.
- **Perfect for quiet, focused play**, allowing children to create and play on their own.
- **Great for family bonding**, especially when putting on puppet shows together.

---

321. Glow Stick Ring Toss

Glow stick ring toss is a fun, nighttime outdoor game where children toss glow stick rings onto a target, such as a glow-in-the-dark bottle. It encourages physical activity, hand-eye coordination, and friendly competition.

How it works:

- **Prepare the rings and target:** Use glow sticks to create rings by connecting the ends, and place a glowing bottle or other object as the target.
- **Start the game:** Let your child toss the rings, aiming to loop them around the target.
- **Add competition:** Encourage them to play with friends or family members, keeping score to see who can land the most rings.

Benefits for kids:

- **Improves hand-eye coordination**, as they aim and toss the rings.
- **Encourages physical activity**, especially during outdoor nighttime play.
- **Promotes friendly competition**, perfect for group or family play.

Benefits for parents:

- **Inexpensive and easy to set up**, using glow sticks and household items.
- **Perfect for outdoor play**, especially after dark.
- **Great for group play**, encouraging teamwork and cooperation.

---

322. DIY Cardboard Castle

Building a DIY cardboard castle is a creative project where children use recycled cardboard boxes to create a castle complete with towers, drawbridges, and windows. It promotes creativity, problem-solving, and imaginative play.

How it works:

- **Collect cardboard boxes:** Gather large and small cardboard boxes to use as the base of the castle.
- **Assemble the castle:** Let your child design and build the castle by cutting and attaching the boxes together, creating towers, walls, and a drawbridge.

- **Decorate the castle:** They can decorate the castle with paint, markers, or construction paper to make it more realistic.
- **Imaginative play:** Once complete, encourage your child to use the castle for imaginative play with toy knights, dragons, and royalty.

Benefits for kids:

- **Encourages creativity and engineering,** as they design and build their own castle.
- **Develops problem-solving skills,** especially in deciding how to construct the castle.
- **Promotes imaginative play,** as they use the castle in different play scenarios.

Benefits for parents:

- **Eco-friendly and inexpensive,** using recycled materials.
- **Perfect for independent or group play,** fostering collaboration and teamwork.
- **Provides hours of entertainment,** offering both a craft project and a play space.

---

323. Water Balloon Piñata

Water balloon piñata is a refreshing outdoor game where children try to pop water balloons hanging from a tree or clothesline using sticks or bats. It's a fun way to cool off on a hot day while promoting physical activity.

How it works:

- **Fill the balloons:** Fill water balloons with water and tie them to a tree branch or clothesline at varying heights.
- **Start the game:** Give your child a plastic bat or a stick and let them take turns trying to hit the water balloons, popping them and getting soaked.
- **Add a challenge:** Blindfold older children or time them to make the game more challenging.

Benefits for kids:

- **Encourages physical activity,** keeping them engaged and moving.
- **Promotes hand-eye coordination,** as they aim to hit the balloons.
- **Provides sensory fun,** especially with the cool water splashing on a hot day.

Benefits for parents:

- **Inexpensive and easy to set up,** using water balloons and a stick or bat.
- **Perfect for outdoor play,** especially on warm days.
- **Great for group play,** encouraging friendly competition.

---

324. Fingerprint Art

Fingerprint art is a simple and creative way for children to use their fingerprints to create pictures and patterns. It's a great way to explore textures, shapes, and creativity while developing fine motor skills.

How it works:

- **Prepare the paint:** Provide washable paint and let your child dip their fingers into the paint.
- **Create art:** Encourage your child to use their fingerprints to make animals, trees, flowers, or abstract designs on paper.
- **Add details:** They can use markers or crayons to add details like eyes, wings, or stems to their fingerprint creations.

Benefits for kids:

- **Promotes creativity**, allowing them to explore new ways of making art.
- **Encourages sensory exploration**, engaging their sense of touch.
- **Develops fine motor skills**, especially through dabbing and pressing their fingers.

Benefits for parents:

- **Inexpensive and easy to set up**, using paint and paper.
- **Perfect for independent play**, fostering quiet, creative exploration.
- **Great for themed crafts**, such as animals or nature scenes.

---

325. Ice Cream in a Bag

Ice cream in a bag is a fun and educational activity where children make their own ice cream using simple ingredients and a bit of shaking. It introduces basic chemistry concepts while offering a delicious treat.

How it works:

- **Prepare the ingredients:** Mix 1 cup of heavy cream, 1 cup of milk, 1/4 cup of sugar, and 1 teaspoon of vanilla extract in a small ziplock bag.
- **Add ice and salt:** Place the small bag inside a larger ziplock bag filled with ice and salt.
- **Shake it up:** Let your child shake the bag for about 5-10 minutes until the mixture turns into ice cream. Enjoy the homemade ice cream as a tasty reward.

Benefits for kids:

- **Teaches basic science concepts**, like freezing and temperature.
- **Promotes physical activity**, as they shake the bag to make the ice cream.
- **Encourages sensory exploration**, especially with the cold temperature and creamy texture.

Benefits for parents:

- **Inexpensive and easy to set up**, using household ingredients.
- **Combines learning with fun**, offering both a science lesson and a treat.
- **Great for group play**, as kids can take turns shaking the bag.

---

326. Q-tip Pointillism Art

Q-tip pointillism is an artistic technique where children use Q-tips to create small dots of paint to form larger pictures. It promotes creativity, fine motor skills, and introduces a new style of painting.

How it works:

- **Prepare the paint:** Provide washable paint and Q-tips for your child to use as their "brushes."
- **Create the art:** Let your child dip the Q-tip in the paint and dab it onto paper to create small dots. They can use these dots to form shapes, animals, or abstract patterns.
- **Experiment with colors:** Encourage them to layer different colors and experiment with spacing to create unique effects.

Benefits for kids:

- **Teaches fine motor control**, as they make small, precise dots.
- **Encourages creativity**, allowing them to experiment with color and pattern.
- **Introduces a new art technique**, giving them a fresh way to express themselves.

Benefits for parents:

- **Inexpensive and easy to set up**, using Q-tips and paint.
- **Great for independent play**, keeping kids focused and engaged.
- **Perfect for themed art**, such as making animals, landscapes, or patterns.

---

327. Rainbow Pasta Sensory Bin

A rainbow pasta sensory bin is a fun, colorful activity where children explore dyed pasta in a sensory bin. It encourages sensory exploration, creativity, and fine motor skills.

How it works:

- **Dye the pasta:** Mix dry pasta with a few drops of food coloring and vinegar in a bag, shake it up, and let it dry.
- **Fill the bin:** Pour the dyed pasta into a large container, adding scoops, cups, or small toys for your child to explore.
- **Encourage play:** Let your child dig, scoop, and sort the pasta, experimenting with the different textures and colors.

Benefits for kids:

- **Encourages sensory exploration**, especially through touch and sight.
- **Develops fine motor skills**, especially through scooping and grasping.
- **Promotes creativity**, as they use the pasta for pretend play or sorting games.

Benefits for parents:

- **Inexpensive and easy to make**, using pasta and food coloring.
- **Perfect for quiet, independent play**, providing a calming sensory experience.
- **Great for sensory development**, especially for younger children.

---

328. Fizzy Rocket Experiment

The fizzy rocket experiment is a fun and exciting science activity where children launch small rockets using a chemical reaction between baking soda and vinegar. It's a thrilling way to introduce basic chemistry concepts.

How it works:

- **Prepare the rocket:** Use a small plastic container or film canister as the rocket. Fill it with a small amount of vinegar.
- **Add the fuel:** Place a baking soda "fuel" packet (wrapped in tissue) inside the container and quickly close the lid.
- **Launch the rocket:** Step back and watch as the rocket blasts off due to the pressure created by the chemical reaction.

Benefits for kids:

- **Teaches basic chemistry concepts**, like chemical reactions and pressure.
- **Encourages curiosity and scientific thinking**, as they observe the launch.
- **Promotes sensory exploration**, especially through the visual excitement of the rocket launch.

Benefits for parents:

- **Inexpensive and easy to set up**, using household materials like baking soda and vinegar.
- **Great for outdoor play**, keeping the mess outside.
- **Perfect for STEM learning**, combining science with hands-on fun.

---

329. Magic Milk Experiment

The magic milk experiment is a colorful and engaging science activity where children explore how soap interacts with milk and food coloring to create swirling patterns. It's a fun way to introduce basic chemistry.

How it works:

- **Prepare the milk:** Pour a shallow layer of milk onto a plate or dish.
- **Add food coloring:** Drop different colors of food coloring onto the milk's surface.
- **Add the magic:** Dip a cotton swab in dish soap and touch it to the surface of the milk, watching as the colors swirl and spread.

Benefits for kids:

- **Teaches basic chemistry concepts**, like how soap breaks down fat molecules.
- **Encourages sensory exploration**, engaging sight and touch.
- **Promotes curiosity**, as they observe the swirling colors and experiment with patterns.

Benefits for parents:

- **Inexpensive and easy to set up**, using household items like milk, food coloring, and soap.
- **Perfect for quick science lessons**, combining education with fun.
- **Great for independent play**, allowing children to experiment with the colors on their own.

---

330. Homemade Paper Kites

Making homemade paper kites is a creative and hands-on activity where children design and build their own kites using paper, string, and sticks. It promotes creativity, engineering skills, and outdoor play.

How it works:

- **Create the kite frame:** Help your child build a simple kite frame using lightweight sticks or straws.
- **Design the kite:** Let them decorate a piece of paper or plastic to use as the kite's body, attaching it to the frame with glue or tape.
- **Fly the kite:** Take the kite outside on a windy day and encourage your child to fly it, experimenting with how high it can go.

Benefits for kids:

- **Teaches basic engineering concepts**, like aerodynamics and flight.
- **Encourages creativity**, allowing them to design and decorate their kite.
- **Promotes outdoor play**, especially on windy days.

Benefits for parents:

- **Inexpensive and eco-friendly**, using household materials like paper and sticks.
- **Great for outdoor activity**, encouraging physical movement.
- **Perfect for family bonding**, as parents can help build and fly the kite.

331. DIY Beaded Wind Chimes

DIY beaded wind chimes are a creative and musical project where children use beads, string, and metal objects to create their own wind chimes. It encourages creativity, fine motor skills, and outdoor sensory play.

How it works:

- **Prepare the materials:** Provide your child with beads, string, and small metal objects like keys or washers to create the chimes.
- **Assemble the chimes:** Let your child thread the beads onto the string and attach the metal objects to the ends, tying them onto a sturdy stick or hoop.
- **Hang the wind chime:** Once complete, hang the wind chime outside and listen to the sounds it makes as the wind blows through.

Benefits for kids:

- **Promotes creativity**, as they design their own wind chime.
- **Develops fine motor skills** through threading beads and tying knots.
- **Encourages sensory exploration**, especially through sound and touch.

Benefits for parents:

- **Inexpensive and eco-friendly**, using recycled materials like beads and metal objects.
- **Perfect for outdoor play**, offering a craft that interacts with nature.
- **Great for family bonding**, especially while making and hanging the chime together.

332. Nature Alphabet Hunt

A nature alphabet hunt is a fun outdoor activity where children search for objects in nature that represent each letter of the alphabet. It encourages outdoor exploration, literacy skills, and creativity.

How it works:

- **Create a checklist:** Write down or draw pictures of each letter of the alphabet and have your child search for natural items that start with each letter (like "A" for acorn, "B" for bark).
- **Start the hunt:** Go on a nature walk and let your child find objects to match each letter on the list.
- **Document the finds:** Encourage them to take pictures, collect small items, or draw the objects they find.

Benefits for kids:

- **Encourages literacy skills**, reinforcing letter recognition and phonics.
- **Promotes outdoor exploration**, connecting them with nature.
- **Develops problem-solving skills**, as they figure out which objects match each letter.

Benefits for parents:

- **Simple and eco-friendly**, requiring only a checklist and outdoor space.
- **Great for outdoor play**, encouraging movement and exploration.
- **Perfect for family bonding**, as parents and children can work together to complete the hunt.

---

333. Water Xylophone

A water xylophone is a simple and educational activity where children fill glasses or jars with different levels of water to create musical notes. It teaches basic science concepts about sound and pitch while promoting sensory play.

How it works:

- **Set up the glasses:** Fill several glasses or jars with varying amounts of water.
- **Make music:** Let your child tap each glass with a spoon or stick, listening to the different pitches created by the water levels.
- **Experiment with pitch:** Encourage them to add or remove water to see how it changes the sound.

Benefits for kids:

- **Teaches basic science concepts**, like sound waves and pitch.
- **Encourages sensory exploration**, especially through sound and touch.
- **Promotes creativity**, allowing them to experiment with different sounds and rhythms.

Benefits for parents:

- **Inexpensive and easy to set up**, using household glasses and water.
- **Great for independent or group play**, as children can create their own music.
- **Perfect for educational play**, combining science with music.

---

334. Glow-in-the-Dark Sensory Bottles

Glow-in-the-dark sensory bottles are visually stimulating and calming tools where children explore glowing objects inside a bottle, helping them relax and focus.

How it works:

- **Fill the bottle:** Use a clear plastic bottle and fill it with water, glow-in-the-dark stars or beads, and a few drops of glow-in-the-dark paint or liquid.
- **Seal the bottle:** Secure the lid tightly to prevent spills, using glue if necessary.
- **Shake and explore:** Let your child shake or roll the bottle in a dark room, watching as the glowing objects move around inside.

Benefits for kids:

- **Promotes sensory exploration**, especially through sight and touch.
- **Encourages calm and focus**, providing a soothing, visual experience.
- **Teaches cause and effect**, as they watch how the objects move inside the bottle.

Benefits for parents:

- **Inexpensive and easy to make**, using glow-in-the-dark items and household materials.
- **Perfect for calming down**, offering a quiet, focused activity.
- **Great for travel or bedtime**, providing a portable sensory tool.

---

335. Pinecone Bird Feeders

Pinecone bird feeders are an eco-friendly craft that encourages children to care for wildlife by making bird feeders using natural materials. It's a great way to connect with nature and promote responsibility.

How it works:

- **Collect pinecones:** Go on a nature walk to collect large pinecones.
- **Add the birdseed:** Spread peanut butter (or a peanut butter alternative) onto the pinecones and roll them in birdseed.
- **Hang the feeders:** Let your child hang the pinecone feeders in the yard or garden, and watch as birds come to eat.

Benefits for kids:

- **Teaches responsibility**, as they care for local wildlife by providing food.
- **Encourages outdoor exploration**, connecting them with nature.
- **Promotes creativity**, as they decorate the feeders with birdseed and other materials.

Benefits for parents:

- **Inexpensive and eco-friendly**, using natural materials like pinecones.
- **Great for outdoor play**, encouraging environmental awareness.
- **Perfect for family bonding**, especially while observing birds together.

---

336. DIY Balloon Animals

Making balloon animals is a creative and fun activity where children learn to twist and shape balloons into animals and other shapes. It encourages fine motor skills, creativity, and problem-solving.

How it works:

- **Provide the balloons:** Use long, twistable balloons for this activity.
- **Teach basic shapes:** Start by teaching your child simple balloon shapes, like a dog or sword, by twisting the balloons into the right form.
- **Experiment with designs:** As they get more confident, encourage them to experiment with creating their own balloon animals or shapes.

Benefits for kids:

- **Teaches problem-solving**, as they figure out how to twist the balloons.
- **Develops fine motor skills**, especially through twisting and shaping.
- **Encourages creativity**, allowing them to design their own balloon animals.

Benefits for parents:

- **Inexpensive and easy to set up**, using twistable balloons.
- **Great for group play**, encouraging creativity and friendly competition.
- **Perfect for parties or outdoor play**, offering an interactive activity.

---

337. DIY Kaleidoscope

A DIY kaleidoscope is a creative craft that teaches children about light and reflection while allowing them to design their own colorful, shifting patterns.

How it works:

- **Create the kaleidoscope:** Use a cardboard tube as the base, and add small pieces of reflective paper or plastic inside to create the kaleidoscope effect.
- **Add colorful beads:** Let your child place small beads, sequins, or pieces of colored paper inside the tube.
- **Look through the kaleidoscope:** Encourage your child to rotate the tube and watch the colorful patterns shift as the light reflects inside.

Benefits for kids:

- **Teaches basic science concepts**, like light reflection and color mixing.
- **Encourages creativity**, allowing them to design their own kaleidoscope patterns.
- **Promotes sensory exploration**, offering a visual and interactive experience.

Benefits for parents:

- **Inexpensive and easy to make**, using household items like cardboard and beads.
- **Great for independent play**, as kids can explore the kaleidoscope on their own.
- **Perfect for educational play**, combining science with art.

---

338. Sock Puppet Theater

Sock puppet theater is a fun and imaginative activity where children create their own sock puppets and use them to perform a puppet show. It promotes creativity, storytelling, and fine motor skills.

How it works:

- **Create the puppets:** Let your child decorate old socks with googly eyes, yarn for hair, and fabric scraps for clothes to create their own characters.
- **Set up the theater:** Use a cardboard box or table as the puppet theater.
- **Put on a show:** Encourage your child to write and perform their own puppet show, using different voices and personalities for each puppet.

Benefits for kids:

- **Encourages creativity and storytelling**, allowing them to create their own characters and stories.
- **Develops fine motor skills**, especially through decorating the puppets.
- **Promotes imaginative play**, helping them act out different roles and scenarios.

Benefits for parents:

- **Inexpensive and eco-friendly**, using old socks and simple craft materials.
- **Great for independent or group play**, fostering collaboration and creativity.
- **Perfect for family bonding**, especially when putting on a puppet show together.

---

339. Foam Cup Towers

Foam cup towers are a simple and creative building activity where children stack foam cups to create tall structures or towers. It promotes creativity, problem-solving, and fine motor skills.

How it works:

- **Provide the cups:** Give your child several foam cups to use as building blocks.
- **Build the towers:** Encourage your child to stack the cups in different ways, creating towers, castles, or other structures.
- **Experiment with designs:** Let them experiment with different shapes and stacking methods to see how tall they can make their tower before it falls.

Benefits for kids:

- **Encourages problem-solving**, as they figure out how to balance the cups.
- **Develops fine motor skills**, especially through stacking and balancing.
- **Promotes creativity**, allowing them to design their own structures.

Benefits for parents:

- **Inexpensive and easy to set up**, using foam cups.
- **Great for independent play**, keeping kids focused and engaged.
- **Perfect for group play**, encouraging teamwork or friendly competition.

---

340. Paper Plate Spinners

Paper plate spinners are a fun craft where children create colorful, spinning toys using paper plates, string, and paint. It promotes creativity, fine motor skills, and sensory play.

How it works:

- **Decorate the plates:** Let your child color or paint a paper plate with bright patterns or designs.
- **Create the spinner:** Punch two holes near the center of the plate and thread a piece of string through. When they pull the string, the plate will spin.
- **Experiment with spinning:** Encourage them to try different designs and see how they look when the plate spins.

Benefits for kids:

- **Encourages creativity**, allowing them to design their own spinning toy.
- **Develops fine motor skills**, especially through threading the string and spinning the plate.
- **Promotes sensory exploration**, especially through sight and movement.

Benefits for parents:

- **Inexpensive and simple to make**, using paper plates and string.
- **Perfect for independent play**, fostering creativity and focus.
- **Great for group play**, encouraging friendly competition or collaboration.

---

341. Scavenger Hunt with Shapes

A scavenger hunt with shapes is an engaging way for children to learn about different shapes by searching for objects that match each shape. It promotes early math skills, problem-solving, and physical activity.

How it works:

- **Create a shape list:** Write or draw different shapes on a piece of paper, such as circles, squares, triangles, and rectangles.
- **Start the hunt:** Ask your child to find objects around the house or yard that match each shape on the list.
- **Identify and discuss:** Once they find each shape, talk about where they found it and what makes it that particular shape.

Benefits for kids:

- **Teaches shape recognition**, reinforcing early math skills.
- **Encourages problem-solving**, as they search for matching objects.
- **Promotes physical activity**, keeping them engaged and moving.

Benefits for parents:

- **Inexpensive and easy to set up**, using a shape list and household items.
- **Perfect for indoor or outdoor play**, offering flexibility.
- **Great for group play**, encouraging teamwork and cooperation.

---

342. DIY Felt Pizza

A DIY felt pizza is a fun, hands-on craft where children create their own pizza using felt pieces for the crust, sauce, and toppings. It encourages creativity, fine motor skills, and pretend play.

How it works:

- **Create the base:** Cut out a large circle from brown felt for the pizza crust, and a smaller red circle for the sauce.
- **Make the toppings:** Let your child cut out toppings from different colored felt, like green for peppers, yellow for cheese, or red for pepperoni.
- **Assemble the pizza:** Your child can assemble and reassemble their pizza, experimenting with different topping combinations.

Benefits for kids:

- **Encourages creativity**, allowing them to design their own pizza.
- **Develops fine motor skills**, through cutting and arranging the felt pieces.
- **Promotes imaginative play**, especially in pretend cooking and serving.

Benefits for parents:

- **Simple and reusable**, providing hours of creative play.
- **Great for themed play**, especially related to food or cooking.

- **Perfect for quiet, independent play**, keeping kids engaged.

---

343. Paper Airplane Competitions

Paper airplane competitions are a fun, active way to engage children in both crafting and physical play. By folding and flying different airplane designs, they learn about physics and aerodynamics.

How it works:

- **Create the airplanes:** Let your child fold paper into different airplane designs, encouraging them to experiment with shapes and folds.
- **Start the competition:** Have them fly their airplanes and see whose design goes the farthest, flies the highest, or stays in the air the longest.
- **Test different designs:** Encourage them to modify their airplanes and test the results to learn what makes a better flying machine.

Benefits for kids:

- **Teaches basic physics concepts**, like aerodynamics and gravity.
- **Encourages problem-solving**, as they figure out how to improve their designs.
- **Promotes friendly competition**, making it perfect for group play.

Benefits for parents:

- **Inexpensive and simple to set up**, using paper and imagination.
- **Perfect for outdoor or indoor play**, offering flexibility.
- **Great for family bonding**, encouraging everyone to join the fun.

---

344. Plastic Bottle Planters

Plastic bottle planters are a creative way for children to recycle plastic bottles while learning about gardening. It teaches responsibility and environmental awareness.

How it works:

- **Prepare the bottle:** Cut a plastic bottle in half or cut an opening along the side, creating a space to plant seeds.
- **Plant the seeds:** Fill the bottle with soil and let your child plant seeds, such as herbs or small flowers.
- **Care for the plant:** Encourage them to water and care for the plant as it grows, teaching them about responsibility.

Benefits for kids:

- **Teaches responsibility**, as they care for their growing plants.
- **Promotes environmental awareness**, especially through recycling.
- **Encourages curiosity about nature**, introducing them to basic gardening.

Benefits for parents:

- **Eco-friendly and inexpensive**, using recycled plastic bottles.
- **Perfect for both indoor and outdoor play**, offering flexibility.
- **Great for educational play**, combining science with hands-on learning.

---

345. Treasure Hunt Maze

A treasure hunt maze is a fun and challenging activity where children follow clues and solve puzzles to find hidden treasure. It encourages problem-solving, critical thinking, and outdoor exploration.

How it works:

- **Set up the maze:** Create a path using objects like chairs, ropes, or cones to form a maze or obstacle course.
- **Hide the clues:** Write clues or riddles and hide them along the path, leading your child toward the "treasure."
- **Find the treasure:** The final clue will lead them to a hidden treasure, such as a small toy or treat.

Benefits for kids:

- **Encourages problem-solving and critical thinking**, through deciphering clues.
- **Promotes physical activity**, keeping them moving as they navigate the maze.
- **Fosters a sense of adventure**, making the hunt exciting and rewarding.

Benefits for parents:

- **Inexpensive and customizable**, using household items and simple clues.
- **Perfect for group play**, encouraging collaboration or friendly competition.
- **Great for indoor or outdoor play**, depending on the setup.

---

346. Miniature Clay Sculptures

Miniature clay sculptures are a creative and tactile craft where children use clay to sculpt small figures, animals, or objects. It promotes creativity, fine motor skills, and sensory exploration.

How it works:

- **Provide the clay:** Give your child air-dry clay or modeling clay and let them shape it into tiny figures or objects.
- **Decorate the sculptures:** Once dry, they can paint or decorate their sculptures to bring them to life.
- **Create a scene:** Encourage them to use their sculptures in imaginative play or to create a mini scene or diorama.

Benefits for kids:

- **Encourages creativity**, allowing them to sculpt whatever they can imagine.
- **Develops fine motor skills**, especially through shaping and molding the clay.
- **Promotes sensory exploration**, engaging their sense of touch.

Benefits for parents:

- **Inexpensive and easy to set up**, using clay and paint.
- **Great for independent play**, fostering focus and creativity.
- **Perfect for quiet play**, offering a calming, tactile experience.

---

347. Tissue Paper Stained Glass Art

Tissue paper stained glass art is a colorful craft where children use tissue paper and contact paper to create window decorations that look like stained glass. It promotes creativity and fine motor skills.

How it works:

- **Prepare the materials:** Cut a piece of clear contact paper and provide different colors of tissue paper cut into shapes.
- **Design the stained glass:** Let your child arrange the tissue paper on the contact paper to create colorful patterns or pictures.
- **Hang it up:** Once complete, hang the art in a sunny window to see the light shine through the "stained glass."

Benefits for kids:

- **Encourages creativity**, allowing them to design their own colorful artwork.
- **Develops fine motor skills**, especially through cutting and arranging the tissue paper.
- **Teaches color mixing and light concepts**, as they observe the colors shining through the window.

Benefits for parents:

- **Inexpensive and simple to make**, using contact paper and tissue paper.
- **Perfect for quiet, independent play**, providing a focused and creative activity.
- **Great for seasonal crafts**, like making autumn leaves or spring flowers.

348. Sponge Stamping Art

Sponge stamping art is a simple and creative activity where children use sponges to create stamped shapes and patterns. It's a fun way to explore textures, colors, and patterns while developing fine motor skills.

How it works:

- **Cut the sponges:** Cut kitchen sponges into different shapes, such as stars, hearts, or animals.
- **Prepare the paint:** Provide washable paint and let your child dip the sponges into the paint.
- **Start stamping:** Encourage them to stamp the sponges onto paper to create patterns, pictures, or scenes.

Benefits for kids:

- **Encourages creativity**, allowing them to experiment with shapes and colors.
- **Promotes sensory exploration**, especially through touch and texture.
- **Develops fine motor skills**, especially through handling and stamping the sponges.

Benefits for parents:

- **Inexpensive and easy to set up**, using sponges and paint.
- **Perfect for independent play**, fostering creativity and focus.
- **Great for group play**, encouraging sharing and collaboration.

---

349. DIY Lava Lamps

A DIY lava lamp is a fun and visually stimulating science activity where children create their own lava lamp using water, oil, and food coloring. It introduces basic chemistry concepts while offering a calming sensory experience.

How it works:

- **Prepare the materials:** Fill a clear bottle with water, add food coloring, and top it off with vegetable oil.
- **Add the "lava":** Drop in an antacid tablet (like Alka-Seltzer) to start the reaction, creating bubbles that move up and down like a real lava lamp.
- **Observe the effects:** Watch as the bubbles rise and fall, creating a soothing, colorful display.

Benefits for kids:

- **Teaches basic chemistry concepts**, like density and chemical reactions.
- **Encourages sensory exploration**, especially through sight and movement.
- **Promotes curiosity**, allowing them to experiment with different effects.

Benefits for parents:

- **Inexpensive and simple to set up**, using household materials.
- **Perfect for STEM learning**, combining science with hands-on play.
- **Great for calming down**, offering a quiet, visually soothing activity.

---

350. Glow Stick Bowling

Glow stick bowling is a fun nighttime activity where children play bowling using glow sticks and water bottles as pins. It promotes physical activity, coordination, and friendly competition.

How it works:

- **Set up the pins:** Fill several empty water bottles with a little water and place a glow stick inside each one to create glowing bowling pins.
- **Prepare the bowling ball:** Use a light ball, such as a beach ball or soccer ball.
- **Start bowling:** Let your child bowl by rolling the ball toward the glowing pins, trying to knock them down.

Benefits for kids:

- **Improves hand-eye coordination**, as they aim and roll the ball.
- **Encourages physical activity**, especially during outdoor nighttime play.
- **Promotes friendly competition**, perfect for group play.

Benefits for parents:

- **Inexpensive and easy to set up**, using glow sticks and water bottles.
- **Perfect for outdoor play**, especially at night.
- **Great for group play**, encouraging teamwork and collaboration.

---

351. DIY Cardboard Tube Rockets

DIY cardboard tube rockets are a creative and educational craft where children design and build rockets using cardboard tubes and craft materials. It encourages creativity, problem-solving, and imaginative play.

How it works:

- **Prepare the materials:** Give your child a cardboard tube (like a toilet paper roll) and other craft materials like construction paper, paint, and glue.
- **Design the rocket:** Let your child decorate the tube to look like a rocket, adding fins, a nose cone, and windows.

- **Launch the rocket:** Once complete, your child can pretend to launch the rocket and use it in space-themed imaginative play.

Benefits for kids:

- **Encourages creativity,** allowing them to design their own rocket.
- **Develops fine motor skills,** through cutting, gluing, and assembling.
- **Promotes imaginative play,** especially in space-themed scenarios.

Benefits for parents:

- **Inexpensive and eco-friendly,** using recycled cardboard tubes.
- **Perfect for themed play,** especially around space or science.
- **Great for independent play,** fostering creativity and focus.

---

352. Nature Suncatchers

Nature suncatchers are a creative way for children to use leaves, flowers, and other natural items to create beautiful decorations that reflect sunlight. It encourages outdoor exploration, creativity, and sensory play.

How it works:

- **Collect materials:** Take your child on a nature walk to gather leaves, flowers, and other small natural objects.
- **Prepare the frame:** Use a cardboard frame or two pieces of clear contact paper to create the base for the suncatcher.
- **Arrange the materials:** Let your child arrange the leaves and flowers between the contact paper or in the frame.
- **Hang the suncatcher:** Once complete, hang the suncatcher in a sunny window and watch as the light shines through the natural objects.

Benefits for kids:

- **Encourages outdoor exploration,** helping them connect with nature.
- **Promotes creativity,** as they design their own suncatcher.
- **Teaches sensory exploration,** especially through sight and touch.

Benefits for parents:

- **Inexpensive and eco-friendly,** using natural materials and simple craft supplies.
- **Great for outdoor and indoor play,** combining art with nature.
- **Perfect for seasonal crafts,** like autumn leaves or spring flowers.

---

353. DIY Fishing Game

The DIY fishing game is a fun and interactive activity where children catch paper or cardboard fish using a magnetized fishing rod. It helps develop hand-eye coordination, fine motor skills, and patience.

How it works:

- **Create the fish:** Cut fish shapes from cardboard or paper and attach a small metal paperclip to each fish.
- **Make the fishing rod:** Attach a magnet to the end of a string, tied to a stick or dowel to serve as the fishing rod.
- **Start fishing:** Let your child use the magnetic fishing rod to "catch" the fish by attracting the paperclip.

Benefits for kids:

- **Improves hand-eye coordination**, as they aim and catch the fish.
- **Encourages patience**, as they wait to hook each fish.
- **Promotes fine motor skills**, especially through using the rod and magnets.

Benefits for parents:

- **Inexpensive and easy to set up**, using simple household materials.
- **Perfect for quiet play**, helping kids focus and practice patience.
- **Great for group play**, encouraging friendly competition or teamwork.

---

354. Pom-Pom Ice Cream Cones

Pom-pom ice cream cones are a fun and simple craft where children create pretend ice cream cones using pom-poms and paper cones. It promotes creativity, fine motor skills, and imaginative play.

How it works:

- **Make the cones:** Let your child roll colored paper into cone shapes and secure with glue or tape.
- **Create the scoops:** Use large colorful pom-poms as the "scoops" of ice cream.
- **Decorate and play:** Encourage them to decorate their cones with glitter or paint, then use them for pretend ice cream shop play.

Benefits for kids:

- **Encourages creativity**, allowing them to design their own ice cream cones.
- **Develops fine motor skills**, especially through rolling and handling the materials.
- **Promotes imaginative play**, fostering pretend play scenarios like running an ice cream shop.

Benefits for parents:

- **Inexpensive and easy to make**, using pom-poms and paper.
- **Perfect for group play**, encouraging sharing and creativity.
- **Great for independent play**, fostering focus and imaginative exploration.

---

355. Magic Wands Craft

Magic wands craft is a whimsical activity where children design and create their own magic wands using sticks, ribbons, and decorations. It encourages creativity, fine motor skills, and imaginative play.

How it works:

- **Create the wand:** Let your child choose a stick from outside or use a dowel, and decorate it with ribbons, paint, glitter, and beads.
- **Add magical touches:** Encourage them to add extra elements like stars, jewels, or feathers to make their wand special.
- **Play with the wand:** Once complete, they can use their wand for pretend play, casting spells, and creating imaginative scenarios.

Benefits for kids:

- **Encourages creativity**, as they design their own unique wand.
- **Develops fine motor skills**, especially through decorating and assembling the wand.
- **Promotes imaginative play**, allowing them to use the wand in make-believe adventures.

Benefits for parents:

- **Inexpensive and simple to make**, using sticks and household craft supplies.
- **Perfect for themed play**, like magic or fantasy-based scenarios.
- **Great for independent play**, fostering creativity and imagination.

---

356. Rice Sensory Bin

A rice sensory bin is a calming and tactile activity where children explore dyed or plain rice with their hands, scooping tools, and small toys. It encourages sensory exploration, fine motor skills, and imaginative play.

How it works:

- **Prepare the bin:** Fill a large container with uncooked rice, either plain or dyed with food coloring.
- **Add scoops and toys:** Let your child use scoops, spoons, cups, or small toys to explore the rice.
- **Encourage sensory play:** Allow them to dig, scoop, pour, and feel the texture of the rice, experimenting with how it moves.

Benefits for kids:

- **Encourages sensory exploration**, engaging their sense of touch.
- **Develops fine motor skills**, through scooping, pouring, and handling the rice.
- **Promotes imaginative play**, especially with added toys or themed elements.

Benefits for parents:

- **Inexpensive and easy to set up**, using uncooked rice and household items.
- **Perfect for calming, independent play**, offering a focused and sensory-rich experience.
- **Great for indoor play**, especially on rainy days.

---

357. Origami Animals

Origami animals is a creative and educational craft where children learn to fold paper into different animal shapes. It helps develop fine motor skills, patience, and creativity while introducing a traditional art form.

How it works:

- **Provide the paper:** Use square sheets of paper, preferably in different colors, to make origami animals.
- **Teach basic folds:** Start with simple animals, like frogs, cranes, or dogs, and guide your child through the folding process.
- **Decorate the animals:** Once folded, let your child use markers, stickers, or googly eyes to add details to their animals.

Benefits for kids:

- **Teaches patience and fine motor skills**, especially through precise folding.
- **Encourages creativity**, allowing them to decorate and personalize their animals.
- **Introduces a traditional art form**, fostering cultural appreciation and learning.

Benefits for parents:

- **Inexpensive and simple to set up**, using just paper.
- **Perfect for quiet play**, fostering focus and concentration.
- **Great for educational play**, combining art with hands-on learning.

---

358. Indoor Obstacle Course

An indoor obstacle course is a fun, physical activity where children navigate through various obstacles set up around the house. It promotes physical activity, problem-solving, and coordination.

How it works:

- **Create the obstacles:** Use pillows, chairs, blankets, and other household items to create an obstacle course with tunnels, jumps, and balance beams.
- **Guide the course:** Give your child challenges, like crawling under tables, hopping over pillows, or balancing on a taped line.
- **Add a timer:** For older children, you can time how fast they complete the course and encourage them to beat their own time.

Benefits for kids:

- **Promotes physical activity,** keeping them engaged and moving.
- **Improves coordination and balance,** especially through different physical challenges.
- **Encourages problem-solving,** as they figure out how to complete each obstacle.

Benefits for parents:

- **Inexpensive and easy to set up,** using household items.
- **Great for indoor play,** especially on rainy or cold days.
- **Perfect for group play,** encouraging teamwork and friendly competition.

---

359. Sock Snowballs

Sock snowballs are a fun and active indoor game where children use rolled-up socks as soft "snowballs" for a playful snowball fight. It encourages physical activity and coordination without the mess of real snow.

How it works:

- **Prepare the snowballs:** Roll up clean socks into balls to create the "snowballs."
- **Set up the game:** Designate areas for teams or individual players to stand, and let the snowball fight begin.
- **Add challenges:** You can also set up targets for your child to aim at, like buckets or boxes, making it a coordination game.

Benefits for kids:

- **Promotes physical activity,** keeping them active and engaged indoors.
- **Improves hand-eye coordination,** through aiming and throwing the socks.
- **Encourages friendly competition,** making it perfect for group play.

Benefits for parents:

- **Inexpensive and easy to set up,** using socks already at home.
- **Great for indoor play,** offering a safe, mess-free alternative to real snowballs.
- **Perfect for rainy days,** keeping kids entertained and active.

360. Clothespin Color Sorting

Clothespin color sorting is a simple, educational activity where children sort colored clothespins onto matching colored cards or containers. It helps develop fine motor skills, color recognition, and early math skills.

How it works:

- **Prepare the clothespins and cards:** Paint or use colored tape to create clothespins in different colors and match them to colored cards or containers.
- **Start sorting:** Let your child clip the clothespins onto the cards or place them in the matching container.
- **Add a challenge:** For older children, you can add numbers to the cards and ask them to match the correct number of clothespins to each card.

Benefits for kids:

- **Teaches color recognition**, reinforcing early learning skills.
- **Develops fine motor skills**, especially through clipping the clothespins.
- **Encourages early math skills**, such as counting and matching.

Benefits for parents:

- **Inexpensive and easy to make**, using simple household materials.
- **Perfect for quiet, independent play**, providing a focused and educational activity.
- **Great for early learning**, combining fun with skill development.

361. Balloon Volleyball

Balloon volleyball is a fun, active indoor or outdoor game where children use a balloon as the volleyball and hit it over an imaginary net. It promotes physical activity, coordination, and teamwork.

How it works:

- **Prepare the balloon:** Inflate a balloon to use as the ball.
- **Set up the court:** Use a string or a piece of tape on the floor to act as the net dividing the court.
- **Start playing:** Let your child and a partner hit the balloon back and forth, trying to keep it in the air and prevent it from touching the ground.

Benefits for kids:

- **Improves hand-eye coordination**, as they aim and hit the balloon.
- **Encourages physical activity**, keeping them active and engaged.

- **Promotes teamwork**, especially when played with friends or siblings.

Benefits for parents:

- **Inexpensive and easy to set up**, using only a balloon.
- **Perfect for indoor or outdoor play**, offering flexibility.
- **Great for group play**, encouraging friendly competition and collaboration.

---

362. Sticky Spider Web Game

The sticky spider web game is a fun indoor activity where children throw small objects, like paper balls, at a "web" made of masking tape, aiming to stick them to the web. It promotes physical activity, coordination, and concentration.

How it works:

- **Create the web:** Use masking tape to create a sticky web on a doorway or a large open space.
- **Prepare the objects:** Crumple up small pieces of paper or use lightweight toys to throw at the web.
- **Start playing:** Let your child throw the paper balls at the web, trying to get them to stick to the tape.

Benefits for kids:

- **Improves hand-eye coordination**, as they aim and throw the objects.
- **Encourages concentration**, focusing on hitting the web.
- **Promotes physical activity**, especially for indoor play.

Benefits for parents:

- **Inexpensive and simple to set up**, using masking tape and paper.
- **Perfect for indoor play**, offering an engaging activity for rainy days.
- **Great for group play**, encouraging friendly competition.

---

363. Button Art

Button art is a creative craft where children use buttons to make colorful pictures and designs on paper. It promotes creativity, fine motor skills, and imaginative expression.

How it works:

- **Prepare the buttons:** Provide a variety of colorful buttons in different sizes and shapes.

- **Create the design:** Let your child glue the buttons onto a piece of paper, arranging them to form animals, flowers, or abstract patterns.
- **Add details:** Encourage them to use markers, paint, or other decorations to enhance their button art.

Benefits for kids:

- **Encourages creativity,** allowing them to design their own art.
- **Develops fine motor skills,** especially through handling and gluing the buttons.
- **Promotes sensory exploration,** especially through the different textures and colors of the buttons.

Benefits for parents:

- **Inexpensive and simple to make,** using buttons and paper.
- **Perfect for quiet, independent play,** offering a focused and creative activity.
- **Great for themed art,** like animals, flowers, or seasonal designs.

---

364. Ice Excavation

Ice excavation is a fun and sensory-rich activity where children dig and melt their way through a block of ice to uncover hidden toys or treasures. It promotes problem-solving, fine motor skills, and scientific exploration.

How it works:

- **Freeze the toys:** Place small toys, like plastic animals or gems, into a container of water and freeze it overnight.
- **Start excavating:** Give your child tools like spoons, salt, or warm water to help them dig through the ice and uncover the treasures.
- **Experiment with methods:** Encourage them to try different methods to see what melts the ice fastest.

Benefits for kids:

- **Teaches basic science concepts,** like states of matter and melting points.
- **Encourages problem-solving,** as they figure out how to free the toys.
- **Promotes sensory exploration,** especially through touch and temperature.

Benefits for parents:

- **Inexpensive and easy to set up,** using ice and small toys.
- **Perfect for outdoor or indoor play,** offering flexibility depending on the weather.
- **Great for group play,** encouraging cooperation and friendly competition.

---

365. Shape Hunt

The shape hunt is a simple educational activity where children search for objects that match specific shapes around the house or outside. It promotes early math skills, problem-solving, and physical activity.

How it works:

- **Create a shape list:** Write down or draw different shapes, such as circles, squares, triangles, and rectangles.
- **Start the hunt:** Ask your child to find objects around the house, yard, or park that match each shape on the list.
- **Identify the shapes:** Once they find an object, have them explain what shape it matches and how they know.

Benefits for kids:

- **Teaches shape recognition**, reinforcing early math skills.
- **Encourages problem-solving**, as they search for matching objects.
- **Promotes physical activity**, keeping them engaged and moving.

Benefits for parents:

- **Inexpensive and easy to set up**, using a simple list and household items.
- **Perfect for indoor or outdoor play**, offering flexibility.
- **Great for family bonding**, as parents and children can work together to find shapes.

---

366. Glow-in-the-Dark Bowling

Glow-in-the-dark bowling is a nighttime version of the classic game where children bowl using glowing pins made from water bottles and glow sticks. It encourages physical activity, coordination, and teamwork.

How it works:

- **Prepare the pins:** Fill several empty water bottles with a little water and insert glow sticks to make glowing bowling pins.
- **Use a light ball:** Provide a lightweight ball, such as a beach ball or foam ball, for bowling.
- **Start bowling:** Let your child bowl and try to knock down the glowing pins, adding a fun twist to traditional bowling.

Benefits for kids:

- **Improves hand-eye coordination**, as they aim and roll the ball.
- **Encourages physical activity**, especially during outdoor nighttime play.
- **Promotes teamwork and friendly competition**, perfect for group play.

Benefits for parents:

- **Inexpensive and easy to set up**, using glow sticks and water bottles.
- **Perfect for outdoor play**, especially at night.
- **Great for family bonding**, offering a fun, engaging game for everyone.

---

367. DIY Pirate Treasure Map

A DIY pirate treasure map is a creative craft where children design their own treasure map using paper and markers, then follow the clues to find hidden treasure. It promotes creativity, problem-solving, and imaginative play.

How it works:

- **Create the map:** Let your child design a pirate-themed treasure map on a piece of paper, marking "X" where the treasure is hidden.
- **Set up the treasure hunt:** Hide small toys or treats around the house or yard as the treasure.
- **Follow the map:** Help your child follow the map and search for the hidden treasure, adding excitement and adventure to the game.

Benefits for kids:

- **Encourages creativity**, allowing them to design their own treasure map.
- **Promotes problem-solving**, as they follow the map and search for the treasure.
- **Fosters imaginative play**, especially in pirate-themed scenarios.

Benefits for parents:

- **Inexpensive and easy to set up**, using paper and small toys or treats.
- **Perfect for indoor or outdoor play**, depending on the weather.
- **Great for family bonding**, offering an adventurous and collaborative activity.

---

368. Tissue Paper Collage

A tissue paper collage is a colorful and tactile art project where children tear and glue tissue paper onto a surface to create patterns, pictures, or abstract designs. It promotes creativity, fine motor skills, and sensory exploration.

How it works:

- **Prepare the materials:** Provide tissue paper in various colors and let your child tear or cut it into pieces.
- **Create the collage:** Let your child glue the tissue paper onto a piece of cardboard or heavy paper, arranging the pieces to form a picture or pattern.

- **Add details:** They can also use markers, paint, or stickers to enhance their collage.

Benefits for kids:

- **Encourages creativity**, allowing them to design their own artwork.
- **Develops fine motor skills**, especially through tearing and gluing the tissue paper.
- **Promotes sensory exploration**, especially through touch and texture.

Benefits for parents:

- **Inexpensive and easy to set up**, using tissue paper and glue.
- **Perfect for quiet, independent play**, offering a focused and creative activity.
- **Great for themed art projects**, like creating animals, flowers, or abstract designs.

---

369. Cardboard Tube Bowling

Cardboard tube bowling is a fun and creative version of bowling where children use cardboard tubes as the pins and a small ball as the bowling ball. It promotes physical activity, coordination, and problem-solving.

How it works:

- **Prepare the pins:** Use empty cardboard tubes, like toilet paper rolls, as the bowling pins. Let your child decorate the tubes if they want.
- **Set up the game:** Arrange the cardboard tubes in a triangle formation at the end of a hallway or on a flat surface.
- **Start bowling:** Let your child roll a small ball, aiming to knock down the cardboard tube pins.

Benefits for kids:

- **Improves hand-eye coordination**, as they aim and roll the ball.
- **Encourages physical activity**, keeping them active and engaged.
- **Promotes problem-solving**, as they figure out how to knock down the pins.

Benefits for parents:

- **Inexpensive and eco-friendly**, using recycled cardboard tubes.
- **Perfect for indoor play**, especially on rainy or cold days.
- **Great for family bonding**, encouraging everyone to join the game.

---

370. Cotton Ball Snowman Craft

Cotton ball snowmen are a simple winter-themed craft where children use cotton balls, glue, and decorations to create fluffy snowmen. It promotes creativity, fine motor skills, and imaginative play.

How it works:

- **Create the snowman base:** Let your child glue cotton balls onto a piece of paper in the shape of a snowman.
- **Add details:** They can decorate the snowman with googly eyes, a paper hat, buttons, and a carrot nose made from colored paper.
- **Display the snowman:** Once complete, they can hang their snowman as a winter decoration or use it in imaginative play.

Benefits for kids:

- **Encourages creativity**, allowing them to design their own snowman.
- **Develops fine motor skills**, especially through gluing and arranging the cotton balls.
- **Promotes imaginative play**, especially during the winter season.

Benefits for parents:

- **Inexpensive and simple to make**, using cotton balls and craft supplies.
- **Perfect for holiday crafts**, making it a fun seasonal activity.
- **Great for independent play**, keeping kids engaged and focused.

---

371. DIY Kaleidoscope Craft

A DIY kaleidoscope is a creative craft where children use reflective materials and colorful objects to make a homemade kaleidoscope. It introduces basic physics concepts while encouraging creativity.

How it works:

- **Prepare the materials:** Use a cardboard tube (like a paper towel roll), reflective paper, and small colorful beads or sequins.
- **Assemble the kaleidoscope:** Line the inside of the tube with reflective paper, and place the colorful beads inside a plastic cap or transparent lid at one end.
- **Look through the kaleidoscope:** Let your child look through the open end of the tube and rotate it to see the colorful patterns change as the light reflects.

Benefits for kids:

- **Teaches basic physics concepts**, like light reflection and color patterns.
- **Encourages creativity**, as they design their own kaleidoscope.

- **Promotes sensory exploration**, offering a visual and interactive experience.

Benefits for parents:

- **Inexpensive and simple to make**, using household items.
- **Great for independent play**, allowing kids to explore the kaleidoscope on their own.
- **Perfect for educational play**, combining science with art.

---

372. Paper Plate Animals

Paper plate animals are a fun and easy craft where children use paper plates to create animals by cutting, painting, and adding decorations. It promotes creativity, fine motor skills, and imaginative play.

How it works:

- **Create the animal base:** Let your child use a paper plate as the base for their animal, such as a lion, cat, or owl.
- **Decorate the animal:** Encourage them to paint or color the plate, adding googly eyes, construction paper ears, and other features like feathers or whiskers.
- **Imaginative play:** Once complete, your child can use the animals in stories, scenes, or as decorations.

Benefits for kids:

- **Encourages creativity**, allowing them to design their own animal.
- **Develops fine motor skills**, especially through cutting, painting, and gluing.
- **Promotes imaginative play**, especially in creating animal-themed stories or scenes.

Benefits for parents:

- **Inexpensive and easy to set up**, using paper plates and simple craft materials.
- **Perfect for quiet, independent play**, fostering creativity and focus.
- **Great for group play**, encouraging collaboration and sharing ideas.

---

373. Puzzle Piece Art

Puzzle piece art is a creative and eco-friendly craft where children use old puzzle pieces to create unique designs, pictures, or even 3D sculptures. It promotes creativity, problem-solving, and fine motor skills.

How it works:

- **Prepare the puzzle pieces:** Use old or incomplete puzzles and provide paint, markers, and glue for decorating.

- **Create the art:** Let your child glue the puzzle pieces together to form shapes, letters, or pictures on a piece of cardboard or paper.
- **Add details:** They can paint or decorate the puzzle pieces to enhance their creation.

Benefits for kids:

- **Encourages creativity**, allowing them to transform puzzle pieces into art.
- **Develops problem-solving skills**, especially in figuring out how to arrange the pieces.
- **Promotes fine motor skills**, especially through handling and gluing the small pieces.

Benefits for parents:

- **Inexpensive and eco-friendly**, using recycled puzzle pieces.
- **Great for quiet, independent play**, offering a focused and creative activity.
- **Perfect for themed art**, such as animals, names, or abstract designs.

---

374. Indoor Scavenger Hunt

An indoor scavenger hunt is an exciting and active game where children search for specific objects or clues hidden around the house. It promotes problem-solving, critical thinking, and physical activity.

How it works:

- **Create a list:** Make a list of objects for your child to find around the house, such as a red sock, a book, or a toy car.
- **Set up the clues:** For older children, you can create a series of clues that lead them from one object to the next.
- **Start the hunt:** Let your child search for the objects, checking off items from the list or following the clues to find the "treasure."

Benefits for kids:

- **Encourages problem-solving and critical thinking**, as they search for and identify the objects.
- **Promotes physical activity**, keeping them engaged and moving around the house.
- **Fosters a sense of adventure**, making the hunt exciting and rewarding.

Benefits for parents:

- **Inexpensive and simple to set up**, using household objects.
- **Perfect for indoor play**, offering an engaging activity for rainy or cold days.
- **Great for family bonding**, especially when parents join in on the fun.

375. Nature Paint Brushes

Nature paint brushes are a creative way for children to explore textures and experiment with art by making their own paintbrushes from natural materials like leaves, twigs, and grass. It combines art and nature in a hands-on project.

How it works:

- **Collect materials:** Take your child on a nature walk to gather leaves, pine needles, grass, or small branches.
- **Make the brushes:** Attach the natural materials to sticks or twigs using rubber bands or string to create paintbrushes with different textures.
- **Start painting:** Let your child dip the brushes into paint and experiment with how each one creates different strokes and textures on paper.

Benefits for kids:

- **Encourages outdoor exploration**, fostering a connection with nature.
- **Teaches about texture and art**, through hands-on experimentation with natural materials.
- **Promotes creativity**, as they create unique artwork using non-traditional tools.

Benefits for parents:

- **Inexpensive and eco-friendly**, using natural materials from outdoors.
- **Encourages outdoor play**, combining art with nature exploration.
- **Great for sensory exploration**, making it a calming and creative activity.

---

376. Bottle Cap Art

Bottle cap art is an eco-friendly craft where children use old bottle caps to create colorful designs and pictures. It encourages creativity, fine motor skills, and an awareness of recycling.

How it works:

- **Collect the bottle caps:** Gather bottle caps of various colors and sizes.
- **Create the design:** Let your child arrange the bottle caps on a piece of cardboard or heavy paper to form shapes, pictures, or patterns.
- **Glue the caps:** Once they're happy with the design, help them glue the bottle caps in place to complete their artwork.

Benefits for kids:

- **Encourages creativity**, allowing them to design with unconventional materials.
- **Develops fine motor skills**, especially through handling and arranging the bottle caps.
- **Promotes environmental awareness**, introducing the concept of recycling.

Benefits for parents:

- **Inexpensive and eco-friendly**, using recycled bottle caps.
- **Perfect for quiet, independent play**, fostering creativity and focus.
- **Great for themed art**, such as making animals, flowers, or abstract designs.

---

377. Felt Storyboard

A felt storyboard is a creative and interactive way for children to use felt pieces to create stories and scenes on a felt board. It promotes storytelling, creativity, and fine motor skills.

How it works:

- **Create the board:** Use a piece of felt as the background, attaching it to a piece of cardboard or a frame.
- **Make the characters:** Cut out characters, animals, and objects from different colors of felt for your child to use in their stories.
- **Tell a story:** Encourage your child to arrange the felt pieces on the board, creating scenes and telling stories using the characters and objects.

Benefits for kids:

- **Encourages storytelling and creativity**, as they create their own scenes and narratives.
- **Develops fine motor skills**, especially through handling and placing the felt pieces.
- **Promotes imaginative play**, allowing them to create endless storylines.

Benefits for parents:

- **Inexpensive and reusable**, providing hours of creative play.
- **Perfect for quiet, independent play**, fostering storytelling and focus.
- **Great for group play**, encouraging collaboration and sharing of stories.

---

378. Rock Painting

Rock painting is a simple and creative activity where children paint designs, animals, or patterns onto smooth rocks. It encourages creativity, fine motor skills, and outdoor exploration.

How it works:

- **Collect the rocks:** Take your child outside to collect smooth rocks of different shapes and sizes.
- **Paint the rocks:** Let them use acrylic paint or paint pens to decorate the rocks with colorful patterns, animals, or messages.

- **Hide or display the rocks:** Your child can hide the painted rocks around the yard or display them in a special garden spot.

Benefits for kids:

- **Encourages creativity**, allowing them to design and paint unique patterns.
- **Develops fine motor skills**, through painting on small, uneven surfaces.
- **Promotes outdoor exploration**, especially when collecting or hiding the rocks.

Benefits for parents:

- **Simple and inexpensive**, using rocks and paint.
- **Perfect for outdoor play**, combining art with nature.
- **Great for family bonding**, especially during rock hunts or garden displays.

---

379. Cardboard Box Train

A cardboard box train is a fun and creative project where children use cardboard boxes to create a train they can sit in or play with. It promotes creativity, problem-solving, and imaginative play.

How it works:

- **Collect the boxes:** Gather several cardboard boxes of various sizes.
- **Assemble the train:** Let your child decorate the boxes with markers, stickers, or paint to create a train with an engine and cars.
- **Imaginative play:** Once complete, they can sit in the boxes and pretend to be the conductor or use the train for toy figurines.

Benefits for kids:

- **Encourages creativity**, allowing them to design and build their own train.
- **Develops problem-solving skills**, especially in deciding how to assemble the train.
- **Promotes imaginative play**, as they use the train for pretend play.

Benefits for parents:

- **Eco-friendly and inexpensive**, using recycled cardboard boxes.
- **Perfect for group play**, encouraging collaboration and teamwork.
- **Provides hours of entertainment**, offering both a craft project and a play space.

---

380. DIY Dreamcatchers

DIY dreamcatchers are a creative craft where children make their own dreamcatchers using string, beads, and decorations. It introduces them to cultural traditions while fostering creativity and fine motor skills.

How it works:

- **Prepare the base:** Use a metal or wooden hoop as the base of the dreamcatcher.
- **Weave the web:** Let your child weave yarn or string across the opening, attaching it to the edges of the hoop to create the "web."
- **Decorate the catcher:** Add beads, feathers, or ribbons to the bottom of the dreamcatcher for decoration.
- **Hang it up:** Once complete, hang the dreamcatcher in their room.

Benefits for kids:

- **Teaches cultural traditions**, introducing them to the history of dreamcatchers.
- **Develops fine motor skills**, through weaving and decorating.
- **Encourages creativity**, as they design their own dreamcatcher.

Benefits for parents:

- **Simple and inexpensive**, using common craft materials.
- **Great for quiet, focused play**, helping kids develop patience and concentration.
- **Provides a lasting decoration**, making it a memorable craft project.

---

381. Bubble Wrap Painting

Bubble wrap painting is a fun, sensory art activity where children use bubble wrap to create textured prints with paint. It encourages creativity, sensory exploration, and fine motor skills.

How it works:

- **Prepare the bubble wrap:** Cut pieces of bubble wrap into manageable sizes and provide washable paint.
- **Start painting:** Let your child dip the bubble wrap into the paint or use a brush to apply paint onto the bubble wrap.
- **Create the prints:** Encourage them to press the bubble wrap onto paper, creating textured, dotted patterns. They can layer colors and experiment with different designs.

Benefits for kids:

- **Encourages sensory exploration**, engaging their sense of touch and sight.
- **Promotes creativity**, as they explore new textures and patterns.
- **Develops fine motor skills**, especially through pressing and handling the bubble wrap.

Benefits for parents:

- **Inexpensive and simple to set up**, using bubble wrap and paint.
- **Perfect for messy, outdoor play**, minimizing cleanup inside.
- **Great for group play**, encouraging collaboration and creative fun.

---

382. Rainbow Water Experiment

The rainbow water experiment is a visually exciting and educational activity where children learn about color mixing by transferring colored water between cups. It introduces basic science concepts while promoting sensory exploration.

How it works:

- **Prepare the cups:** Fill three cups with water and add different food coloring to each (e.g., red, yellow, and blue).
- **Set up the experiment:** Place two empty cups between the colored cups. Use paper towels, folding them into strips, and place one end of each strip into a colored cup and the other end into the empty cup.
- **Watch the colors mix:** Over time, the colored water will travel along the paper towel into the empty cups, mixing to form new colors like orange, green, and purple.

Benefits for kids:

- **Teaches basic science concepts**, like color mixing and capillary action.
- **Encourages curiosity and experimentation**, as they watch the colors change.
- **Promotes sensory exploration**, especially through sight and color.

Benefits for parents:

- **Inexpensive and easy to set up**, using water and food coloring.
- **Great for educational play**, combining science with hands-on learning.
- **Perfect for quiet, independent play**, allowing children to observe and experiment on their own.

---

383. Cardboard Box Fort

A cardboard box fort is a fun and imaginative project where children build a fort using large cardboard boxes, turning them into a play space. It encourages creativity, problem-solving, and imaginative play.

How it works:

- **Collect the boxes:** Gather large cardboard boxes and let your child design their fort.
- **Assemble the fort:** Help them cut windows, doors, and other features, then decorate the fort with markers, stickers, or paint.
- **Imaginative play:** Once the fort is built, they can use it as a clubhouse, castle, or cozy reading nook.

Benefits for kids:

- **Encourages creativity and problem-solving**, as they design and build their own fort.
- **Promotes imaginative play**, creating a special space for pretend adventures.
- **Develops spatial awareness**, especially through the construction process.

Benefits for parents:

- **Inexpensive and eco-friendly**, using recycled cardboard boxes.
- **Perfect for group play**, encouraging teamwork and collaboration.
- **Provides hours of entertainment**, offering both a craft project and a play space.

---

384. Yarn Wrapped Letters

Yarn wrapped letters is a creative craft where children wrap yarn around cardboard cutouts of letters to create personalized decorations. It promotes fine motor skills, creativity, and concentration.

How it works:

- **Create the letters:** Cut large letter shapes out of cardboard, either representing your child's initials or spelling out their name.
- **Wrap with yarn:** Let your child choose their favorite yarn colors and wrap the yarn tightly around each letter, securing the ends with glue.
- **Decorate and display:** Once complete, they can add beads or small decorations and display the letters on a wall or shelf.

Benefits for kids:

- **Develops fine motor skills**, especially through wrapping and handling the yarn.
- **Encourages creativity**, allowing them to personalize their letters with colors and decorations.
- **Promotes concentration and patience**, as they carefully wrap the yarn.

Benefits for parents:

- **Inexpensive and easy to set up**, using cardboard and yarn.
- **Perfect for quiet, focused play**, fostering creativity and focus.
- **Great for personalized room decor**, making it a long-lasting craft project.

---

385. Glowing Firefly Jars

Glowing firefly jars are a magical nighttime craft where children create their own glowing "fireflies" using glow sticks and mason jars. It promotes creativity and sensory exploration.

How it works:

- **Prepare the jars:** Use mason jars or other clear containers.
- **Create the glow:** Cut open glow sticks and pour the glowing liquid into the jars. You can also use glow-in-the-dark paint to achieve a similar effect.
- **Decorate the jar:** Let your child decorate the outside of the jar with stickers, glitter, or paint to make it even more magical.

Benefits for kids:

- **Encourages creativity,** as they design their glowing jars.
- **Promotes sensory exploration,** especially through sight and light.
- **Teaches basic science concepts,** like light and luminescence.

Benefits for parents:

- **Inexpensive and simple to set up,** using glow sticks and jars.
- **Perfect for outdoor play,** especially at night.
- **Great for group play,** offering a fun, collaborative craft activity.

---

386. Sticky Note Wall Art

Sticky note wall art is a creative and interactive activity where children use colorful sticky notes to create large-scale designs on a wall or window. It promotes creativity, problem-solving, and fine motor skills.

How it works:

- **Choose a surface:** Let your child pick a blank wall or window as their canvas.
- **Create the design:** Provide colorful sticky notes and encourage your child to arrange them in patterns, pictures, or abstract designs.
- **Change it up:** The sticky notes can easily be rearranged, allowing them to experiment with different designs.

Benefits for kids:

- **Encourages creativity,** allowing them to design and build large-scale art.
- **Promotes problem-solving,** especially in figuring out how to arrange the sticky notes.
- **Develops fine motor skills,** through handling and placing the sticky notes.

Benefits for parents:

- **Inexpensive and easy to set up,** using sticky notes.
- **Great for independent play,** fostering focus and creativity.
- **Perfect for quiet play,** offering a low-mess, reusable activity.

---

387. Button Collage

Button collages are a simple and colorful art project where children use buttons to create pictures, patterns, or abstract designs. It promotes creativity, fine motor skills, and sensory exploration.

How it works:

- **Collect buttons:** Provide a variety of buttons in different colors and sizes.
- **Create the collage:** Let your child glue the buttons onto a piece of cardboard or paper, arranging them to form a picture, pattern, or abstract design.
- **Add details:** They can use paint, markers, or glitter to enhance their collage.

Benefits for kids:

- **Encourages creativity**, allowing them to design their own button art.
- **Develops fine motor skills**, especially through handling and gluing the buttons.
- **Promotes sensory exploration**, engaging their sense of touch and sight.

Benefits for parents:

- **Inexpensive and simple to set up**, using buttons and glue.
- **Perfect for quiet, independent play**, fostering creativity and focus.
- **Great for themed art projects**, like making animals, flowers, or geometric designs.

---

388. Egg Carton Flowers

Egg carton flowers are a fun, eco-friendly craft where children use old egg cartons to create beautiful, colorful flowers. It promotes creativity, fine motor skills, and imaginative play.

How it works:

- **Prepare the egg cartons:** Cut apart the sections of an egg carton to form the petals of each flower.
- **Paint and decorate:** Let your child paint the petals in bright colors, adding glitter or other decorations if they like.
- **Assemble the flowers:** Attach a pipe cleaner or straw as the stem and glue the petals together to form the flower.

Benefits for kids:

- **Encourages creativity**, as they design their own colorful flowers.
- **Develops fine motor skills**, especially through painting and assembling the flowers.
- **Promotes imaginative play**, especially in creating a garden or flower shop.

Benefits for parents:

- **Inexpensive and eco-friendly**, using recycled egg cartons.

- **Perfect for quiet, focused play**, offering a creative and calming activity.
- **Great for themed projects**, like spring or garden-related crafts.

---

389. Foil Art

Foil art is a creative activity where children use aluminum foil to create shiny, textured art by molding and shaping the foil into patterns or pictures. It promotes creativity, fine motor skills, and sensory exploration.

How it works:

- **Prepare the foil:** Provide sheets of aluminum foil and let your child crumple, fold, or mold the foil into different shapes and textures.
- **Create the art:** Encourage them to glue the foil pieces onto a piece of cardboard or heavy paper to create a shiny, textured picture or design.
- **Decorate:** They can add paint, markers, or glitter to enhance their foil art.

Benefits for kids:

- **Encourages creativity**, allowing them to explore new textures and shapes.
- **Develops fine motor skills**, especially through handling and shaping the foil.
- **Promotes sensory exploration**, engaging their sense of touch and sight.

Benefits for parents:

- **Inexpensive and easy to set up**, using aluminum foil and glue.
- **Perfect for independent play**, fostering creativity and focus.
- **Great for themed art**, such as making stars, animals, or abstract designs.

---

390. Paper Chain Wall Decor

Paper chain wall decor is a fun and simple craft where children create colorful paper chains to decorate their room or celebrate a special occasion. It encourages creativity, fine motor skills, and concentration.

How it works:

- **Prepare the paper strips:** Provide strips of colored paper for your child to use.
- **Create the chains:** Let your child glue or staple the strips together, forming loops and connecting them into a long chain.
- **Decorate the room:** Once complete, they can hang the paper chain as room decor, for a party, or just for fun.

Benefits for kids:

- **Encourages creativity**, as they design their own colorful chains.
- **Develops fine motor skills**, through cutting, gluing, and connecting the strips.
- **Promotes concentration**, especially through the repetitive nature of making the chain.

Benefits for parents:

- **Inexpensive and easy to make**, using paper and glue.
- **Great for quiet, focused play**, providing a calming activity.
- **Perfect for party decorations**, offering a homemade and personalized touch.

---

391. Shadow Puppets

Shadow puppets are a fun and creative way for children to tell stories using shadows cast on a wall or screen. It promotes creativity, storytelling, and fine motor skills.

How it works:

- **Create the puppets:** Cut out shapes of animals, people, or objects from cardboard or paper and attach them to sticks.
- **Set up a light source:** Use a flashlight or lamp to cast light on a wall or behind a thin sheet or curtain.
- **Tell a story:** Let your child move the puppets in front of the light to cast shadows on the wall, creating a story or scene with the shadows.

Benefits for kids:

- **Encourages creativity and storytelling**, allowing them to create their own narratives.
- **Promotes fine motor skills**, especially through handling and moving the puppets.
- **Teaches cause and effect**, as they observe how shadows are formed.

Benefits for parents:

- **Inexpensive and simple to set up**, using basic household materials.
- **Perfect for quiet, imaginative play**, offering a calming and engaging activity.
- **Great for family bonding**, as parents and children can create stories together.

---

392. Cotton Swab Painting

Cotton swab painting is a simple and creative activity where children use cotton swabs to create small dots of paint to form larger pictures. It introduces a new technique for making art and promotes fine motor skills.

How it works:

- **Prepare the paint:** Provide washable paint and cotton swabs for your child to use as painting tools.
- **Create the art:** Let your child dip the cotton swabs in the paint and dab them onto paper to form small dots. They can use the dots to create pictures, animals, or abstract designs.
- **Experiment with patterns:** Encourage them to try different patterns and colors for unique effects.

Benefits for kids:

- **Promotes fine motor control**, especially through precise dabbing with the swabs.
- **Encourages creativity**, allowing them to experiment with colors and patterns.
- **Introduces a new painting technique**, offering a fresh way to express themselves.

Benefits for parents:

- **Inexpensive and easy to set up**, using cotton swabs and paint.
- **Great for independent play**, keeping kids focused and engaged.
- **Perfect for themed art**, such as creating animals, landscapes, or abstract designs.

393. Leaf Rubbing Art

Leaf rubbing art is a nature-inspired activity where children place paper over leaves and use crayons to reveal the leaf's texture and pattern. It encourages outdoor exploration, creativity, and sensory play.

How it works:

- **Collect leaves:** Take your child outside to gather leaves of different shapes and sizes.
- **Create the rubbings:** Place the leaves under a piece of paper and let your child rub a crayon or colored pencil over the top, revealing the leaf's texture.
- **Experiment with designs:** Encourage them to layer different leaves and colors to create unique art.

Benefits for kids:

- **Encourages outdoor exploration**, connecting them with nature.
- **Promotes sensory exploration**, especially through touch and texture.
- **Teaches about patterns and shapes**, as they observe the details of each leaf.

Benefits for parents:

- **Inexpensive and eco-friendly**, using leaves and simple art supplies.
- **Great for outdoor and indoor play**, combining art with nature.
- **Perfect for seasonal crafts**, like autumn leaf rubbings or spring flowers.

394. Pasta Jewelry

Pasta jewelry is a fun and simple craft where children use colored pasta to create necklaces, bracelets, and other accessories. It promotes creativity, fine motor skills, and early math concepts like patterns and sorting.

How it works:

- **Dye the pasta:** Use food coloring to dye uncooked pasta in different colors, such as penne or macaroni.
- **Thread the pasta:** Let your child string the pasta onto yarn or string to create patterns or designs.
- **Wear the jewelry:** Once complete, they can wear their handmade necklaces or bracelets or give them as gifts.

Benefits for kids:

- **Teaches pattern recognition and color sorting**, reinforcing early math skills.
- **Develops fine motor skills**, especially through threading the pasta onto the string.
- **Encourages creativity**, allowing them to design their own accessories.

Benefits for parents:

- **Inexpensive and easy to make**, using pasta and string.
- **Great for independent play**, allowing kids to explore their creativity at their own pace.
- **Perfect for themed crafts**, like creating rainbow jewelry or holiday-themed accessories.

---

395. DIY Pop-Up Cards

DIY pop-up cards are a fun and creative craft where children make their own greeting cards with pop-up designs inside. It promotes creativity, fine motor skills, and imaginative play.

How it works:

- **Create the card:** Fold a piece of paper or cardstock in half to make the card.
- **Make the pop-up:** Help your child cut small slits into the fold and fold a section inward to create the pop-up feature.
- **Decorate the card:** Let them draw, color, and decorate the inside and outside of the card, adding messages or decorations to make it special.

Benefits for kids:

- **Encourages creativity**, allowing them to design their own cards.
- **Develops fine motor skills**, especially through cutting and folding the paper.
- **Promotes imaginative play**, especially in creating pop-up scenes or characters.

- **Inexpensive and easy to set up**, using paper and simple craft supplies.
- **Perfect for personalized gifts**, allowing children to create special cards for friends and family.
- **Great for themed occasions**, such as birthdays, holidays, or thank-you notes.

---

396. Sand Art Bottles

Sand art bottles are a creative and colorful craft where children layer different colors of sand in clear bottles to create beautiful patterns and designs. It promotes creativity, fine motor skills, and sensory play.

How it works:

- **Prepare the materials:** Provide colored sand and small clear bottles or containers.
- **Create the layers:** Let your child use a funnel to pour different colors of sand into the bottle, creating layers and patterns.
- **Display the bottle:** Once complete, they can display their sand art as a decoration or gift it to someone special.

Benefits for kids:

- **Encourages creativity**, allowing them to design their own colorful patterns.
- **Develops fine motor skills**, especially through pouring and layering the sand.
- **Promotes sensory exploration**, engaging their sense of touch and sight.

Benefits for parents:

- **Inexpensive and easy to make**, using colored sand and bottles.
- **Perfect for quiet, focused play**, offering a calming and creative activity.
- **Great for personalized gifts**, allowing children to create unique keepsakes.

---

397. Fingerprint Animals

Fingerprint animals are a creative and easy art project where children use their fingerprints to create animal shapes, then add details with markers. It promotes creativity, fine motor skills, and imaginative play.

How it works:

- **Create the fingerprints:** Let your child dip their fingers into washable paint or stamp ink and press them onto paper to make different shapes.
- **Add details:** Once the paint is dry, encourage them to use markers to add eyes, legs, and other details to turn their fingerprints into animals like dogs, birds, or fish.

- **Create a scene:** They can use the animals to create a whole scene, like a farm or underwater world.

Benefits for kids:

- **Encourages creativity**, allowing them to design their own animal characters.
- **Develops fine motor skills**, especially through adding details with markers.
- **Promotes imaginative play**, especially in creating scenes and stories for their animals.

Benefits for parents:

- **Inexpensive and easy to set up**, using washable paint or ink.
- **Perfect for themed crafts**, like making jungle animals or sea creatures.
- **Great for independent play**, fostering focus and creativity.

---

398. Foam Cup Snowmen

Foam cup snowmen are a simple winter-themed craft where children use foam cups to create snowman characters. It promotes creativity, fine motor skills, and imaginative play.

How it works:

- **Create the snowman:** Let your child stack foam cups and glue them together to form the snowman's body.
- **Add decorations:** They can use markers, googly eyes, pipe cleaners, and felt to create the snowman's face, arms, and hat.
- **Display the snowmen:** Once complete, they can display their snowmen as winter decorations or use them in imaginative play.

Benefits for kids:

- **Encourages creativity**, allowing them to design their own snowmen.
- **Develops fine motor skills**, through decorating and assembling the cups.
- **Promotes imaginative play**, especially during the winter season.

Benefits for parents:

- **Inexpensive and easy to make**, using foam cups and craft materials.
- **Perfect for holiday crafts**, offering a fun seasonal activity.
- **Great for group play**, encouraging sharing and collaboration.

---

399. DIY Snow Globe

A DIY snow globe is a magical craft where children create their own snow globes using small jars, water, and glitter. It promotes creativity, fine motor skills, and sensory play.

How it works:

- **Prepare the materials:** Use a small jar with a lid, water, glitter, and a small figurine or decoration to go inside the globe.
- **Assemble the globe:** Help your child glue the figurine to the inside of the jar lid, fill the jar with water and glitter, and screw the lid back on tightly.
- **Shake and enjoy:** Let your child shake the globe and watch as the glitter swirls around, creating a snow-like effect.

Benefits for kids:

- **Encourages creativity**, allowing them to design their own snow globe.
- **Develops fine motor skills**, especially through assembling the globe.
- **Promotes sensory exploration**, especially through sight and movement.

Benefits for parents:

- **Inexpensive and easy to set up**, using simple materials like jars and glitter.
- **Perfect for seasonal crafts**, making it a great holiday project.
- **Great for personalized gifts**, offering a handmade keepsake for friends and family.

400. Pinecone Bird Feeders

Pinecone bird feeders are an eco-friendly craft where children use natural pinecones, peanut butter, and birdseed to make feeders for birds. It encourages outdoor exploration, responsibility, and caring for nature.

How it works:

- **Collect pinecones:** Take your child on a nature walk to collect large pinecones.
- **Spread the birdseed:** Spread peanut butter or a peanut butter alternative onto the pinecones, then roll them in birdseed.
- **Hang the feeders:** Let your child hang the feeders in the yard or garden and observe the birds that come to eat.

Benefits for kids:

- **Teaches responsibility**, as they care for local wildlife by providing food.
- **Encourages outdoor exploration**, fostering a connection with nature.
- **Promotes creativity**, as they design and decorate the feeders.

Benefits for parents:

- **Inexpensive and eco-friendly**, using natural materials.
- **Perfect for outdoor play**, encouraging environmental awareness.

- **Great for family bonding**, especially while observing birds together.

---

401. DIY Water Xylophone

A DIY water xylophone is a fun and educational activity where children use glasses filled with different levels of water to create musical notes. It introduces basic science concepts about sound and pitch.

How it works:

- **Set up the glasses:** Line up several glasses or jars and fill each one with a different amount of water.
- **Make music:** Let your child tap each glass with a spoon or stick, listening to the different pitches created by the water levels.
- **Experiment with pitch:** Encourage them to add or remove water to see how it changes the sound.

Benefits for kids:

- **Teaches basic science concepts**, like sound waves and pitch.
- **Encourages sensory exploration**, especially through sound and movement.
- **Promotes creativity**, as they experiment with different sounds and rhythms.

Benefits for parents:

- **Inexpensive and simple to set up**, using household glasses and water.
- **Perfect for quick, educational play**, combining science with music.
- **Great for group play**, encouraging kids to create music together.

---

402. DIY Jellyfish in a Bottle

DIY jellyfish in a bottle is a fascinating sensory craft where children create a floating jellyfish using a plastic bag and water in a clear bottle. It promotes creativity, curiosity, and sensory exploration.

How it works:

- **Create the jellyfish:** Cut a plastic bag into the shape of a jellyfish, leaving long tentacles. Fill the head with a small amount of water and tie it closed with a string.
- **Assemble the bottle:** Fill a clear bottle with water and gently place the jellyfish inside.
- **Watch it swim:** Let your child shake or move the bottle to watch the jellyfish float and swirl inside, mimicking how it moves in the ocean.

Benefits for kids:

- **Teaches about marine life**, introducing them to how jellyfish move in water.
- **Encourages sensory exploration**, especially through sight and movement.
- **Promotes creativity**, as they design their own jellyfish.

Benefits for parents:

- **Inexpensive and eco-friendly**, using plastic bags and household items.
- **Perfect for quiet play**, providing a soothing, sensory-rich experience.
- **Great for educational play**, combining science with hands-on crafting.

---

403. Pom-Pom Drop Game

The pom-pom drop game is a fun and simple activity where children drop pom-poms through tubes and watch them fall into containers. It promotes hand-eye coordination, fine motor skills, and problem-solving.

How it works:

- **Create the drop station:** Attach cardboard tubes to a wall or door at various angles.
- **Start dropping:** Let your child drop pom-poms into the tubes and watch them travel down into containers placed at the bottom.
- **Experiment with angles:** Encourage them to adjust the tubes and try different angles to see how the pom-poms move through the tubes.

Benefits for kids:

- **Develops hand-eye coordination**, as they aim and drop the pom-poms.
- **Teaches problem-solving**, as they experiment with different tube setups.
- **Promotes fine motor skills**, especially through handling and dropping the pom-poms.

Benefits for parents:

- **Inexpensive and easy to set up**, using household materials like cardboard tubes.
- **Perfect for quiet, independent play**, offering a focused and engaging activity.
- **Great for sensory play**, especially for younger children.

---

404. Coffee Filter Butterflies

Coffee filter butterflies are a creative and colorful craft where children turn coffee filters into vibrant butterflies using markers and water. It promotes creativity, fine motor skills, and sensory exploration.

How it works:

- **Color the filters:** Let your child use markers to color a coffee filter with bright designs.
- **Spray with water:** Lightly spray the filter with water to make the colors blend and spread.
- **Create the butterfly:** Once the filter is dry, pinch it in the middle and twist a pipe cleaner around it to form the butterfly's body and antennae.

Benefits for kids:

- **Encourages creativity,** allowing them to design colorful patterns.
- **Teaches color mixing,** as the water helps blend the colors on the filter.
- **Develops fine motor skills,** especially through assembling the butterfly.

Benefits for parents:

- **Inexpensive and simple to set up,** using coffee filters and markers.
- **Great for sensory exploration,** engaging sight and touch.
- **Perfect for themed crafts,** like spring or garden projects.

---

405. Paper Plate Clocks

Paper plate clocks are a fun and educational craft where children create their own clocks using paper plates and movable hands. It teaches time-telling skills while promoting creativity and fine motor development.

How it works:

- **Create the clock face:** Let your child decorate a paper plate with the numbers 1 to 12 to represent the hours on a clock.
- **Add the hands:** Cut out clock hands from cardboard and attach them to the center of the plate using a brad or pin.
- **Practice telling time:** Once the clock is complete, you can use it to help your child practice telling time by moving the hands to different positions.

Benefits for kids:

- **Teaches time-telling skills,** reinforcing numbers and clock reading.
- **Encourages creativity,** as they design their own clock face.
- **Develops fine motor skills,** especially through assembling the clock.

Benefits for parents:

- **Inexpensive and educational,** using paper plates and simple materials.
- **Perfect for early learning,** offering a hands-on approach to teaching time.
- **Great for independent play,** allowing children to practice and explore at their own pace.

406. Salt Dough Ornaments

Salt dough ornaments are a creative and hands-on craft where children make their own ornaments using a simple dough mixture of salt, flour, and water. It promotes creativity, fine motor skills, and sensory play.

How it works:

- **Make the dough:** Mix 1 cup of flour, 1/2 cup of salt, and 1/2 cup of water to form a dough.
- **Create the ornaments:** Let your child roll out the dough and use cookie cutters to cut out shapes like stars, hearts, or trees.
- **Decorate and bake:** Once the ornaments are baked and hardened, they can be painted and decorated with glitter, sequins, or beads.

Benefits for kids:

- **Encourages creativity**, allowing them to design their own ornaments.
- **Develops fine motor skills**, through rolling, cutting, and decorating the dough.
- **Promotes sensory exploration**, especially through the texture of the dough.

Benefits for parents:

- **Inexpensive and easy to make**, using simple household ingredients.
- **Perfect for holiday crafts**, creating personalized keepsakes.
- **Great for family bonding**, especially during decorating and painting.

407. Cupcake Liner Flowers

Cupcake liner flowers are a fun and easy craft where children use colorful cupcake liners to create beautiful flower decorations. It promotes creativity, fine motor skills, and imaginative play.

How it works:

- **Create the flowers:** Let your child stack and flatten different colored cupcake liners to form the petals of the flower.
- **Assemble the flowers:** Glue the cupcake liners together, add a paper circle or button for the center, and attach a pipe cleaner or straw as the stem.
- **Display the flowers:** Once complete, they can use the flowers as decorations or in pretend play.

Benefits for kids:

- **Encourages creativity**, allowing them to design colorful flowers.

- **Develops fine motor skills**, through assembling and gluing the liners.
- **Promotes imaginative play**, especially in creating pretend gardens or bouquets.

Benefits for parents:

- **Inexpensive and simple to make**, using cupcake liners and craft supplies.
- **Perfect for spring or garden-themed crafts**, offering a cheerful project.
- **Great for group play**, encouraging sharing and collaboration.

---

408. Dinosaur Fossil Dig

A dinosaur fossil dig is a fun, educational activity where children pretend to be paleontologists by digging for dinosaur "fossils" in a sensory bin filled with sand or dirt. It promotes curiosity, fine motor skills, and scientific exploration.

How it works:

- **Prepare the dig site:** Fill a container with sand, dirt, or rice and hide small dinosaur toys or plastic bones inside.
- **Start digging:** Give your child tools like brushes, spoons, or small shovels to dig for the fossils.
- **Learn about dinosaurs:** Encourage them to identify the dinosaurs or bones they find, introducing basic paleontology concepts.

Benefits for kids:

- **Teaches basic science concepts**, like paleontology and fossil discovery.
- **Promotes fine motor skills**, especially through digging and brushing.
- **Encourages curiosity and exploration**, making it an educational adventure.

Benefits for parents:

- **Inexpensive and easy to set up**, using small toys and sand or dirt.
- **Perfect for outdoor play**, offering a mess-free sensory activity.
- **Great for group play**, encouraging collaboration and discovery.

---

409. Egg Carton Caterpillars

Egg carton caterpillars are a simple and fun craft where children turn an old egg carton into a colorful caterpillar by painting and decorating it. It promotes creativity, fine motor skills, and imaginative play.

How it works:

- **Cut the egg carton:** Cut a strip of the egg carton to form the caterpillar's body.

- **Paint and decorate:** Let your child paint the caterpillar and add googly eyes, pipe cleaner antennae, and other decorations.
- **Use in play:** Once complete, they can use the caterpillar in stories or imaginative play.

Benefits for kids:

- **Encourages creativity**, as they design their own caterpillar.
- **Develops fine motor skills**, through painting and decorating the carton.
- **Promotes imaginative play**, allowing them to create stories with their caterpillar.

Benefits for parents:

- **Inexpensive and eco-friendly**, using recycled egg cartons.
- **Perfect for themed crafts**, like spring or insect-related projects.
- **Great for independent play**, fostering focus and creativity.

---

410. Paper Towel Roll Binoculars

Paper towel roll binoculars are a creative craft where children make their own binoculars using empty paper towel rolls and decorations. It promotes creativity, imaginative play, and fine motor skills.

How it works:

- **Create the binoculars:** Let your child tape or glue two empty paper towel rolls together side by side.
- **Decorate the binoculars:** Encourage them to decorate the binoculars with paint, stickers, or markers.
- **Imaginative play:** Once complete, they can use the binoculars for pretend adventures, like a safari or nature walk.

Benefits for kids:

- **Encourages creativity**, allowing them to design their own binoculars.
- **Promotes imaginative play**, especially in adventure or exploration scenarios.
- **Develops fine motor skills**, through decorating and assembling the binoculars.

Benefits for parents:

- **Inexpensive and eco-friendly**, using recycled materials.
- **Perfect for themed play**, like nature, adventure, or exploration games.
- **Great for independent play**, fostering creativity and imagination.

---

411. Nature Weaving

Nature weaving is an eco-friendly craft where children collect leaves, flowers, and grass and weave them into a simple loom made from cardboard or sticks. It promotes creativity, fine motor skills, and outdoor exploration.

How it works:

- **Create the loom:** Use a piece of cardboard or sticks tied together with string to make a simple loom.
- **Collect natural materials:** Take your child outside to gather leaves, flowers, and grass for weaving.
- **Weave the materials:** Let your child weave the natural materials through the strings of the loom, creating a nature-inspired design.

Benefits for kids:

- **Encourages outdoor exploration**, helping them connect with nature.
- **Develops fine motor skills**, especially through weaving.
- **Promotes creativity**, allowing them to design their own nature art.

Benefits for parents:

- **Inexpensive and eco-friendly**, using natural materials.
- **Perfect for outdoor play**, combining art with nature exploration.
- **Great for independent play**, offering a calming, mindful activity.

---

412. Straw Rockets

Straw rockets are a fun and simple science activity where children create their own mini rockets using straws and paper. It promotes creativity, problem-solving, and introduces basic concepts of physics and motion.

How it works:

- **Create the rocket:** Cut out small paper triangles or rectangles for the rocket's fins and attach them to a straw.
- **Prepare the launcher:** Place the straw rocket inside a wider straw or tube. Blow into the tube to launch the rocket into the air.
- **Experiment with distance:** Let your child experiment with different sizes of rockets and see how far they can launch each one.

Benefits for kids:

- **Teaches basic physics concepts**, like force and motion.
- **Encourages problem-solving**, as they test different rocket designs.
- **Promotes creativity**, allowing them to design their own rockets.

Benefits for parents:

- **Inexpensive and simple to make,** using paper and straws.
- **Perfect for STEM learning,** combining science with hands-on play.
- **Great for group play,** encouraging friendly competition.

---

413. DIY Suncatchers

DIY suncatchers are a creative and colorful craft where children use tissue paper and clear plastic to make decorations that catch and reflect sunlight. It promotes creativity, fine motor skills, and sensory exploration.

How it works:

- **Prepare the base:** Use clear contact paper or plastic to create the base for the suncatcher.
- **Create the design:** Let your child tear or cut colorful tissue paper into small pieces and arrange them on the plastic or contact paper.
- **Hang it up:** Once the suncatcher is complete, hang it in a sunny window and watch the colors light up as the sunlight passes through.

Benefits for kids:

- **Encourages creativity,** allowing them to design their own colorful suncatcher.
- **Promotes fine motor skills,** especially through cutting and arranging the tissue paper.
- **Teaches sensory exploration,** as they observe how light interacts with color.

Benefits for parents:

- **Inexpensive and easy to make,** using simple craft materials.
- **Great for seasonal or holiday decorations,** adding a personal touch to your home.
- **Perfect for quiet, independent play,** fostering creativity and focus.

---

414. DIY Mini Greenhouses

DIY mini greenhouses are a hands-on gardening activity where children learn how plants grow by creating small greenhouses using plastic containers and seeds. It promotes responsibility, science learning, and environmental awareness.

How it works:

- **Create the greenhouse:** Use a clear plastic container with a lid, such as a recycled food container, to act as the greenhouse.
- **Plant the seeds:** Let your child plant seeds in small pots or directly in the container, then cover it with the lid to trap moisture.
- **Watch them grow:** Place the mini greenhouse in a sunny spot and encourage your child to water and care for the seeds as they sprout.

Benefits for kids:

- **Teaches responsibility**, as they care for and nurture the growing plants.
- **Introduces basic science concepts**, like plant life cycles and photosynthesis.
- **Encourages environmental awareness**, helping them understand how plants grow.

Benefits for parents:

- **Inexpensive and eco-friendly**, using recycled containers and seeds.
- **Perfect for hands-on science learning**, combining nature with education.
- **Great for family bonding**, especially when caring for the plants together.

---

415. Toilet Paper Roll Owls

Toilet paper roll owls are a creative craft where children turn empty toilet paper rolls into cute owl decorations using paint, paper, and markers. It promotes creativity, fine motor skills, and imaginative play.

How it works:

- **Create the owl body:** Let your child paint the toilet paper roll to form the owl's body.
- **Add details:** Cut out paper shapes for the owl's wings, eyes, and beak, and let your child glue them onto the roll.
- **Display the owls:** Once complete, they can display the owls as decorations or use them in imaginative play.

Benefits for kids:

- **Encourages creativity**, allowing them to design their own owls.
- **Develops fine motor skills**, through painting, cutting, and gluing.
- **Promotes imaginative play**, especially in creating woodland scenes or stories.

Benefits for parents:

- **Inexpensive and eco-friendly**, using recycled toilet paper rolls.
- **Perfect for themed crafts**, like autumn or woodland creatures.
- **Great for independent play**, fostering focus and creativity.

---

416. DIY Kaleidoscope

A DIY kaleidoscope is a creative and scientific craft where children use reflective materials and colorful objects to make their own kaleidoscope. It promotes creativity, curiosity, and an understanding of light and reflection.

How it works:

- **Create the kaleidoscope:** Use a cardboard tube, reflective paper, and small beads or sequins. Line the inside of the tube with reflective paper, and add colorful objects inside a clear lid at one end.
- **Look through the kaleidoscope:** Encourage your child to look through the tube and rotate it, watching how the patterns change as light reflects inside.

Benefits for kids:

- **Teaches basic physics concepts,** like light reflection and symmetry.
- **Encourages curiosity and creativity,** allowing them to design their own kaleidoscope.
- **Promotes sensory exploration,** offering a visual and interactive experience.

Benefits for parents:

- **Inexpensive and easy to make,** using household materials.
- **Great for educational play,** combining science with creativity.
- **Perfect for quiet, focused play,** fostering concentration and discovery.

---

417. DIY Lava Lamp

A DIY lava lamp is a fun and educational activity where children create their own bubbling "lava lamp" using oil, water, and food coloring. It introduces basic chemistry concepts while promoting sensory exploration.

How it works:

- **Set up the lamp:** Fill a clear bottle with water and vegetable oil. Add food coloring and drop in an antacid tablet, like Alka-Seltzer, to start the reaction.
- **Watch the bubbles:** Let your child observe how the oil and water interact, and how the antacid creates bubbles that float through the liquid.

Benefits for kids:

- **Teaches basic chemistry concepts,** like density and chemical reactions.
- **Encourages sensory exploration,** through sight and movement.
- **Promotes curiosity and experimentation,** as they watch the "lava" bubble up.

Benefits for parents:

- **Inexpensive and easy to set up,** using household materials.
- **Perfect for STEM learning,** combining science with hands-on play.
- **Great for group play,** encouraging kids to explore science together.

---

418. Rock Tic-Tac-Toe

Rock tic-tac-toe is a fun outdoor craft and game where children paint rocks to create a reusable tic-tac-toe set. It promotes creativity, problem-solving, and fine motor skills.

How it works:

- **Create the rocks:** Let your child paint rocks with "X"s and "O"s to use as the game pieces.
- **Prepare the game board:** Use chalk to draw a tic-tac-toe grid on the ground or create a portable board using cardboard or a small wooden tray.
- **Play the game:** Encourage your child to play tic-tac-toe with friends or family, using the painted rocks as the game pieces.

Benefits for kids:

- **Teaches problem-solving and strategy**, through playing the game.
- **Encourages creativity**, as they design and paint the rocks.
- **Develops fine motor skills**, through painting and handling the rocks.

Benefits for parents:

- **Inexpensive and eco-friendly**, using natural materials like rocks.
- **Perfect for outdoor or indoor play**, offering flexibility.
- **Great for family bonding**, encouraging fun and friendly competition.

---

419. Sensory Cloud Dough

Sensory cloud dough is a soft, moldable dough made from flour and oil that children can squish, mold, and play with. It promotes sensory exploration, creativity, and fine motor skills.

How it works:

- **Make the cloud dough:** Mix 8 cups of flour with 1 cup of vegetable oil to create the dough. You can also add food coloring or glitter for a fun twist.
- **Start molding:** Let your child mold the dough into different shapes, using cookie cutters or their hands to explore the texture.
- **Experiment with textures:** Encourage them to squeeze, press, and shape the dough, noticing how it feels and moves.

Benefits for kids:

- **Promotes sensory exploration**, engaging their sense of touch.
- **Encourages creativity**, as they mold and shape the dough.
- **Develops fine motor skills**, through squeezing and handling the dough.

Benefits for parents:

- **Inexpensive and easy to make**, using simple household ingredients.
- **Perfect for quiet, independent play**, offering a calming sensory experience.
- **Great for indoor play**, especially on rainy days.

---

420. DIY Balloon Hovercraft

A DIY balloon hovercraft is a fun science experiment where children create a hovercraft using a balloon and a CD. It introduces basic physics concepts like air pressure and motion.

How it works:

- **Create the hovercraft:** Attach a bottle cap to the center of a CD. Inflate a balloon and place it over the bottle cap, then let go to see the hovercraft glide across a flat surface.
- **Experiment with movement:** Encourage your child to experiment with different surfaces and see how far the hovercraft can glide.

Benefits for kids:

- **Teaches basic physics concepts**, like air pressure and motion.
- **Encourages curiosity and experimentation**, as they explore how the hovercraft moves.
- **Promotes creativity**, allowing them to decorate the CD or design their own hovercraft.

Benefits for parents:

- **Inexpensive and easy to set up**, using household materials like CDs and balloons.
- **Perfect for STEM learning**, combining science with play.
- **Great for group play**, encouraging collaboration and friendly competition.

---

421. DIY Dream Catchers

DIY dream catchers are a creative craft where children make their own dream catchers using string, beads, and decorations. It introduces them to cultural traditions while fostering creativity and fine motor skills.

How it works:

- **Prepare the base:** Use a metal or wooden hoop as the base of the dream catcher.
- **Weave the web:** Let your child weave yarn or string across the opening, attaching it to the edges of the hoop to create the "web."
- **Decorate the catcher:** Add beads, feathers, or ribbons to the bottom of the dream catcher for decoration.
- **Hang it up:** Once complete, hang the dream catcher in their room.

Benefits for kids:

- **Teaches cultural traditions**, introducing them to the history of dreamcatchers.
- **Develops fine motor skills**, through weaving and decorating.
- **Encourages creativity**, as they design their own dreamcatcher.

Benefits for parents:

- **Simple and inexpensive**, using common craft materials.
- **Great for quiet, focused play**, helping kids develop patience and concentration.
- **Provides a lasting decoration**, making it a memorable craft project.

---

422. Balloon Tennis

Balloon tennis is an exciting and active indoor game where children use homemade paddles to hit a balloon back and forth like tennis. It promotes physical activity, coordination, and teamwork.

How it works:

- **Create the paddles:** Let your child make paddles by attaching paper plates to sticks or cardboard handles.
- **Set up the game:** Inflate a balloon and use the paddles to hit the balloon across an imaginary net, or create a net using string or tape on the floor.
- **Start playing:** Encourage your child to keep the balloon in the air as long as possible, taking turns hitting it with their paddle.

Benefits for kids:

- **Improves hand-eye coordination**, as they aim and hit the balloon.
- **Encourages physical activity**, keeping them engaged and moving.
- **Promotes teamwork and cooperation**, especially when played in pairs or groups.

Benefits for parents:

- **Inexpensive and easy to set up**, using balloons and paper plates.
- **Perfect for indoor play**, especially on rainy or cold days.
- **Great for group play**, encouraging friendly competition.

---

423. Paper Bag Puppets

Paper bag puppets are a fun and creative craft where children turn paper bags into puppet characters by decorating them with paint, paper, and other materials. It promotes creativity, fine motor skills, and imaginative play.

How it works:

- **Create the puppets:** Let your child decorate paper lunch bags to create animals, people, or fictional characters, using markers, paint, googly eyes, and other craft materials.
- **Put on a show:** Once the puppets are complete, they can use them in a puppet show, acting out stories or creating their own skits.
- **Add voices and personalities:** Encourage your child to give each puppet a unique voice or personality for more engaging play.

Benefits for kids:

- **Encourages creativity**, allowing them to design and create their own puppets.
- **Promotes fine motor skills**, through cutting, gluing, and decorating the bags.
- **Fosters imaginative play**, as they act out scenes and stories with the puppets.

Benefits for parents:

- **Inexpensive and easy to set up**, using paper bags and craft supplies.
- **Perfect for quiet, independent play**, offering a focused and creative activity.
- **Great for family bonding**, especially when putting on puppet shows together.

---

424. Rainbow Noodle Sensory Bin

A rainbow noodle sensory bin is a fun and colorful activity where children explore dyed pasta in a sensory bin, engaging their senses while developing fine motor skills. It promotes sensory exploration, creativity, and early learning.

How it works:

- **Dye the pasta:** Use food coloring to dye uncooked pasta in different colors.
- **Fill the bin:** Pour the dyed pasta into a large container, adding scoops, cups, or small toys for your child to explore.
- **Encourage play:** Let your child dig, scoop, pour, and sort the pasta, experimenting with the different textures and colors.

Benefits for kids:

- **Encourages sensory exploration**, especially through touch and sight.
- **Develops fine motor skills**, particularly through scooping and grasping.
- **Promotes creativity**, as they use the pasta for pretend play or sorting games.

Benefits for parents:

- **Inexpensive and easy to make**, using pasta and food coloring.
- **Perfect for quiet, independent play**, providing a calming sensory experience.
- **Great for sensory development**, especially for younger children.

425. Sticky Note Mosaics

Sticky note mosaics are a simple yet creative way for children to design colorful patterns or pictures by arranging sticky notes on a wall, door, or window. It promotes creativity, problem-solving, and fine motor skills.

How it works:

- **Choose a surface:** Allow your child to choose a blank wall, door, or window as their canvas.
- **Create the mosaic:** Provide colorful sticky notes and let them arrange them in patterns, pictures, or abstract designs.
- **Experiment with designs:** Encourage your child to try different layouts and colors, experimenting with how they look when arranged together.

Benefits for kids:

- **Encourages creativity**, as they design and build large-scale mosaics.
- **Promotes problem-solving**, as they figure out how to arrange the sticky notes.
- **Develops fine motor skills**, especially through handling and placing the sticky notes.

Benefits for parents:

- **Inexpensive and easy to set up**, using sticky notes.
- **Perfect for quiet, independent play**, fostering creativity and focus.
- **Great for themed projects**, like making seasonal or holiday decorations.

426. Shaving Cream Sensory Play

Shaving cream sensory play is a fun and tactile activity where children use shaving cream to explore textures and create art on a smooth surface. It promotes sensory exploration, creativity, and fine motor skills.

How it works:

- **Prepare the surface:** Spread shaving cream on a tray, table, or baking sheet.
- **Start exploring:** Let your child use their hands to explore the shaving cream, drawing pictures, letters, or patterns in it.
- **Experiment with textures:** You can also add food coloring or small toys to the shaving cream for extra sensory play.

Benefits for kids:

- **Promotes sensory exploration**, engaging their sense of touch.
- **Encourages creativity**, allowing them to draw and experiment with patterns.

- **Develops fine motor skills**, especially through squeezing and manipulating the shaving cream.

Benefits for parents:

- **Inexpensive and easy to clean up**, using shaving cream.
- **Great for calming, independent play**, providing a soothing sensory experience.
- **Perfect for indoor play**, offering a mess-free tactile activity.

---

427. DIY Monster Rocks

DIY monster rocks are a fun and creative craft where children paint rocks to look like silly or scary monsters. It promotes creativity, fine motor skills, and imaginative play.

How it works:

- **Collect the rocks:** Take your child outside to collect smooth rocks of various shapes and sizes.
- **Paint the monsters:** Let them use acrylic paint or paint pens to turn the rocks into monsters, adding googly eyes, teeth, or horns.
- **Use in play:** Once the rocks are dry, they can use them in imaginative play or as decorations.

Benefits for kids:

- **Encourages creativity**, allowing them to design unique monster characters.
- **Develops fine motor skills**, especially through painting on uneven surfaces.
- **Promotes imaginative play**, as they create stories and adventures with their monster rocks.

Benefits for parents:

- **Inexpensive and eco-friendly**, using rocks and paint.
- **Perfect for outdoor play**, combining art with nature exploration.
- **Great for themed crafts**, like Halloween or monster-related activities.

---

428. Ball Drop Race

The ball drop race is an exciting and simple physics-based activity where children race to drop small balls or marbles through tubes or funnels into a container. It promotes hand-eye coordination, fine motor skills, and problem-solving.

How it works:

- **Set up the tubes:** Use paper towel tubes, funnels, or other household objects to create a track or course for the balls.
- **Start the race:** Let your child drop balls or marbles through the tubes, racing to see how fast they can get the balls to the bottom.
- **Experiment with speed:** Encourage them to try different ball sizes and tube angles to see how it affects the speed of the balls.

Benefits for kids:

- **Develops hand-eye coordination**, as they aim and drop the balls.
- **Teaches problem-solving**, through experimenting with different setups.
- **Encourages fine motor skills**, especially through handling small balls and marbles.

Benefits for parents:

- **Inexpensive and easy to set up**, using household materials.
- **Perfect for STEM learning**, combining physics with play.
- **Great for group play**, encouraging friendly competition.

---

429. Washi Tape Art

Washi tape art is a fun and colorful craft where children use decorative tape to create patterns, pictures, or abstract designs on paper or canvas. It promotes creativity, fine motor skills, and concentration.

How it works:

- **Choose a surface:** Let your child choose paper, canvas, or even a notebook as the base for their artwork.
- **Create the design:** Provide different colors and patterns of washi tape and encourage them to create pictures, geometric patterns, or abstract designs by layering and arranging the tape.
- **Experiment with texture:** They can also experiment with overlapping the tape or adding other materials, like stickers or paint.

Benefits for kids:

- **Encourages creativity**, allowing them to explore patterns and textures.
- **Develops fine motor skills**, especially through handling and placing the tape.
- **Promotes concentration**, as they focus on creating their design.

Benefits for parents:

- **Inexpensive and easy to set up**, using washi tape and paper.
- **Perfect for quiet, focused play**, providing a calming and creative outlet.
- **Great for personalized gifts or room decor**, making it a versatile craft project.

---

430. Sensory Water Beads Play

Sensory water beads play is a calming and tactile activity where children explore squishy water beads in a sensory bin, helping them develop fine motor skills and sensory awareness.

How it works:

- **Prepare the beads:** Soak water beads in water for a few hours until they expand.
- **Fill the bin:** Pour the water beads into a sensory bin and provide scoops, cups, or small toys for your child to explore.
- **Encourage play:** Let your child dig, scoop, pour, and feel the texture of the water beads, experimenting with how they move and feel.

Benefits for kids:

- **Promotes sensory exploration**, especially through touch.
- **Develops fine motor skills**, through grasping and scooping the beads.
- **Encourages creativity**, allowing them to experiment with textures and materials.

Benefits for parents:

- **Inexpensive and easy to set up**, using water beads and household items.
- **Perfect for calming, independent play**, providing a soothing sensory experience.
- **Great for group play**, encouraging cooperative exploration.

---

431. Lego Printing Art

Lego printing art is a creative activity where children use Lego blocks dipped in paint to create prints and patterns on paper. It promotes creativity, fine motor skills, and sensory exploration.

How it works:

- **Prepare the paint:** Provide washable paint in shallow containers and a variety of Lego blocks.
- **Start printing:** Let your child dip the Lego blocks in paint and press them onto paper, creating colorful prints and patterns.
- **Experiment with designs:** Encourage them to try different block shapes and colors to see how they affect the prints.

Benefits for kids:

- **Encourages creativity**, allowing them to explore new textures and patterns.
- **Promotes sensory exploration**, especially through touch and sight.
- **Develops fine motor skills**, through handling and pressing the blocks.

Benefits for parents:

- **Inexpensive and simple to set up**, using Lego blocks and paint.
- **Perfect for themed art**, such as creating cityscapes or abstract designs.
- **Great for group play**, encouraging collaboration and sharing ideas.

---

432. Foil Boats Experiment

Foil boats is a fun and educational activity where children create small boats from aluminum foil and test how many objects they can hold before sinking. It introduces basic physics concepts such as buoyancy and weight distribution.

How it works:

- **Create the boat:** Let your child shape a piece of aluminum foil into a boat, encouraging them to experiment with different shapes.
- **Test the boat:** Place the boat in a tub of water and add small objects, such as coins or buttons, to see how many the boat can hold before it sinks.
- **Experiment with designs:** Encourage your child to try different boat designs to see which one can hold the most weight.

Benefits for kids:

- **Teaches basic physics concepts**, such as buoyancy and balance.
- **Encourages problem-solving**, as they figure out how to improve their boat design.
- **Promotes creativity**, allowing them to experiment with different shapes and structures.

Benefits for parents:

- **Inexpensive and easy to set up**, using aluminum foil and household objects.
- **Perfect for STEM learning**, combining science with hands-on experimentation.
- **Great for independent play**, fostering curiosity and exploration.

---

433. Bubble Wrap Stomp Painting

Bubble wrap stomp painting is a fun and energetic art activity where children paint with their feet by stomping on bubble wrap covered in paint. It promotes creativity, sensory exploration, and physical activity.

How it works:

- **Prepare the bubble wrap:** Lay out a large piece of bubble wrap and pour washable paint onto it.

- **Stomp and create:** Let your child step on the bubble wrap and stomp around, creating unique prints on a large piece of paper underneath.
- **Experiment with colors:** Encourage them to try different colors of paint to see how the prints change.

Benefits for kids:

- **Promotes sensory exploration,** engaging their sense of touch and movement.
- **Encourages physical activity,** as they stomp and move around.
- **Fosters creativity,** allowing them to create unique, large-scale art.

Benefits for parents:

- **Inexpensive and easy to set up,** using bubble wrap and paint.
- **Perfect for outdoor play,** minimizing indoor mess.
- **Great for group play,** encouraging collaboration and shared fun.

---

434. DIY Memory Game

A DIY memory game is a creative and educational activity where children make their own memory cards using drawings, stickers, or photos, then play a memory-matching game. It promotes cognitive development, concentration, and creativity.

How it works:

- **Create the cards:** Let your child draw pairs of matching pictures on small cards or use stickers or photos to create pairs.
- **Start the game:** Lay the cards face down and have your child flip over two at a time, trying to find matching pairs.
- **Experiment with difficulty:** You can add more pairs to make the game more challenging or change the theme, such as animals or colors.

Benefits for kids:

- **Develops memory and concentration,** through matching the cards.
- **Encourages creativity,** as they design their own game pieces.
- **Promotes problem-solving,** especially as the game becomes more challenging.

Benefits for parents:

- **Inexpensive and personalized,** using simple materials like paper or cardboard.
- **Perfect for quiet, independent play,** helping kids focus and develop cognitive skills.
- **Great for family bonding,** as parents and children can play together.

---

435. Pom-Pom Sorting by Color

Pom-pom sorting is a simple yet educational activity where children sort colorful pom-poms into different containers based on their color. It promotes fine motor skills, color recognition, and early math skills.

How it works:

- **Prepare the materials:** Provide a variety of colored pom-poms and matching containers or cups.
- **Start sorting:** Let your child use tweezers or their fingers to sort the pom-poms into the containers by color.
- **Add a challenge:** For older children, you can add a timer to see how fast they can complete the sorting or introduce patterns to follow.

Benefits for kids:

- **Teaches color recognition,** reinforcing early learning skills.
- **Develops fine motor skills,** especially through handling small pom-poms.
- **Encourages early math skills,** such as sorting, counting, and pattern recognition.

Benefits for parents:

- **Inexpensive and easy to set up,** using pom-poms and cups.
- **Perfect for quiet, independent play,** offering a focused and educational activity.
- **Great for early learning,** combining fun with skill development.

---

436. Tissue Paper Hot Air Balloons

Tissue paper hot air balloons are a creative craft where children use tissue paper and glue to create colorful hot air balloons for decoration. It promotes creativity, fine motor skills, and imaginative play.

How it works:

- **Create the balloon shape:** Let your child cut pieces of colorful tissue paper and glue them onto a balloon to create the balloon's colorful surface.
- **Make the basket:** Attach a small paper cup or box to the bottom as the hot air balloon's basket, using string to connect it to the balloon.
- **Display the balloon:** Once the tissue paper is dry, your child can display their hot air balloon as room decor or use it in pretend play.

Benefits for kids:

- **Encourages creativity,** allowing them to design their own colorful balloon.
- **Develops fine motor skills,** especially through cutting and gluing.
- **Promotes imaginative play,** particularly in creating flying adventures.

Benefits for parents:

- **Inexpensive and simple to make**, using tissue paper and glue.
- **Perfect for themed crafts**, like travel or sky-related activities.
- **Great for group play**, encouraging collaboration and shared creativity.

---

437. Miniature Garden in a Box

A miniature garden in a box is a hands-on and eco-friendly craft where children design and plant a tiny garden using natural materials. It promotes creativity, responsibility, and a connection with nature.

How it works:

- **Create the garden base:** Use a small box, tray, or shallow container as the base for the garden.
- **Design the garden:** Let your child collect small plants, rocks, twigs, and moss to create a miniature garden. They can also add small toys or figures as decorations.
- **Take care of the garden:** Encourage your child to water and care for the garden, teaching them about plant life and responsibility.

Benefits for kids:

- **Teaches responsibility**, as they care for their garden.
- **Encourages creativity**, allowing them to design their own natural space.
- **Promotes environmental awareness**, fostering a connection with nature.

Benefits for parents:

- **Inexpensive and eco-friendly**, using natural materials and simple supplies.
- **Perfect for educational play**, teaching about plants and gardening.
- **Great for family bonding**, as parents and children can garden together.

---

438. Glow Stick Ring Toss

Glow stick ring toss is an exciting nighttime game where children toss glow stick rings onto glowing targets, combining fun with physical activity and hand-eye coordination.

How it works:

- **Create the rings:** Connect glow sticks into rings by attaching the ends together.
- **Set up the target:** Use a glowing bottle or other glowing object as the target.
- **Start the game:** Let your child toss the glowing rings, aiming to loop them onto the target.

Benefits for kids:

- **Improves hand-eye coordination**, as they aim and toss the rings.
- **Encourages physical activity**, keeping them engaged in movement.
- **Promotes friendly competition**, making it perfect for group play.

Benefits for parents:

- **Inexpensive and easy to set up**, using glow sticks and simple household items.
- **Perfect for outdoor play**, especially at night or in low-light settings.
- **Great for group play**, encouraging teamwork and collaboration.

---

439. Nature Scavenger Hunt

A nature scavenger hunt is a fun and educational outdoor activity where children search for specific items in nature, such as leaves, rocks, or flowers, based on a checklist. It promotes outdoor exploration, problem-solving, and environmental awareness.

How it works:

- **Create a checklist:** Write down or draw pictures of different natural items for your child to find, such as a pinecone, a feather, or a specific type of leaf.
- **Start the hunt:** Take your child on a nature walk and have them search for the items on the list.
- **Document the finds:** Encourage them to take photos, collect small items, or draw what they find.

Benefits for kids:

- **Encourages outdoor exploration**, connecting them with nature.
- **Teaches problem-solving and observation skills**, as they search for specific items.
- **Promotes environmental awareness**, helping them learn about different elements of nature.

Benefits for parents:

- **Inexpensive and eco-friendly**, requiring only a checklist and outdoor space.
- **Great for family bonding**, offering an adventure for parents and children.
- **Perfect for educational play**, teaching about the natural world.

---

440. Cardboard Box Robot

A cardboard box robot is a creative craft where children use cardboard boxes to build and design their own robot, adding decorations and movable parts. It promotes creativity, problem-solving, and imaginative play.

How it works:

- **Collect the boxes:** Use small and large cardboard boxes to build the robot's body, head, and arms.
- **Decorate the robot:** Let your child paint, color, and add details like buttons, wires, or tin foil to make their robot come to life.
- **Imaginative play:** Once complete, they can use their robot in pretend play or as a room decoration.

Benefits for kids:

- **Encourages creativity and problem-solving**, as they design and build their own robot.
- **Promotes imaginative play**, especially in creating robot-themed adventures.
- **Develops fine motor skills**, through assembling and decorating the boxes.

Benefits for parents:

- **Inexpensive and eco-friendly**, using recycled cardboard boxes.
- **Perfect for themed crafts**, like space or technology-related projects.
- **Great for independent play**, fostering creativity and focus.

441. DIY Bird Feeders with Toilet Paper Rolls

DIY bird feeders made from toilet paper rolls are a fun and eco-friendly craft where children create simple bird feeders using peanut butter (or a peanut butter alternative) and birdseed. It promotes environmental awareness, creativity, and responsibility.

How it works:

- **Prepare the roll:** Spread peanut butter onto an empty toilet paper roll.
- **Add birdseed:** Roll the peanut butter-covered toilet paper roll in birdseed until it's fully coated.
- **Hang the feeder:** Thread a string through the roll and hang it in a tree. Watch as birds come to enjoy the treat.

Benefits for kids:

- **Teaches responsibility and caring for wildlife**, as they help feed local birds.
- **Encourages outdoor exploration**, getting children involved in nature.
- **Promotes fine motor skills**, through spreading peanut butter and handling birdseed.

Benefits for parents:

- **Inexpensive and eco-friendly**, using recycled toilet paper rolls.
- **Great for outdoor play**, offering an engaging, nature-focused activity.
- **Perfect for family bonding**, especially while observing birds together.

442. Spaghetti Towers

Spaghetti towers are a fun STEM-based activity where children use uncooked spaghetti and marshmallows to build tall structures. It promotes problem-solving, creativity, and basic engineering skills.

How it works:

- **Provide the materials:** Give your child a box of uncooked spaghetti and a bag of marshmallows.
- **Build the tower:** Encourage them to use the marshmallows to connect the spaghetti sticks, building a tower as tall and stable as possible.
- **Experiment with designs:** Let them try different building techniques to see which creates the most stable tower.

Benefits for kids:

- **Teaches basic engineering concepts**, like structure and balance.
- **Encourages problem-solving and experimentation**, as they figure out how to make their tower stand.
- **Promotes creativity**, allowing them to design unique structures.

Benefits for parents:

- **Inexpensive and easy to set up**, using spaghetti and marshmallows.
- **Perfect for STEM learning**, combining fun with hands-on science.
- **Great for group play**, encouraging teamwork and friendly competition.

---

443. Crayon Resist Art

Crayon resist art is a simple and magical art technique where children use white crayons and watercolor paint to create hidden designs. It promotes creativity, fine motor skills, and early art exploration.

How it works:

- **Draw with the crayon:** Let your child draw a picture or pattern on white paper using a white crayon.
- **Add watercolor:** Have them paint over the entire paper with watercolor paint. The crayon design will resist the paint, creating a colorful background with a hidden design.
- **Experiment with colors:** Encourage them to experiment with different color combinations and designs.

Benefits for kids:

- **Teaches color theory**, as they see how colors interact with each other.
- **Encourages creativity**, allowing them to design their own artwork.

- **Develops fine motor skills**, through drawing and painting.

Benefits for parents:

- **Inexpensive and easy to set up**, using crayons and watercolor paint.
- **Perfect for independent play**, fostering creativity and exploration.
- **Great for themed art**, like making hidden messages or seasonal designs.

---

444. DIY Friendship Bracelets

DIY friendship bracelets are a creative and meaningful craft where children use colorful threads to weave and create bracelets for friends or family. It promotes fine motor skills, creativity, and social connection.

How it works:

- **Choose the thread:** Let your child pick out colorful embroidery thread or yarn for their bracelet.
- **Start weaving:** Teach them how to braid or knot the thread to create different patterns.
- **Give the bracelet:** Once complete, they can give the bracelet to a friend or family member as a gift.

Benefits for kids:

- **Develops fine motor skills**, especially through weaving and knotting.
- **Encourages creativity**, allowing them to design their own unique bracelets.
- **Promotes social connection**, as they make and give bracelets to friends.

Benefits for parents:

- **Inexpensive and simple to set up**, using thread or yarn.
- **Perfect for quiet, focused play**, fostering concentration and creativity.
- **Great for group play**, encouraging sharing and gift-giving.

---

445. Mirror Symmetry Drawing

Mirror symmetry drawing is a creative art activity where children draw half of an object or picture and use a mirror to reflect the other half, teaching symmetry and balance. It promotes spatial awareness, creativity, and fine motor skills.

How it works:

- **Start the drawing:** Let your child draw half of an object, such as a butterfly or a face, on one side of the paper.

- **Use the mirror:** Place a small mirror along the center of the drawing to reflect the other half, showing how the picture looks when completed symmetrically.
- **Finish the picture:** Encourage your child to complete the drawing by adding the other half or experimenting with different shapes and designs.

Benefits for kids:

- **Teaches spatial awareness and symmetry**, helping them understand balance in art.
- **Encourages creativity**, allowing them to experiment with shapes and designs.
- **Develops fine motor skills**, through drawing and completing the picture.

Benefits for parents:

- **Inexpensive and easy to set up**, using paper and a mirror.
- **Perfect for early learning**, especially in teaching symmetry and balance.
- **Great for independent play**, fostering creativity and focus.

---

446. Pipe Cleaner Sculptures

Pipe cleaner sculptures are a fun and tactile craft where children use bendable pipe cleaners to create 3D shapes, animals, or objects. It promotes creativity, fine motor skills, and imaginative play.

How it works:

- **Provide the pipe cleaners:** Let your child choose different colored pipe cleaners to use as the base for their sculptures.
- **Start shaping:** Encourage them to twist, bend, and shape the pipe cleaners into different animals, flowers, or abstract designs.
- **Experiment with structures:** They can add beads or other small decorations to enhance their sculptures.

Benefits for kids:

- **Encourages creativity**, as they design their own 3D sculptures.
- **Develops fine motor skills**, through twisting and shaping the pipe cleaners.
- **Promotes imaginative play**, especially in creating animals or characters.

Benefits for parents:

- **Inexpensive and easy to set up**, using simple craft supplies like pipe cleaners.
- **Perfect for independent play**, fostering creativity and focus.
- **Great for group play**, encouraging collaboration and sharing ideas.

---

447. Moon Sand Sensory Play

Moon sand is a soft, moldable sensory material made from flour and oil that children can shape, mold, and play with. It promotes sensory exploration, creativity, and fine motor skills.

How it works:

- **Make the moon sand:** Mix 8 cups of flour with 1 cup of baby oil or vegetable oil to create a soft, crumbly texture.
- **Start molding:** Let your child use their hands or molds to shape the moon sand into different structures, like castles or animals.
- **Experiment with textures:** Encourage them to squish, press, and shape the moon sand, exploring how it moves and feels.

Benefits for kids:

- **Promotes sensory exploration**, engaging their sense of touch.
- **Encourages creativity**, as they mold and shape the moon sand.
- **Develops fine motor skills**, especially through squeezing and handling the sand.

Benefits for parents:

- **Inexpensive and easy to make**, using household ingredients.
- **Perfect for calming, independent play**, providing a soothing sensory experience.
- **Great for indoor play**, especially on rainy days.

---

448. Glow-in-the-Dark Slime

Glow-in-the-dark slime is a fun and sensory-rich activity where children create slime that glows in the dark, adding an extra element of excitement to traditional slime play. It promotes creativity, sensory exploration, and early science learning.

How it works:

- **Make the slime:** Mix glue, baking soda, and contact lens solution to create slime. Add glow-in-the-dark paint or glow powder to the mixture to make it glow.
- **Explore the slime:** Let your child squish, stretch, and play with the glowing slime in a dark room.
- **Experiment with light:** Encourage them to expose the slime to light and see how it glows in the dark afterward.

Benefits for kids:

- **Promotes sensory exploration**, especially through touch and sight.
- **Teaches basic science concepts**, like how materials can glow in the dark.
- **Encourages creativity**, as they experiment with stretching and shaping the slime.

Benefits for parents:

- **Inexpensive and easy to make**, using common household ingredients.

- **Perfect for sensory play**, offering a fun and engaging tactile experience.
- **Great for group play**, encouraging collaboration and shared fun.

---

449. Shadow Drawing

Shadow drawing is an engaging outdoor activity where children use the shadows of objects to create unique drawings. It promotes creativity, problem-solving, and fine motor skills while teaching about light and shadows.

How it works:

- **Set up the objects:** Place toys or other objects outside in the sun so that they cast clear shadows on a piece of paper.
- **Trace the shadows:** Let your child trace the shadows of the objects onto the paper using a pencil or marker.
- **Complete the drawings:** Encourage them to turn the traced shadows into animals, people, or abstract designs by adding details and colors.

Benefits for kids:

- **Teaches basic science concepts**, like light and shadows.
- **Encourages creativity**, allowing them to transform shadows into art.
- **Develops fine motor skills**, through tracing and adding details.

Benefits for parents:

- **Inexpensive and simple to set up**, using toys and sunlight.
- **Perfect for outdoor play**, combining art with nature exploration.
- **Great for early learning**, teaching about shadows and light.

---

450. Cup Stacking Challenge

The cup stacking challenge is a fun and physical activity where children try to build and dismantle pyramids of plastic cups as fast as possible. It promotes hand-eye coordination, problem-solving, and fine motor skills.

How it works:

- **Prepare the cups:** Provide a set of plastic cups for stacking.
- **Start stacking:** Let your child build a pyramid by stacking the cups in rows, then have them dismantle it as quickly as possible.
- **Add a timer:** For added excitement, you can time how fast they can complete the stacking and challenge them to beat their previous time.

Benefits for kids:

- **Develops hand-eye coordination**, through precise stacking and handling.
- **Encourages problem-solving and critical thinking**, as they figure out the best way to stack and unstack the cups.
- **Promotes friendly competition**, especially when played with friends or siblings.

Benefits for parents:

- **Inexpensive and easy to set up**, using plastic cups.
- **Perfect for indoor play**, offering a fast-paced, engaging activity.
- **Great for group play**, encouraging teamwork and friendly challenges.

---

451. Giant Paper Mural

A giant paper mural is a collaborative art project where children create a large-scale piece of artwork on a big sheet of paper. It promotes creativity, teamwork, and fine motor skills.

How it works:

- **Set up the mural:** Tape a large sheet of paper to a wall or floor.
- **Start drawing and painting:** Let your child use markers, paint, crayons, or colored pencils to create a giant mural. They can work alone or invite friends or siblings to join in.
- **Create a theme:** Encourage them to work on a theme, such as an underwater scene, outer space, or a jungle, allowing for creativity and collaboration.

Benefits for kids:

- **Encourages creativity and imagination**, allowing them to design a large-scale artwork.
- **Promotes teamwork**, especially when working on the mural with others.
- **Develops fine motor skills**, through drawing, painting, and coloring.

Benefits for parents:

- **Inexpensive and simple to set up**, using paper and art supplies.
- **Perfect for group play**, encouraging collaboration and shared creativity.
- **Great for independent or family bonding**, making it a versatile activity.

---

452. Magnetic Fishing Game

The magnetic fishing game is a fun, hands-on activity where children "catch" fish with a magnetized fishing rod. It promotes fine motor skills, hand-eye coordination, and patience.

How it works:

- **Create the fish:** Cut out fish shapes from cardboard or paper and attach a small metal paperclip to each fish.
- **Make the fishing rod:** Attach a magnet to the end of a string tied to a stick or dowel to serve as the fishing rod.
- **Start fishing:** Let your child use the magnetic rod to "catch" the fish by attracting the paperclip, promoting both fun and concentration.

Benefits for kids:

- **Improves hand-eye coordination**, as they aim and catch the fish.
- **Encourages patience and focus**, as they wait to hook the fish.
- **Promotes fine motor skills**, especially through using the rod and magnets.

Benefits for parents:

- **Inexpensive and easy to make**, using household materials like cardboard and magnets.
- **Perfect for quiet, independent play**, fostering focus and patience.
- **Great for group play**, encouraging friendly competition or collaboration.

---

453. Pom-Pom Catapult

The pom-pom catapult is a playful STEM activity where children build a simple catapult using craft sticks and launch soft pom-poms. It introduces basic physics concepts like force and motion while promoting problem-solving.

How it works:

- **Build the catapult:** Let your child stack and secure craft sticks with rubber bands to create a simple catapult base. Attach a spoon to the top as the launching arm.
- **Launch the pom-poms:** Place a pom-pom in the spoon, press down, and release to launch it through the air.
- **Experiment with distance:** Encourage them to experiment with different angles and forces to see how far they can launch the pom-poms.

Benefits for kids:

- **Teaches basic physics concepts**, like force and motion.
- **Encourages problem-solving and experimentation**, as they test how the catapult works.
- **Promotes fine motor skills**, through assembling and using the catapult.

Benefits for parents:

- **Inexpensive and easy to set up**, using craft sticks and rubber bands.
- **Perfect for STEM learning**, combining science with hands-on play.
- **Great for group play**, encouraging collaboration and friendly competition.

454. Homemade Storybook

A homemade storybook is a creative writing and art project where children write and illustrate their own story. It promotes literacy, creativity, and fine motor skills.

How it works:

- **Create the book:** Fold pieces of paper in half to form the pages of the book. Staple or tape them together.
- **Write the story:** Let your child write their own story, whether it's about animals, adventures, or anything they can imagine.
- **Illustrate the book:** Encourage them to draw pictures to go along with their story, creating a fully illustrated book.

Benefits for kids:

- **Promotes literacy and storytelling**, encouraging them to create their own narratives.
- **Encourages creativity**, allowing them to write and illustrate their own book.
- **Develops fine motor skills**, through writing and drawing.

Benefits for parents:

- **Inexpensive and simple to make**, using paper and basic supplies.
- **Perfect for quiet, independent play**, fostering creativity and concentration.
- **Great for early learning**, especially in literacy and writing skills.

---

455. Cotton Ball Sensory Bin

A cotton ball sensory bin is a calming and tactile activity where children explore soft cotton balls in a sensory bin, enhancing their sensory awareness while promoting fine motor skills.

How it works:

- **Fill the bin:** Place cotton balls in a large container or bin.
- **Add toys and tools:** Provide scoops, cups, and small toys for your child to explore the texture and movement of the cotton balls.
- **Encourage play:** Let your child dig, scoop, pour, and feel the softness of the cotton balls, experimenting with how they move and feel.

Benefits for kids:

- **Promotes sensory exploration**, engaging their sense of touch.
- **Encourages fine motor skills**, especially through scooping and handling the cotton balls.
- **Provides a calming sensory experience**, perfect for quiet play.

Benefits for parents:

- **Inexpensive and easy to set up**, using cotton balls and household tools.
- **Perfect for calming, independent play**, offering a soothing sensory activity.
- **Great for younger children**, helping them explore texture and movement.

---

456. Nature Collage

A nature collage is a creative outdoor activity where children collect natural items like leaves, flowers, and twigs, and use them to create a collage on paper or cardboard. It promotes creativity, fine motor skills, and an appreciation for nature.

How it works:

- **Collect natural items:** Take your child outside to gather leaves, flowers, twigs, or seeds.
- **Create the collage:** Let your child glue the collected items onto paper or cardboard, arranging them to form patterns, pictures, or abstract designs.
- **Add details:** They can use markers or paint to enhance their collage with additional drawings or colors.

Benefits for kids:

- **Encourages outdoor exploration**, helping them connect with nature.
- **Promotes creativity**, as they design their own nature-inspired artwork.
- **Develops fine motor skills**, through arranging and gluing natural items.

Benefits for parents:

- **Inexpensive and eco-friendly**, using natural materials from outdoors.
- **Perfect for educational play**, teaching about different plants and seasons.
- **Great for family bonding**, combining art with nature exploration.

---

457. Sticker Scene Creation

Sticker scene creation is a simple yet engaging activity where children use stickers to create scenes and stories on paper. It promotes creativity, fine motor skills, and imaginative play.

How it works:

- **Choose a theme:** Provide themed stickers, such as animals, cars, or space, and let your child choose a theme for their scene.
- **Create the scene:** Encourage them to arrange the stickers on paper to create a story or picture.

- **Add details:** They can draw backgrounds, add speech bubbles, or write captions to enhance their sticker scene.

Benefits for kids:

- **Encourages creativity**, allowing them to design their own stories and scenes.
- **Develops fine motor skills**, especially through peeling and placing stickers.
- **Promotes imaginative play**, helping them create narratives with their stickers.

Benefits for parents:

- **Inexpensive and easy to set up**, using stickers and paper.
- **Perfect for quiet, independent play**, fostering focus and creativity.
- **Great for group play**, encouraging collaboration and story-sharing.

---

458. Cardboard Box Maze

A cardboard box maze is a large-scale, interactive craft where children use cardboard boxes to build a maze or tunnel system for toys or even themselves. It promotes problem-solving, creativity, and physical activity.

How it works:

- **Collect the boxes:** Gather large cardboard boxes and cut out doors and windows to form the pathways of the maze.
- **Assemble the maze:** Let your child help design and arrange the boxes to create a connected maze, adding tunnels and turns.
- **Explore the maze:** Once complete, they can crawl through the maze or send toys through to see how they navigate the twists and turns.

Benefits for kids:

- **Encourages problem-solving and creativity**, as they design and explore the maze.
- **Promotes physical activity**, especially through crawling and moving through the maze.
- **Fosters imaginative play**, turning the maze into an adventure.

Benefits for parents:

- **Inexpensive and eco-friendly**, using recycled cardboard boxes.
- **Perfect for indoor or outdoor play**, offering flexibility in setup.
- **Great for group play**, encouraging teamwork and exploration.

---

459. Foam Sticker Puzzles

Foam sticker puzzles are a simple craft where children use foam stickers to create their own puzzles, enhancing creativity, problem-solving, and fine motor skills.

How it works:

- **Create the puzzle:** Let your child stick foam shapes or designs onto a piece of cardboard or sturdy paper.
- **Cut the puzzle:** Once the design is complete, cut the foam-covered cardboard into puzzle pieces.
- **Solve the puzzle:** Encourage your child to put the puzzle back together, enjoying the process of creating and solving their own design.

Benefits for kids:

- **Develops problem-solving skills**, as they figure out how to complete the puzzle.
- **Encourages creativity**, allowing them to design their own puzzle.
- **Promotes fine motor skills**, through handling the foam stickers and puzzle pieces.

Benefits for parents:

- **Inexpensive and easy to make**, using foam stickers and cardboard.
- **Perfect for quiet, independent play**, fostering creativity and focus.
- **Great for group play**, allowing kids to swap and solve each other's puzzles.

---

460. Marble Run with Cardboard Tubes

A marble run is a fun, hands-on engineering activity where children build a track out of cardboard tubes for marbles to roll through. It promotes creativity, problem-solving, and fine motor skills.

How it works:

- **Create the track:** Cut cardboard tubes, such as toilet paper or paper towel rolls, into pieces and tape them to a wall or board at different angles to create a marble track.
- **Start the run:** Let your child drop a marble at the top of the track and watch it roll through the tubes.
- **Experiment with design:** Encourage them to adjust the angles of the tubes and add different paths to see how it affects the marble's speed and movement.

Benefits for kids:

- **Teaches basic engineering concepts**, like gravity and motion.
- **Encourages problem-solving and experimentation**, as they design and test the track.
- **Promotes fine motor skills**, through assembling and adjusting the marble run.

Benefits for parents:

- **Inexpensive and eco-friendly**, using recycled cardboard tubes.
- **Perfect for STEM learning**, combining science with hands-on play.
- **Great for group play**, encouraging collaboration and friendly competition.

---

461. Homemade Playdough

Homemade playdough is a classic sensory activity where children mix and play with soft dough that they can mold and shape into different creations. It promotes fine motor skills, creativity, and sensory exploration.

How it works:

- **Make the playdough:** Mix 2 cups of flour, 1 cup of salt, 1 cup of water, and 2 tablespoons of vegetable oil. You can add food coloring to create different colors.
- **Start playing:** Let your child use cookie cutters, rolling pins, or their hands to shape the playdough into different objects like animals, flowers, or abstract forms.
- **Store for later:** Keep the playdough in an airtight container for future play.

Benefits for kids:

- **Promotes sensory exploration**, engaging their sense of touch and sight.
- **Encourages creativity**, as they mold and shape the dough into different designs.
- **Develops fine motor skills**, especially through squeezing, rolling, and shaping the dough.

Benefits for parents:

- **Inexpensive and easy to make**, using household ingredients.
- **Perfect for quiet, independent play**, offering a calming sensory experience.
- **Great for group play**, allowing kids to share tools and ideas.

---

462. Balloon Rockets

Balloon rockets are a fun and simple science activity where children launch balloons along a string, learning about force and motion. It promotes problem-solving, creativity, and introduces basic physics concepts.

How it works:

- **Set up the rocket:** Tie a piece of string between two objects (like chairs) and thread a straw through the string. Inflate a balloon and tape it to the straw.
- **Launch the rocket:** Let your child release the balloon, watching it zoom along the string as it deflates.
- **Experiment with distance:** Encourage your child to experiment with different balloon sizes and amounts of air to see how far the rocket travels.

Benefits for kids:

- **Teaches basic physics concepts**, like force and motion.
- **Encourages problem-solving and experimentation**, as they test different balloon sizes.
- **Promotes creativity**, allowing them to modify and improve the design of their balloon rocket.

Benefits for parents:

- **Inexpensive and easy to set up**, using balloons and string.
- **Perfect for STEM learning**, combining science with hands-on fun.
- **Great for group play**, encouraging friendly competition and collaboration.

---

463. Paper Plate Weaving

Paper plate weaving is a fun and creative craft where children use yarn to weave patterns on a paper plate. It promotes fine motor skills, creativity, and patience.

How it works:

- **Prepare the plate:** Cut small slits around the edges of a paper plate and wrap yarn across the plate to create the warp (the base threads for weaving).
- **Start weaving:** Let your child weave different colored yarn through the warp, creating a circular pattern or design.
- **Experiment with colors:** Encourage them to try different yarn colors and textures for unique designs.

Benefits for kids:

- **Develops fine motor skills**, especially through handling and weaving the yarn.
- **Encourages creativity**, allowing them to design their own woven patterns.
- **Promotes patience and concentration**, as they carefully weave the yarn.

Benefits for parents:

- **Inexpensive and simple to set up**, using paper plates and yarn.
- **Perfect for quiet, focused play**, fostering concentration and creativity.
- **Great for educational play**, introducing basic weaving techniques.

---

464. Water Balloon Painting

Water balloon painting is a fun and messy outdoor art activity where children throw paint-filled water balloons at a canvas or paper to create colorful splatter art. It promotes creativity, physical activity, and sensory exploration.

How it works:

- **Fill the balloons:** Fill small water balloons with water and a little bit of washable paint.
- **Set up the canvas:** Place a large sheet of paper or canvas on the ground or against a wall outside.
- **Start painting:** Let your child throw the balloons at the canvas, creating colorful splatters and abstract designs.

Benefits for kids:

- **Encourages physical activity**, as they throw and aim the balloons.
- **Promotes creativity**, allowing them to create unique, abstract art.
- **Provides sensory exploration**, through the feel and sound of the balloons bursting.

Benefits for parents:

- **Inexpensive and easy to set up**, using balloons and washable paint.
- **Perfect for outdoor play**, minimizing indoor mess.
- **Great for group play**, encouraging collaboration and shared fun.

---

465. Edible Necklaces

Edible necklaces are a fun and tasty craft where children thread cereal or candy onto string to create wearable snacks. It promotes fine motor skills, creativity, and early math skills like pattern recognition.

How it works:

- **Prepare the materials:** Provide string and different types of cereal or candy with holes (like O-shaped cereal or gummy rings).
- **Start threading:** Let your child thread the cereal or candy onto the string, creating patterns or random designs.
- **Wear and eat:** Once complete, they can wear their necklace and enjoy eating it too.

Benefits for kids:

- **Develops fine motor skills**, especially through threading the cereal or candy.
- **Teaches pattern recognition and sorting**, reinforcing early math skills.
- **Encourages creativity**, allowing them to design their own edible jewelry.

Benefits for parents:

- **Inexpensive and simple to set up**, using cereal or candy.
- **Perfect for themed parties or snacks**, offering a fun and tasty activity.
- **Great for group play**, encouraging sharing and creativity.

466. Ice Block Treasure Hunt

The ice block treasure hunt is a cool and sensory-rich activity where children dig through a block of ice to uncover hidden toys or treasures. It promotes problem-solving, fine motor skills, and sensory exploration.

How it works:

- **Prepare the ice block:** Freeze small toys, gems, or other treasures inside a large block of ice.
- **Start excavating:** Let your child use tools like spoons, salt, or warm water to help melt the ice and uncover the hidden treasures.
- **Experiment with methods:** Encourage them to try different ways to melt the ice faster, like adding more salt or warm water.

Benefits for kids:

- **Teaches basic science concepts**, like melting and states of matter.
- **Encourages problem-solving**, as they figure out how to free the treasures.
- **Promotes fine motor skills**, especially through handling the ice and tools.

Benefits for parents:

- **Inexpensive and easy to set up**, using ice and small toys.
- **Perfect for outdoor or indoor play**, offering flexibility depending on the weather.
- **Great for sensory play**, engaging their sense of touch and temperature.

---

467. DIY Kaleidoscope Craft

A DIY kaleidoscope is a creative and scientific craft where children use reflective materials and colorful objects to make their own kaleidoscope. It promotes creativity, curiosity, and an understanding of light and reflection.

How it works:

- **Create the kaleidoscope:** Use a cardboard tube, reflective paper, and small beads or sequins. Line the inside of the tube with reflective paper, and add colorful objects inside a clear lid at one end.
- **Look through the kaleidoscope:** Encourage your child to look through the tube and rotate it, watching how the patterns change as light reflects inside.

Benefits for kids:

- **Teaches basic physics concepts**, like light reflection and symmetry.
- **Encourages curiosity and creativity**, allowing them to design their own kaleidoscope.
- **Promotes sensory exploration**, offering a visual and interactive experience.

Benefits for parents:

- **Inexpensive and easy to make**, using household materials.
- **Great for educational play**, combining science with creativity.
- **Perfect for quiet, focused play**, fostering concentration and discovery.

---

468. Sock Puppets

Sock puppets are a classic and creative craft where children turn old socks into fun puppets with eyes, hair, and decorations. It promotes creativity, fine motor skills, and imaginative play.

How it works:

- **Create the puppets:** Let your child decorate old socks with googly eyes, yarn for hair, and other craft materials like fabric, buttons, and markers.
- **Put on a show:** Once the puppets are complete, they can use them in a puppet show, creating stories and acting out scenes.
- **Add voices and personalities:** Encourage your child to give each puppet a unique voice and personality for more engaging play.

Benefits for kids:

- **Encourages creativity**, as they design and create their own puppets.
- **Promotes fine motor skills**, through decorating and handling the socks.
- **Fosters imaginative play**, as they act out scenes and stories with the puppets.

Benefits for parents:

- **Inexpensive and eco-friendly**, using old socks and household materials.
- **Perfect for quiet, independent play**, fostering creativity and focus.
- **Great for family bonding**, especially during puppet shows.

---

469. Sponge Water Bombs

Sponge water bombs are a fun and refreshing outdoor activity where children make water bombs from sponges for a water fight. It promotes physical activity, teamwork, and sensory play.

How it works:

- **Create the water bombs:** Cut sponges into strips and tie them together in the middle with string to form a star-shaped water bomb.
- **Soak in water:** Let your child soak the sponge bombs in water.

- **Start the water fight:** Throw the sponge bombs at targets or play a water fight, enjoying a fun and refreshing activity on a hot day.

Benefits for kids:

- **Encourages physical activity**, keeping them active and engaged.
- **Promotes teamwork**, especially in group water fights.
- **Provides sensory exploration**, through the feel and splash of the water.

Benefits for parents:

- **Inexpensive and easy to make**, using sponges and string.
- **Perfect for outdoor play**, especially on hot days.
- **Great for group play**, encouraging collaboration and friendly competition.

---

470. Nature Paint Brushes

Nature paint brushes are a creative way for children to explore textures and experiment with art by making their own paintbrushes from natural materials like leaves, twigs, and grass. It combines art and nature in a hands-on project.

How it works:

- **Collect materials:** Take your child on a nature walk to gather leaves, pine needles, grass, or small branches.
- **Make the brushes:** Attach the natural materials to sticks or twigs using rubber bands or string to create paintbrushes with different textures.
- **Start painting:** Let your child dip the brushes into paint and experiment with how each one creates different strokes and textures on paper.

Benefits for kids:

- **Encourages outdoor exploration**, fostering a connection with nature.
- **Teaches about texture and art**, through hands-on experimentation with natural materials.
- **Promotes creativity**, as they create unique artwork using non-traditional tools.

Benefits for parents:

- **Inexpensive and eco-friendly**, using natural materials from outdoors.
- **Encourages outdoor play**, combining art with nature exploration.
- **Great for sensory exploration**, making it a calming and creative activity.

471. Obstacle Course with Household Items

Create a fun indoor obstacle course using pillows, chairs, and blankets for children to crawl under, jump over, and weave around. It promotes physical activity, coordination, and problem-solving.

How it works:

- **Set up the course:** Arrange household items like chairs to crawl under, pillows to jump over, and a blanket tunnel.
- **Add challenges:** Include tasks like hopping on one foot or balancing on a line of tape.
- **Start the race:** Let your child navigate the course and time them to add excitement.

Benefits for kids:

- **Encourages physical activity**, keeping them moving and engaged.
- **Promotes problem-solving**, as they figure out how to navigate the obstacles.
- **Improves coordination and balance**, through various physical challenges.

Benefits for parents:

- **Inexpensive and simple to set up**, using household items.
- **Great for indoor play**, especially on rainy days.
- **Perfect for group play**, encouraging friendly competition and teamwork.

472. Bubble Snake Maker

Create a fun bubble snake maker using a plastic bottle, an old sock, and dish soap. It promotes sensory play, creativity, and coordination.

How it works:

- **Create the snake maker:** Cut the bottom off a plastic bottle and place a sock over the cut end. Secure it with a rubber band.
- **Dip and blow:** Dip the sock-covered end in dish soap and blow through the bottle to create a long bubble snake.
- **Experiment with bubbles:** Encourage your child to experiment with different blowing techniques to make longer or shorter bubble snakes.

Benefits for kids:

- **Promotes sensory exploration**, engaging their sense of touch and sight.
- **Encourages creativity**, as they experiment with bubble sizes.
- **Improves coordination**, through controlling their breath while blowing bubbles.

Benefits for parents:

- **Inexpensive and easy to make**, using household materials.
- **Perfect for outdoor play**, minimizing mess.
- **Great for group play**, encouraging friendly competition for the longest bubble snake.

---

473. Paper Plate Mask Making

Paper plate masks are a fun and creative craft where children turn paper plates into masks with paint, markers, and decorations. It promotes creativity, fine motor skills, and imaginative play.

How it works:

- **Create the mask base:** Let your child cut eye holes in a paper plate.
- **Decorate the mask:** Encourage them to paint or color the mask, adding feathers, glitter, or yarn for hair.
- **Imaginative play:** Once the mask is complete, they can use it in pretend play, creating characters and acting out stories.

Benefits for kids:

- **Encourages creativity**, allowing them to design their own masks.
- **Promotes fine motor skills**, through cutting, painting, and gluing.
- **Fosters imaginative play**, especially in creating characters and stories.

Benefits for parents:

- **Inexpensive and easy to set up**, using paper plates and craft materials.
- **Perfect for themed play**, like animals, superheroes, or fantasy characters.
- **Great for group play**, encouraging sharing and collaboration.

---

474. Balloon Car Race

Balloon car races are a fun, hands-on STEM activity where children use air-powered balloon cars to race. It promotes creativity, problem-solving, and basic physics concepts.

How it works:

- **Build the cars:** Help your child attach a balloon to a lightweight toy car or create one from cardboard.
- **Inflate the balloon:** Inflate the balloon and release it to see how far the car travels.
- **Experiment with designs:** Encourage them to try different car shapes and balloon sizes to see which goes fastest.

Benefits for kids:

- **Teaches basic physics concepts**, like force and motion.
- **Encourages creativity**, as they design their own balloon-powered car.
- **Promotes problem-solving**, through experimenting with different designs.

Benefits for parents:

- **Inexpensive and easy to make**, using balloons and toy cars or cardboard.
- **Perfect for STEM learning**, combining science with play.
- **Great for group play**, encouraging friendly competition.

---

475. Nature Bracelets

Nature bracelets are a creative outdoor craft where children collect leaves, flowers, and small twigs to make wearable art. It promotes creativity, fine motor skills, and a connection to nature.

How it works:

- **Create the bracelet base:** Wrap masking tape or double-sided tape around your child's wrist, sticky side out.
- **Collect nature materials:** Let them explore the yard or park to find leaves, flowers, or small twigs to attach to their bracelet.
- **Wear the bracelet:** Once complete, they can wear their nature bracelet or use it as a decoration.

Benefits for kids:

- **Encourages outdoor exploration**, fostering a connection with nature.
- **Promotes creativity**, allowing them to design their own nature bracelet.
- **Develops fine motor skills**, through handling and attaching small items.

Benefits for parents:

- **Inexpensive and eco-friendly**, using natural materials from outdoors.
- **Perfect for outdoor play**, combining craft with nature exploration.
- **Great for family bonding**, especially during nature walks.

---

476. Rainbow Milk Experiment

The rainbow milk experiment is a visually exciting science activity where children watch colors swirl in milk when soap is added. It promotes sensory exploration, curiosity, and early science learning.

How it works:

- **Prepare the milk:** Pour milk into a shallow dish and add drops of food coloring.
- **Add soap:** Dip a cotton swab into dish soap and touch it to the milk. Watch as the colors swirl and mix.
- **Experiment with designs:** Encourage your child to try different patterns and color combinations to see how the colors move.

Benefits for kids:

- **Teaches basic science concepts,** like surface tension and chemical reactions.
- **Encourages sensory exploration,** through sight and color movement.
- **Promotes curiosity and experimentation,** as they observe how colors interact.

Benefits for parents:

- **Inexpensive and easy to set up,** using household materials.
- **Perfect for quick, educational play,** combining science with fun.
- **Great for sensory play,** offering a colorful, hands-on experience.

---

477. Jelly Bean Building

Jelly bean building is a fun and creative STEM activity where children use jelly beans and toothpicks to build structures. It promotes problem-solving, creativity, and basic engineering skills.

How it works:

- **Create the structure:** Let your child use jelly beans as connecting points and toothpicks as the beams to build different structures like towers or bridges.
- **Experiment with designs:** Encourage them to try different shapes and structures to see which is the most stable.
- **Add a challenge:** See who can build the tallest or most creative structure.

Benefits for kids:

- **Teaches basic engineering concepts,** like stability and structure.
- **Encourages creativity,** allowing them to design their own buildings.
- **Promotes problem-solving,** through experimenting with different designs.

Benefits for parents:

- **Inexpensive and edible,** making it a tasty and engaging activity.
- **Perfect for STEM learning,** combining science with hands-on play.
- **Great for group play,** encouraging collaboration and competition.

---

478. Paper Plate Frisbee

Paper plate frisbee is a simple outdoor game where children decorate paper plates and use them as frisbees. It promotes physical activity, coordination, and creativity.

How it works:

- **Decorate the frisbee:** Let your child decorate paper plates with markers, stickers, or paint.
- **Start playing:** Use the decorated paper plates as frisbees and play a game of catch or aim for targets.
- **Experiment with throwing techniques:** Encourage them to try different ways of throwing the frisbee to see how it flies.

Benefits for kids:

- **Encourages physical activity**, keeping them engaged and moving.
- **Improves hand-eye coordination**, as they aim and throw the frisbee.
- **Promotes creativity**, through decorating the frisbees.

Benefits for parents:

- **Inexpensive and simple to make**, using paper plates.
- **Perfect for outdoor play**, offering a fun and active game.
- **Great for group play**, encouraging friendly competition.

---

479. Glow-in-the-Dark Sensory Bottles

Glow-in-the-dark sensory bottles are a calming and visually engaging activity where children create bottles filled with glowing water and glitter. It promotes sensory exploration, creativity, and focus.

How it works:

- **Prepare the bottle:** Fill a clear plastic bottle with water, add glow-in-the-dark paint or liquid, and sprinkle in glitter or small objects.
- **Shake and observe:** Let your child shake the bottle and watch how the glitter and glowing liquid swirl around in the dark.
- **Experiment with light:** Encourage them to experiment with how long the glow lasts after exposure to light.

Benefits for kids:

- **Promotes sensory exploration**, especially through sight and movement.
- **Encourages creativity**, allowing them to design their own glowing bottle.
- **Provides a calming sensory experience**, perfect for quiet play.

Benefits for parents:

- **Inexpensive and easy to set up**, using bottles and glow-in-the-dark materials.
- **Perfect for sensory play**, offering a soothing and engaging activity.
- **Great for group play**, encouraging kids to compare their designs.

---

480. Paper Airplane Target Game

Paper airplane target games are a fun way for children to improve their paper-folding and aiming skills. It promotes hand-eye coordination, problem-solving, and creativity.

How it works:

- **Create the targets:** Set up rings or hoops as targets at different distances.
- **Make the planes:** Let your child fold paper airplanes, encouraging them to try different designs.
- **Aim for the targets:** Have your child throw their planes through the targets, experimenting with throwing techniques to improve accuracy.

Benefits for kids:

- **Develops hand-eye coordination**, as they aim and throw the planes.
- **Encourages problem-solving and creativity**, through experimenting with different plane designs.
- **Promotes friendly competition**, making it a fun group activity.

Benefits for parents:

- **Inexpensive and simple to set up**, using paper and household items.
- **Perfect for indoor or outdoor play**, offering flexibility.
- **Great for group play**, encouraging friendly challenges and teamwork.

---

481. Nature Art Mandalas

Nature art mandalas are a calming outdoor activity where children arrange natural items like leaves, stones, and flowers in circular, symmetrical patterns. It promotes creativity, mindfulness, and an appreciation of nature.

How it works:

- **Collect natural materials:** Take your child outside to gather leaves, stones, flowers, and other natural items.
- **Create the mandala:** Encourage them to arrange the items in a circular, symmetrical pattern, working from the center outward.
- **Experiment with patterns:** Let them try different designs and patterns, creating beautiful mandalas in different colors and textures.

Benefits for kids:

- **Encourages outdoor exploration and creativity**, connecting them with nature.
- **Promotes mindfulness**, through the calming and focused activity.
- **Develops fine motor skills**, through arranging and handling small items.

Benefits for parents:

- **Inexpensive and eco-friendly**, using natural materials.
- **Perfect for outdoor play**, combining art with nature.
- **Great for family bonding**, as parents and children can create together.

---

482. DIY Kite Making

DIY kite making is a fun craft where children create and decorate their own kites before flying them. It promotes creativity, engineering skills, and outdoor play.

How it works:

- **Build the kite:** Help your child create a simple kite using lightweight materials like paper, string, and sticks.
- **Decorate the kite:** Encourage them to paint or color the kite with their favorite designs.
- **Fly the kite:** Take it outside on a windy day and let them experience the joy of flying their handmade kite.

Benefits for kids:

- **Teaches basic engineering concepts**, like balance and wind resistance.
- **Encourages creativity**, as they design and decorate their own kite.
- **Promotes physical activity**, through outdoor play and running with the kite.

Benefits for parents:

- **Inexpensive and easy to make**, using household or craft materials.
- **Perfect for outdoor play**, offering a fun way to explore nature.
- **Great for family bonding**, especially while flying the kite together.

---

483. Frozen Dinosaur Eggs

Frozen dinosaur eggs are a sensory-rich and exciting activity where children excavate small toy dinosaurs from frozen ice eggs. It promotes problem-solving, sensory exploration, and basic science concepts.

How it works:

- **Prepare the eggs:** Freeze small dinosaur toys in water-filled balloons to create "eggs."
- **Excavate the dinosaurs:** Let your child use tools like warm water, salt, or small hammers to break open the eggs and find the dinosaurs inside.
- **Experiment with methods:** Encourage them to try different ways of melting the ice faster, like using salt or warm water.

Benefits for kids:

- **Teaches basic science concepts,** like melting and states of matter.
- **Encourages problem-solving,** as they figure out how to free the dinosaurs.
- **Promotes sensory exploration,** through the feel and texture of the ice.

Benefits for parents:

- **Inexpensive and easy to set up,** using water balloons and small toys.
- **Perfect for outdoor or indoor play,** depending on the weather.
- **Great for sensory play,** offering a cool, hands-on activity.

---

484. Sensory Bags

Sensory bags are a calming and exploratory activity where children squish and manipulate sealed plastic bags filled with different textures like gel, beads, or rice. It promotes sensory play, creativity, and fine motor skills.

How it works:

- **Prepare the bags:** Fill sealable plastic bags with materials like hair gel, water beads, glitter, or small toys, and seal them tightly.
- **Start exploring:** Let your child squish, press, and manipulate the bags, feeling the textures inside without the mess.
- **Experiment with textures:** Encourage them to explore the different materials and describe how they feel.

Benefits for kids:

- **Promotes sensory exploration,** especially through touch.
- **Develops fine motor skills,** through squeezing and pressing the bags.
- **Encourages creativity,** allowing them to explore textures and designs.

Benefits for parents:

- **Inexpensive and mess-free,** using household materials.
- **Perfect for sensory play,** offering a calming and engaging experience.
- **Great for quiet, independent play,** fostering focus and relaxation.

---

485. Shape Hunt

A shape hunt is an interactive educational activity where children search for specific shapes around the house or yard. It promotes shape recognition, problem-solving, and physical activity.

How it works:

- **Create a checklist:** Make a list of shapes for your child to find, such as circles, squares, and triangles.
- **Start the hunt:** Let your child search the house or yard for objects that match the shapes on the list.
- **Experiment with levels:** Add more complex shapes like stars or hexagons for older children.

Benefits for kids:

- **Teaches shape recognition and classification**, reinforcing early math skills.
- **Encourages problem-solving**, as they identify objects by shape.
- **Promotes physical activity**, keeping them moving and engaged.

Benefits for parents:

- **Inexpensive and educational**, using household objects.
- **Perfect for quiet, independent play**, helping kids focus and explore.
- **Great for early learning**, especially for preschoolers and young children.

---

486. DIY Stamps with Potatoes

DIY potato stamps are a creative craft where children carve shapes into potatoes and use them to stamp designs onto paper. It promotes creativity, fine motor skills, and early art exploration.

How it works:

- **Create the stamps:** Cut potatoes in half and carve simple shapes like hearts, stars, or circles into the flat surface.
- **Start stamping:** Let your child dip the potato stamps into paint and press them onto paper to create patterns and designs.
- **Experiment with colors:** Encourage them to try different colors and stamps to create unique art.

Benefits for kids:

- **Encourages creativity**, allowing them to design their own stamps.
- **Develops fine motor skills**, through handling and stamping the potatoes.
- **Teaches early art techniques**, like stamping and color mixing.

Benefits for parents:

- **Inexpensive and easy to set up**, using potatoes and paint.
- **Perfect for quiet, independent play**, fostering creativity and focus.
- **Great for themed art projects**, like creating cards or wrapping paper.

---

487. Lava Lamp Experiment

The lava lamp experiment is a visually exciting science activity where children create a lava lamp effect using water, oil, and an antacid tablet. It promotes curiosity, creativity, and basic chemistry concepts.

How it works:

- **Prepare the materials:** Fill a clear glass with water, then add vegetable oil and food coloring.
- **Add the tablet:** Drop an antacid tablet into the glass and watch as bubbles rise, creating a lava lamp effect.
- **Experiment with colors:** Encourage your child to try different color combinations to see how the effect changes.

Benefits for kids:

- **Teaches basic chemistry concepts**, like density and chemical reactions.
- **Encourages sensory exploration**, through sight and movement.
- **Promotes curiosity and experimentation**, as they watch the bubbles rise and fall.

Benefits for parents:

- **Inexpensive and easy to set up**, using household materials.
- **Perfect for STEM learning**, combining science with play.
- **Great for quick, educational play**, offering a simple yet engaging activity.

---

488. Mini Ice Cream Shop Play

Mini ice cream shop play is a pretend-play activity where children set up their own "ice cream shop" using playdough, pom-poms, or other craft materials to represent ice cream. It promotes creativity, social skills, and imaginative play.

How it works:

- **Set up the shop:** Provide your child with materials like playdough or pom-poms to represent different flavors of ice cream.
- **Create the menu:** Let them create a menu with different "flavors" and prices.

- **Start serving:** Encourage your child to serve pretend ice cream to family members or stuffed animals, acting as both the server and the customer.

Benefits for kids:

- **Encourages imaginative play**, allowing them to role-play as shopkeepers.
- **Promotes creativity**, through designing their own ice cream flavors.
- **Teaches social skills**, through interaction with "customers."

Benefits for parents:

- **Inexpensive and simple to set up**, using household craft materials.
- **Perfect for indoor play**, offering a quiet and imaginative activity.
- **Great for group play**, encouraging teamwork and role-playing.

---

489. Button Sorting by Size

Button sorting by size is a simple educational activity where children sort a collection of buttons into groups based on their size. It promotes fine motor skills, early math skills, and problem-solving.

How it works:

- **Prepare the buttons:** Provide a variety of buttons in different sizes and shapes.
- **Start sorting:** Let your child sort the buttons into groups by size, from smallest to largest.
- **Add challenges:** For older children, add a timer or ask them to create patterns with the buttons.

Benefits for kids:

- **Teaches size recognition and sorting**, reinforcing early math skills.
- **Develops fine motor skills**, through handling and sorting small buttons.
- **Encourages problem-solving**, as they figure out how to classify the buttons.

Benefits for parents:

- **Inexpensive and easy to set up**, using household buttons.
- **Perfect for quiet, independent play**, fostering focus and concentration.
- **Great for early learning**, especially for preschoolers.

---

490. DIY T-Shirt Design

DIY T-shirt design is a creative craft where children decorate plain T-shirts using fabric paint, markers, or tie-dye. It promotes creativity, fine motor skills, and self-expression.

How it works:

- **Choose a design:** Let your child decide on a design or pattern for their T-shirt.
- **Decorate the shirt:** Encourage them to use fabric markers, paint, or tie-dye to create their design on a plain T-shirt.
- **Wear their creation:** Once the shirt is dry, they can proudly wear their handmade design.

Benefits for kids:

- **Encourages creativity and self-expression,** allowing them to design their own clothing.
- **Promotes fine motor skills,** through drawing, painting, or tie-dyeing.
- **Provides a sense of accomplishment,** as they wear their personalized creation.

Benefits for parents:

- **Inexpensive and easy to set up,** using plain T-shirts and fabric paint.
- **Perfect for themed projects,** like creating custom shirts for special events.
- **Great for family bonding,** especially when designing shirts together.

---

491. DIY Puzzle Creation

DIY puzzle creation is a fun craft where children design their own pictures and then turn them into puzzles. It promotes creativity, problem-solving, and fine motor skills.

How it works:

- **Create the picture:** Let your child draw or paint a picture on a piece of cardboard or thick paper.
- **Cut the puzzle pieces:** Once the picture is finished, cut the cardboard into puzzle pieces (simple shapes for younger children, more complex ones for older kids).
- **Solve the puzzle:** Encourage your child to put the puzzle back together, helping develop problem-solving skills.

Benefits for kids:

- **Encourages creativity,** as they design their own puzzle.
- **Develops fine motor skills,** through cutting and handling the pieces.
- **Teaches problem-solving,** as they figure out how to complete the puzzle.

Benefits for parents:

- **Inexpensive and easy to make,** using cardboard and art supplies.
- **Perfect for quiet, independent play,** fostering concentration.
- **Great for themed learning,** such as creating puzzles based on animals, seasons, or family.

492. Indoor Scavenger Hunt

An indoor scavenger hunt is an exciting game where children search for specific items hidden around the house. It promotes problem-solving, physical activity, and attention to detail.

How it works:

- **Create a list:** Make a list of items for your child to find around the house, such as a red sock, a spoon, or a book with animals on the cover.
- **Start the hunt:** Let them search the house for the items on the list, checking them off as they go.
- **Add a challenge:** You can add a timer or offer clues to make the hunt more exciting.

Benefits for kids:

- **Teaches problem-solving**, as they figure out where to find the items.
- **Promotes attention to detail**, as they search for specific objects.
- **Encourages physical activity**, keeping them moving and engaged.

Benefits for parents:

- **Inexpensive and easy to set up**, using household items.
- **Perfect for rainy days**, offering indoor entertainment.
- **Great for family bonding**, as parents can join in or offer hints.

493. DIY Paper Windmills

Paper windmills are a creative and hands-on craft where children make their own wind-powered toys. It promotes creativity, fine motor skills, and basic science learning.

How it works:

- **Create the windmill:** Cut a square piece of paper and fold it to form the blades of the windmill. Attach the center to a stick with a pin or tack.
- **Decorate the windmill:** Let your child decorate the blades with markers, stickers, or paint.
- **Test the windmill:** Take it outside or blow on it to see how the windmill spins.

Benefits for kids:

- **Teaches basic physics concepts**, like wind and motion.
- **Encourages creativity**, allowing them to design their own windmill.
- **Develops fine motor skills**, through cutting, folding, and assembling the windmill.

Benefits for parents:

- **Inexpensive and easy to set up**, using paper and simple craft materials.
- **Perfect for outdoor play**, especially on windy days.
- **Great for STEM learning**, combining science with crafting.

---

494. Animal Yoga

Animal yoga is a playful way for children to practice yoga poses while pretending to be different animals. It promotes physical activity, mindfulness, and body awareness.

How it works:

- **Teach the poses:** Show your child different yoga poses that mimic animals, such as the "cat-cow" pose, "downward dog," or "cobra" pose.
- **Pretend to be animals:** As they hold each pose, encourage them to make the sounds of the animals or act like them.
- **Create a sequence:** Let them create their own yoga routine by linking different animal poses together.

Benefits for kids:

- **Encourages physical activity**, helping develop strength and flexibility.
- **Promotes mindfulness and body awareness**, as they focus on movement and breath.
- **Fosters creativity**, allowing them to pretend and act like animals.

Benefits for parents:

- **Inexpensive and easy to do**, requiring no special equipment.
- **Perfect for indoor play**, offering a calm, relaxing activity.
- **Great for family bonding**, as parents and children can practice yoga together.

---

495. Fingerprint Family Tree

A fingerprint family tree is a creative art project where children use their fingerprints to represent family members on a tree. It promotes creativity, fine motor skills, and family bonding.

How it works:

- **Create the tree:** Let your child draw or paint the trunk and branches of a tree on a large piece of paper.
- **Add fingerprints:** Use ink or paint to let your child press their fingerprints onto the branches to represent each family member.
- **Label the tree:** They can write the names of family members next to each fingerprint.

Benefits for kids:

- **Encourages creativity**, allowing them to design their own family tree.
- **Promotes fine motor skills**, through pressing and handling the ink or paint.
- **Teaches family connections**, helping them learn about family relationships.

Benefits for parents:

- **Inexpensive and easy to set up**, using basic art supplies.
- **Perfect for family bonding**, as parents can help with names and stories.
- **Great for keepsakes**, creating a meaningful piece of artwork to display.

---

496. Glow-in-the-Dark Bowling

Glow-in-the-dark bowling is a fun, nighttime activity where children knock down glowing pins using a ball. It promotes physical activity, coordination, and excitement.

How it works:

- **Create the pins:** Place glow sticks inside clear plastic bottles to make the glowing pins.
- **Set up the bowling lane:** Line up the glowing pins in a triangle formation.
- **Start bowling:** Use a soft ball to knock down the pins, keeping score for extra fun.

Benefits for kids:

- **Encourages physical activity**, through running and rolling the ball.
- **Improves hand-eye coordination**, as they aim for the pins.
- **Provides sensory play**, through the glowing lights in the dark.

Benefits for parents:

- **Inexpensive and easy to make**, using glow sticks and plastic bottles.
- **Perfect for outdoor play**, especially at night or in low-light settings.
- **Great for group play**, encouraging friendly competition.

---

497. Paper Plate Maze

Paper plate mazes are a fun and hands-on craft where children create mazes by gluing straws or yarn onto paper plates. It promotes creativity, problem-solving, and fine motor skills.

How it works:

- **Create the maze:** Let your child glue straws, yarn, or string onto a paper plate to form a maze path.
- **Add a marble:** Provide a marble or small ball for your child to navigate through the maze by tilting the plate.

- **Experiment with designs:** Encourage them to try different maze patterns and paths.

Benefits for kids:

- **Encourages problem-solving**, as they figure out how to navigate the maze.
- **Develops fine motor skills**, through handling the marble and tilting the plate.
- **Promotes creativity**, allowing them to design unique mazes.

Benefits for parents:

- **Inexpensive and easy to set up**, using paper plates and straws.
- **Perfect for quiet, independent play**, fostering focus and concentration.
- **Great for STEM learning**, introducing basic concepts of motion and balance.

---

498. Emoji Storytelling

Emoji storytelling is a creative writing and speaking activity where children use emojis to create and tell stories. It promotes creativity, communication skills, and social interaction.

How it works:

- **Create the story prompts:** Write or draw different emojis on paper, representing different elements like characters, settings, and actions.
- **Start the story:** Let your child pick a few emojis and use them as inspiration to create and tell a story.
- **Add a challenge:** Encourage them to act out the story or draw a picture to go along with it.

Benefits for kids:

- **Encourages creativity**, as they build stories from emoji prompts.
- **Promotes communication skills**, especially through storytelling.
- **Fosters social interaction**, when shared with others.

Benefits for parents:

- **Inexpensive and easy to set up**, using emojis or printed images.
- **Perfect for quiet, independent play**, fostering creative thinking.
- **Great for family bonding**, as parents can listen and engage with the stories.

---

499. Sensory Rice Bin

A sensory rice bin is a calming and exploratory activity where children play with colored rice, digging, pouring, and scooping. It promotes sensory play, creativity, and fine motor skills.

How it works:

- **Prepare the rice:** Dye uncooked rice with food coloring and let it dry.
- **Fill the bin:** Place the rice in a large container or sensory bin.
- **Start playing:** Let your child explore the texture of the rice with scoops, cups, and small toys, experimenting with how it moves.

Benefits for kids:

- **Promotes sensory exploration**, engaging their sense of touch.
- **Develops fine motor skills**, through scooping, pouring, and digging.
- **Encourages creativity**, as they use the rice in imaginative play.

Benefits for parents:

- **Inexpensive and easy to make**, using rice and food coloring.
- **Perfect for calming, independent play**, offering a soothing sensory experience.
- **Great for sensory development**, especially for younger children.

---

500. Rock Painting

Rock painting is a creative outdoor or indoor craft where children paint rocks with designs, patterns, or characters. It promotes creativity, fine motor skills, and imaginative play.

How it works:

- **Collect the rocks:** Let your child collect smooth rocks from outside.
- **Paint the rocks:** Provide acrylic paint or paint pens for them to decorate the rocks with designs, animals, or patterns.
- **Use in play:** Once dry, the painted rocks can be used for decoration or in imaginative play.

Benefits for kids:

- **Encourages creativity**, as they design and paint their own rocks.
- **Develops fine motor skills**, especially through painting on uneven surfaces.
- **Promotes imaginative play**, especially when using the painted rocks in storytelling or pretend play.

Benefits for parents:

- **Inexpensive and eco-friendly**, using natural materials.
- **Perfect for outdoor or indoor play**, offering flexibility in setup.
- **Great for family bonding**, especially during the painting and collecting process.

501. Create Sensory Bins

Sensory bins are a fantastic way to let kids explore new textures, sounds, and sights. These bins are simply containers filled with various materials that children can manipulate with their hands, helping them develop sensory awareness and fine motor skills.

How it works:

- **Choose your fillers:** Sensory bins can be filled with just about anything! Popular options include colored rice, aquarium gravel, moon dough, feathers, buttons, beads, or even sand and dirt. You can also make it themed by using objects that fit your child's interests, like plastic dinosaurs or ocean animals.
- **Add tools:** To make the experience even more interactive, add small tools like tweezers, scoops, or small containers for your child to sort and explore the materials.
- **Let them explore:** Allow your child to sift, pour, and play freely with the materials. It's a great opportunity to talk with them about the different textures and sounds they are experiencing.

Benefits for kids:

- **Stimulates multiple senses** like touch, sight, and hearing, which helps children better understand their environment.
- **Improves fine motor skills** as they scoop, sort, and manipulate small objects.
- **Encourages independent play** and exploration, promoting creativity and focus.
- Helps with **sensory processing issues** by allowing children to engage with different textures in a controlled way.

Benefits for parents:

- **Customizable:** You can easily change the contents of the bin to match your child's interests, keeping them engaged and excited.
- **Educational opportunities:** Parents can use sensory bins as an opportunity to introduce concepts like sorting, counting, and color recognition.
- **Calming effect:** Sensory play is often soothing, making it a great activity for children who need to wind down or manage their emotions.

502. Pool Noodles Play

Pool noodles aren't just for the pool—they're fantastic, affordable tools for all kinds of play therapy! These foam noodles can spark endless creativity, whether you're indoors or outdoors. With just a few simple modifications, they can be turned into learning tools that encourage physical development and problem-solving skills.

How it works:

- **Building blocks:** Cut the noodles into smaller sections and let your child stack them like blocks. They can create towers or imaginative buildings.
- **Alphabet practice:** Label each noodle piece with a letter and have your child stack them in alphabetical order. This can be a fun way to practice spelling!
- **Obstacle course:** Cut the noodles in half and use them to create a simple balance beam. You can arrange them in different ways to create a fun obstacle course in the backyard or living room.
- **Creative crafts:** Use noodles to create boats, bugs, or even DIY lightsabers. Your child can decorate the noodles with markers, googly eyes, and more.

Benefits for kids:

- **Boosts fine motor skills** as they build, balance, and manipulate the noodles.
- **Improves gross motor coordination** with activities like balancing or obstacle courses.
- **Encourages creativity and problem-solving** by transforming simple materials into imaginative crafts.
- Helps with **letter and shape recognition** when used in educational games.

Benefits for parents:

- **Affordable and versatile:** Pool noodles are inexpensive and can be repurposed for a wide range of activities.
- **Easy setup:** The activities don't require much preparation, making them perfect for busy days.
- **Builds confidence:** Parents can help guide their child's play, reinforcing learning concepts in a fun and hands-on way.

Superhero Play

Superhero Play is all about creativity and imagination! For this activity, ask your child to draw their favorite superhero, complete with all their special powers. The key here is to help your child connect with the strengths these superheroes have and to talk about how they can use their personal "superpowers" in real life.

How it works:

- **Set up the activity:** You only need some paper and coloring supplies. You can ask questions like, "What's your superhero's name?" or "What powers do they have?"

- **Discussion:** While your child is drawing, have a casual conversation about what their superhero would do in different situations. Relating the superhero's powers to real-life scenarios helps them feel empowered and confident.

Benefits for kids:

- Encourages **creative expression**.
- Helps with **emotional regulation** by turning abstract emotions into tangible characters.
- Teaches **problem-solving** as they think through how their superhero can help in tough situations.

Benefits for parents:

- **Insight into your child's emotions:** How they draw and describe their superhero can give you a glimpse into their thoughts and feelings.
- **Connection-building:** Talking through these stories helps open up communication in a fun and relaxed way.

List of Activities :

- **Sand Tray Therapy**: Children create scenes using miniature figures in a sandbox.

- **Art Drawing**: Provide various art supplies for free drawing or guided themes.

- **Puppet Play**: Use puppets to act out stories or emotions.

- **Dollhouse Play**: Children use dollhouses to reenact family dynamics.

- **Clay Modeling**: Sculpting with clay to express feelings.

- **Storytelling**: Encourage children to tell or write their own stories.

- **Role-Playing**: Act out different scenarios to explore feelings.

- **Music Therapy**: Use instruments to create music expressing emotions.

- **Emotion Charades**: Guess emotions based on acted-out cues.

- **Finger Painting**: Express feelings through tactile art.

- **Therapeutic Board Games**: Play games designed to address specific issues.

- **Building Blocks**: Construct structures to represent thoughts or feelings.

- **Bubble Blowing**: Teach deep breathing and relaxation techniques.

- **Coloring Mandalas**: Promote mindfulness through intricate coloring.

- **Emotion Masks**: Create masks that represent different feelings.

- **Sensory Bins**: Explore textures with rice, beans, or sand.

- **Guided Imagery**: Lead children through calming visualizations.

- **Yoga for Kids**: Introduce basic poses to promote relaxation.

- **Feelings Chart**: Use charts to help identify and express emotions.

- **Journaling**: Encourage writing or drawing in a personal journal.

- **Treasure Hunts**: Scavenger hunts with therapeutic themes.

- **Obstacle Courses**: Physical activities that require problem-solving.

- **Emotion Matching Games**: Match emotion cards to facial expressions.

- **Story Stones**: Painted stones used as storytelling prompts.

- **Animal-Assisted Therapy**: Interact with therapy animals.

- **Emotion Thermometers**: Visual tool to gauge emotional intensity.

- **Balloon Messages**: Write feelings on balloons and release them.

- **Nature Walks**: Explore outdoors to promote mindfulness.

- **Sensory Bottles**: Create calming bottles with glitter and liquid.

- **Mirror Drawing**: Draw self-portraits to explore self-image.

- **Face Painting**: Use face art to express different emotions.

- **Dance Therapy**: Use movement to express feelings.

- **Cooking Activities**: Prepare simple recipes to build confidence.

- **Magic Wand Play**: Imagine changing situations with a magic wand.

- **Emotion Dominoes**: Match emotions instead of numbers.

- **Build a Safe Place**: Create a model of a place where they feel secure.

- **Positive Affirmation Stones**: Paint stones with encouraging words.

- **Emotion Pie Charts**: Visualize the proportion of different feelings.

- **Group Mural**: Collaborate on a large art project.

- **Trust Falls**: Partner activities to build trust.

- **Emotion Bingo**: Use emotion words or faces on bingo cards.

- **Sensory Walks**: Barefoot walks on different textures.

- **Bubble Wrap Stomp**: Pop bubble wrap to relieve stress.

- **Emotion Puppets**: Puppets designed to express specific feelings.

- **Lego Therapy**: Build creations to facilitate discussion.

- **Shadow Play**: Use shadows to tell stories.

- **Paper Airplane Messages**: Write and fly messages about feelings.

- **Emotion Puzzles**: Assemble puzzles that reveal emotion words or faces.

- **Feelings Matching Eggs**: Match plastic eggs with emotion faces.

- **Stress Balls**: Squeeze balls to manage anxiety.

- **Emotion Stoplight**: Use red, yellow, green signals to express readiness to talk.

- **Dream Catchers**: Create crafts to discuss hopes and fears.

- **Finger Puppets**: Small puppets for individual storytelling.

- **Emotion Thermometer Craft**: Make a thermometer to measure feelings.

- **Worry Boxes**: Decorate boxes to "store" worries.

- **Friendship Bracelets**: Make bracelets to represent relationships.

- **Emotion Charades with Props**: Act out feelings using objects.

- **Rain Stick Craft**: Create instruments to explore sounds.

- **Emotion Scavenger Hunt**: Find items that represent different feelings.

- **Paper Plate Masks**: Craft masks from paper plates.

- **Mindfulness Coloring**: Focus on the present while coloring.

- **Sensory Play with Slime**: Explore textures with homemade slime.

- **Feelings Hopscotch**: Jump on squares labeled with emotions.

- **Emotion Wheel**: Create a wheel to identify complex feelings.

- **Role-Reversal Games**: Swap roles with the therapist.

- **Emotion Flashcards**: Use cards to identify and discuss feelings.

- **Nature Collage**: Collect natural items to create art.

- **Emotion Freeze Dance**: Freeze when the music stops and express a feeling.

- **Positive Affirmation Mirror**: Decorate a mirror with uplifting words.

- **Sensory Balloons**: Balloons filled with different textures (rice, beans).

- **Emotion Road Map**: Draw a map representing life's emotional journey.

- **Feelings Memory Game**: Match pairs of emotion cards.

- **Sensory Play with Kinetic Sand**: Moldable sand for tactile exploration.

- **Emotion Volcano**: Create a volcano to symbolize anger release.

- **Emotion Jenga**: Write emotions on blocks; discuss when pulled.

- **Guided Story Completion**: Finish a story started by the therapist.

- **Emotion Relay Race**: Physical activity combined with expressing feelings.

- **Build a Fort**: Create a safe space using blankets and pillows.

- **Emotion Word Search**: Find emotion words in a puzzle.

- **Create a Personal Flag**: Design a flag that represents the self.

- **Emotion Socks**: Decorate socks to express different feelings.

- **Positive Message Chain**: Add links with kind words or deeds.

- **Emotion Treasure Box**: Keep items that make them feel good.

- **Puppet Making**: Craft puppets to represent different aspects of self.

- **Emotion Dice**: Roll dice with emotions to prompt discussions.

- **Feelings Garden**: Plant seeds to represent growth and emotions.

- **Sensory Path**: Walk along a path with varied textures.

- **Emotion Traffic Lights**: Visual cues for comfort levels in sharing.

- **Create a Comic Book**: Draw a story featuring themselves as the hero.

- **Emotion Music Playlist**: Compile songs that evoke different feelings.

- **Body Outline Drawing**: Trace and draw emotions on body outlines.

- **Emotion Origami**: Fold paper into shapes representing feelings.

- **Worry Dolls**: Make dolls to "hold" worries.

- **Emotion Story Cubes**: Dice with images to inspire storytelling.

- **Emotion Bracelets**: Use colored beads to represent different feelings.

- **Create a Vision Board**: Collage of goals and positive images.

- **Feelings Tic-Tac-Toe**: Replace Xs and Os with emotion symbols.

- **Emotion Treasure Hunt**: Find hidden items that lead to discussions.

- **Create a Mood Journal**: Daily entries about emotions.

- **Emotion Masks Parade**: Show off masks in a fun parade.

- **Sensory Play with Water Beads**: Tactile exploration with gel beads.

- **Feelings Alphabet**: Associate each letter with an emotion word.

- **Emotion Matching Game with Photos**: Use personal photos to discuss feelings.

- **Build a Time Capsule**: Collect items to open in the future.

- **Emotion Bingo with Sounds**: Use sounds to represent different feelings.

- **Create a Scrapbook**: Compile memories and discuss them.

- **Emotion Treasure Map**: Draw maps leading to "emotional treasures."

- **Sensory Play with Shaving Cream**: Messy play to reduce anxiety.

- **Feelings Musical Chairs**: Discuss emotions when landing on a chair.

- **Create a Gratitude Jar**: Add notes about things they are thankful for.

- **Emotion Storytelling with Puppets**: Use puppets to narrate feelings.

- **Build a Dream Catcher**: Craft to discuss sleep and dreams.

- **Emotion Charades with Music**: Express feelings through movement to music.

- **Create a Family Tree**: Visualize family relationships.

- **Emotion Dominoes with Faces**: Match dominoes based on emotion expressions.

- **Sensory Play with Rice**: Hide objects in rice for tactile search.

- **Feelings Collage**: Assemble images representing various emotions.

- **Emotion Matching with Objects**: Associate items with feelings.

- **Create a Life Timeline**: Highlight significant life events.

- **Emotion Hot Potato**: Pass an object and share feelings when music stops.

- **Build a Lego Self-Portrait**: Represent themselves using blocks.

- **Emotion Bingo with Stories**: Share experiences when certain emotions are called.

- **Create a "Me" Box**: Decorate a box with personal significance.

- **Emotion Walk**: Move around the room expressing different feelings.

- **Sensory Play with Foam**: Explore textures with soap foam.

- **Emotion Guess Who**: Modify the classic game to include emotions.

- **Create a Personal Shield**: Symbols representing strengths and values.

- **Feelings Pictionary**: Draw emotions for others to guess.

- **Emotion Balloon Toss**: Catch balloons labeled with feelings and discuss.

- **Make Friendship Tokens**: Craft items to give to friends.

- **Emotion Simon Says**: Incorporate feelings into the classic game.

- **Create a Weather Chart**: Relate emotions to different weather conditions.

- **Sensory Play with Feathers**: Soft textures to promote calm.

- **Emotion Charms**: Make charms representing different feelings.

- **Build a Cardboard City**: Use boxes to create a miniature town.

- **Emotion Hangman**: Use emotion words in the game.

- **Create a Story Quilt**: Each square represents a different feeling or event.

- **Feelings Scavenger Hunt Outdoors**: Find natural items that symbolize emotions.

- **Emotion Jeopardy**: Game show format to discuss feelings.

- **Sensory Play with Beads**: String beads for tactile stimulation.

- **Create an Emotion Diary**: Daily entries focused on feelings.

- **Emotion Charades in Groups**: Team-based expression games.

- **Build a Miniature Garden**: Create a small garden representing peace.

- **Emotion Puzzles with Personal Photos**: Turn photos into puzzles.

- **Create a Worry Tree**: Hang written worries on a tree model.

- **Sensory Play with Fabrics**: Explore different textures.

- **Emotion Role-Play with Costumes**: Dress up to explore identities.

- **Make a Peace Corner**: Designate a space for calm activities.

- **Emotion Board Game Creation**: Design a game based on feelings.

- **Feelings Relay**: Pass items that symbolize emotions.

- **Create a Dream Journal**: Record and discuss dreams.

- **Emotion Memory Cards with Words and Faces**: Match words to expressions.

- **Build a Birdhouse**: Crafting to promote patience and focus.

- **Emotion Musical Statues**: Freeze in poses representing feelings.

- **Sensory Play with Nature Items**: Leaves, pinecones, and more.

- **Emotion Charades with Animals**: Express feelings as different animals.

- **Create a Personal Motto**: Develop a phrase that inspires them.

- **Feelings Fishing Game**: "Catch" emotions and talk about them.

- **Build a Marble Run**: Cooperative construction activity.

- **Emotion Sticker Chart**: Collect stickers representing daily feelings.

- **Create an Affirmation Collage**: Assemble positive statements and images.

- **Emotion Dance-Off**: Express feelings through dance moves.

- **Sensory Play with Dough**: Manipulate dough for stress relief.

- **Emotion Ladder**: Visualize steps to move from one feeling to another.

- **Build a Puzzle Together**: Promote teamwork and communication.

- **Create a Calm Down Bottle**: Glitter and water in a bottle to watch and relax.

- **Emotion Art with Music**: Paint while listening to different genres.

- **Feelings Hop**: Jump on mats labeled with emotions and discuss.

- **Sensory Play with Bubbles**: Blowing and catching bubbles to relax.

- **Emotion Telephone Game**: Whisper emotions down a line to see how they change.

- **Create a Self-Portrait**: Draw themselves expressing an emotion.

- **Emotion Wheel of Fortune**: Spin to land on feelings to explore.

- **Build a Fairy Garden**: Create a miniature garden to nurture.

- **Emotion Role-Play in Pairs**: Practice social interactions.

- **Sensory Play with Seeds**: Plant seeds and discuss growth.

- **Emotion Word Collage**: Cut out words from magazines.

- **Create a Time Capsule Letter**: Write to their future self.

- **Feelings Balloon Pop**: Pop balloons to reveal emotion prompts.

- **Emotion Mask Painting**: Decorate masks to represent inner feelings.

- **Build a Friendship Tree**: Add leaves with friends' names.

- **Create a Mindfulness Jar**: Fill with items that promote calm.

- **Emotion Relay with Art**: Draw or sculpt emotions in a relay race.

- **Sensory Play with Glitter**: Use glitter for art projects.

- **Emotion Story Circle**: Each person adds to a story about feelings.

- **Make a Positivity Poster**: Display affirmations and uplifting images.

- **Build a Card Tower**: Patience and focus activity.

- **Emotion Pictionary with Teams**: Group drawing game.

- **Create a Gratitude Tree**: Add notes of gratitude to branches.

- **Feelings Hot Seat**: Answer questions from the perspective of an emotion.

- **Sensory Play with Water Play Tables**: Pouring and measuring.

- **Emotion Mimes**: Silent acting to express feelings.

- **Build a Memory Box**: Decorate a box for keepsakes.

- **Create a "My Strengths" Booklet**: Highlight personal strengths.

- **Emotion Simon Says with Feelings**: Follow commands that express emotions.

- **Sensory Play with Sand Art**: Layer colored sand in containers.

- **Emotion Guessing Game with Drawings**: Interpret peers' artwork.

- **Make Friendship Coupons**: Vouchers for kind acts.

- **Create a Safety Plan Poster**: Visual steps for coping.

- **Emotion Balloon Volleyball**: Cooperative play while discussing feelings.

- **Build a Puppet Theater**: Stage for puppet shows.

- **Emotion Treasure Box with Locks**: Secure place for personal items.

- **Create a Hope Collage**: Images and words that represent hope.

- **Sensory Play with Sponges**: Absorbent materials for tactile fun.

- **Emotion Face Cookies**: Decorate cookies with different expressions.

- **Build a Miniature Zoo**: Use toys to represent different traits.

- **Emotion Walk with Signs**: Hold signs expressing feelings during a walk.

- **Create a Family Crest**: Symbols representing family values.

- **Feelings Matching Game with Music**: Match songs to emotions.

- **Sensory Play with Magnets**: Explore magnetic properties.

- **Emotion Role-Play with Scenarios**: Act out given situations.

- **Make a "Calm Down" Kit**: Assemble tools for self-soothing.

- **Create an Achievement Wall**: Display accomplishments.

- **Emotion Bingo with Real-Life Examples**: Share personal experiences.

- **Build a Model Vehicle**: Craft cars or planes from materials.

- **Sensory Play with Ice Cubes**: Explore temperature sensations.

- **Emotion Storytelling with Props**: Use items to enhance narratives.

- **Create a Personal Anthem**: Write or choose a song that represents them.

- **Feelings Sculpture with Recyclables**: Use materials to build.

- **Emotion Relay with Words**: Race to arrange words into sentences.

- **Build a Maze**: Design and navigate mazes.

- **Create a "Secret Handshake"**: Develop a unique greeting.

- **Emotion Word Search Puzzle Creation**: Make their own puzzles.

- **Sensory Play with Edible Materials**: Safe exploration with taste.

- **Emotion Poster with Handprints**: Use handprints to express feelings.

- **Make a Comic Strip About Emotions**: Draw a sequence of events.

- **Build a Tower with Cups**: Stack cups to represent building resilience.

- **Emotion Mask Dance**: Choreograph movements while wearing masks.

- **Create a Future Goals Chart**: Visualize aspirations.

- **Feelings Finger Puppets**: Small puppets for each emotion.

- **Sensory Play with Light Tables**: Explore colors and shapes.

- **Emotion Alphabet Book**: Create pages for each letter and feeling.

- **Build a Floating Device**: Experiment with buoyancy.

- **Create a Personal Logo**: Design a symbol that represents them.

- **Emotion Word Collage on Canvas**: Art project with emotion words.

- **Sensory Play with Balloons**: Static electricity experiments.

- **Emotion Role-Play with Puppets**: Puppets interact to explore feelings.

- **Make a Personal Calendar**: Mark important dates and emotions.

- **Create a "Thankful Jar"**: Collect notes of gratitude.

- **Feelings Telephone with Drawings**: Pass along a drawing to see changes.

- **Build a Musical Instrument**: Craft simple instruments.

- **Emotion Hop with Hula Hoops**: Jump into hoops labeled with feelings.

- **Sensory Play with Finger Paints**: Express emotions through color.

- **Create a Superhero Alter Ego**: Develop a character with special traits.

- **Emotion Matching Game with Smells**: Associate scents with feelings.

- **Build a Rain Shelter**: Use materials to create a small shelter.

- **Emotion Storytelling with Music**: Narrate stories while playing instruments.

- **Make a Mood Bracelet**: Use color-changing beads.

- **Create a "My Favorites" Collage**: Display preferred things.

- **Sensory Play with Play Foam**: Moldable material for creativity.

- **Emotion Relay with Drawings**: Pass drawings to build on each other's work.

- **Build a Card House**: Focus and patience activity.

- **Emotion Musical Chairs with Questions**: Answer prompts when seated.

- **Create a Personal Dictionary**: Define important words.

- **Sensory Play with Leaves**: Explore textures and sounds.

- **Emotion Bingo with Colors**: Use colors to represent feelings.

- **Make a Puzzle of Their Name**: Personalize a puzzle.

- **Build a Castle with Blocks**: Imaginative play and construction.

- **Create a "Steps to Success" Ladder**: Visualize goals.

- **Emotion Story Swap**: Exchange stories and discuss.

- **Sensory Play with Wind Chimes**: Explore sounds and breezes.

- **Emotion Guessing Game with Emoji Cards**: Use modern symbols.

- **Build a Dream Board**: Display hopes and aspirations.

- **Create a Family Portrait**: Draw or collage family members.

- **Sensory Play with Water Tables**: Experiment with floating and sinking.

- **Emotion Relay with Words and Actions**: Combine physical activity with expression.

- **Make a Gratitude Garland**: String together notes of thanks.

- **Build a Lego Emotion Tower**: Each block represents a feeling.

- **Create a Story Using Only Pictures**: Visual storytelling.

- **Emotion Charades with Animals**: Mimic animals to express feelings.

- **Sensory Play with Clay**: Mold to express emotions.

- **Emotion Hot Air Balloon Craft**: Write feelings on balloon shapes.

- **Build a Model Neighborhood**: Discuss community and relationships.

- **Create a Time Capsule Drawing**: Illustrate current life to revisit later.

- **Sensory Play with Textured Balls**: Tactile exploration.

- **Emotion Relay with Ball Toss**: Share feelings when catching a ball.

- **Make a Family Crest Shield**: Symbols representing family traits.

- **Create a "Wish Box"**: Store wishes and dreams.

- **Build a Friendship Web**: Use yarn to connect group members.

- **Emotion Walk with Chalk**: Draw paths representing different feelings.

- **Sensory Play with Musical Instruments**: Explore sounds and rhythms.

- **Emotion Matching with Socks**: Pair socks representing feelings.

- **Create a "My Day" Comic Strip**: Illustrate daily events.

- **Build a Paper Airplane Fleet**: Decorate planes with messages.

- **Sensory Play with Texture Cards**: Feel and describe different surfaces.

- **Emotion Role-Play with Storybooks**: Act out parts of a story.

- **Make a "Calm Corner"**: Designate a space for relaxation.

- **Create a "Feeling Faces" Poster**: Draw various emotional expressions.

- **Build a Collaborative Art Piece**: Group creativity project.

- **Emotion Hopscotch with Numbers**: Combine math and feelings.

- **Sensory Play with Scented Playdough**: Engage multiple senses.

- **Emotion Matching with Colors**: Assign feelings to colors.

- **Create a "Circle of Support" Diagram**: Visualize supportive relationships.

- **Build a Cardboard Robot**: Imaginative construction.

- **Sensory Play with Bubble Wrap Painting**: Use bubble wrap as a stamp.

- **Emotion Storytelling with Masks**: Hide behind masks to express freely.

- **Make a "My Strengths" Shield**: Highlight personal abilities.

- **Create a "Path of Life" Board Game**: Map out life events.

- **Emotion Hot Potato with Questions**: Answer when holding the object.

- **Build a Dream Catcher Mobile**: Combine crafts for visual appeal.

- **Sensory Play with Rain Sticks**: Listen to soothing sounds.

- **Emotion Matching Game with Animals**: Link animals to feelings.

- **Create a "Feelings Flower"**: Each petal represents a different emotion.

- **Build a Miniature Landscape**: Use materials to create scenes.

- **Sensory Play with Fabric Squares**: Different textures and colors.

- **Emotion Storytelling with Drawings**: Illustrate narratives.

- **Make a "Feelings Clock"**: Assign emotions to clock numbers.

- **Create a "Safe Space" Drawing**: Visualize a place of comfort.

- **Build a Model Bridge**: Symbolize overcoming obstacles.

- **Emotion Matching with Weather Symbols**: Link feelings to weather.

- **Sensory Play with Sounds**: Identify objects by their noises.

- **Emotion Relay with Hats**: Wear hats representing different feelings.

- **Create a Personal Timeline**: Map significant life events.

- **Build a House of Cards**: Focus on balance and patience.

- **Sensory Play with Colored Lights**: Explore how colors affect mood.

- **Emotion Word Association**: Quickly say words that come to mind.

- **Make a "Tree of Life" Drawing**: Represent growth and life stages.

- **Create a "Feelings Recipe"**: Mix "ingredients" of emotions.

- **Build a Paper Chain of Emotions**: Add links representing feelings.

- **Emotion Storytelling with Puppets and Props**: Enhance narratives.

- **Sensory Play with Bubbles and Light**: Use bubble machines and flashlights.

- **Emotion Matching with Storybooks**: Identify feelings in stories.

- **Create a "Wish Upon a Star" Craft**: Write wishes on star shapes.

- **Build a Maze with Blocks**: Navigate challenges.

- **Sensory Play with Nature Sounds**: Listen and identify.

- **Emotion Role-Play with Scripts**: Read prepared dialogues.

- **Make a "Hope Jar"**: Fill with messages of hope.

- **Create a "Feelings Thermometer" Poster**: Visual scale of emotions.

- **Build a Dream House Model**: Design their ideal home.

- **Emotion Charades with Emoticons**: Use digital symbols.

- **Sensory Play with Taste Tests**: Safe exploration of flavors.

- **Emotion Word Puzzles**: Unscramble letters to find emotion words.

- **Create a "Future Self" Portrait**: Imagine themselves years ahead.

- **Build a Balloon Tower**: Cooperative construction.

- **Sensory Play with Snow (Real or Fake)**: Explore cold textures.

- **Emotion Storytelling with Photos**: Use images as prompts.

- **Make a "Comfort Object"**: Craft something to hold when upset.

- **Create a "Friendship Map"**: Visualize social connections.

- **Build a Vehicle from Recyclables**: Encourage creativity.

- **Emotion Matching with Food**: Associate foods with feelings.

- **Sensory Play with Aromatherapy**: Use scents to promote calm.

- **Emotion Role-Play with News Anchors**: Report "news" about feelings.

- **Create a "Feelings Collage" with Magazines**: Cut and paste images.

- **Build a Puzzle Together**: Collaborative effort.

- **Sensory Play with Soap Bubbles**: Blow and observe bubbles.

- **Emotion Matching with Seasons**: Link feelings to times of year.

- **Make a "Coping Skills" Wheel**: Strategies for managing emotions.

- **Create a "Book of Me"**: Compile pages about themselves.

- **Build a Model Planet**: Discuss feelings associated with exploration.

- **Emotion Relay with Storytelling**: Continue a story in turns.

- **Sensory Play with Watercolors**: Paint and watch colors blend.

- **Emotion Hot Seat with Costumes**: Dress up and answer questions.

- **Create a "Memory Lane" Drawing**: Illustrate past events.

- **Build a Domino Chain Reaction**: Focus and anticipation.

- **Sensory Play with Dry Pasta**: Sort and organize shapes.

- **Emotion Word Ladder**: Create word chains linked by feelings.

- **Make a "Calm Down" Playlist**: Choose soothing music.

- **Create a "Feelings Garden" Drawing**: Flowers represent emotions.

- **Build a Paper Airplane Obstacle Course**: Navigate challenges.

- **Emotion Matching with Colors and Shapes**: Combine visual elements.

- **Sensory Play with Marbles**: Observe movement and patterns.

- **Emotion Role-Play with Superheroes**: Use characters to explore traits.

- **Create a "Feelings Diary"**: Regular entries about emotions.

- **Build a Kite**: Craft and fly, discussing freedom.

- **Sensory Play with Finger Puppets**: Small-scale storytelling.

- **Emotion Word Scramble**: Solve mixed-up letters.

- **Make a "Treasure Map"**: Draw paths to personal treasures.

- **Create a "Friendship Bracelet" Exchange**: Share crafts.

- **Build a Bridge with Popsicle Sticks**: Symbolize connection.

- **Emotion Charades with Silly Faces**: Encourage humor.

- **Sensory Play with Colored Rice**: Visual and tactile stimulation.

- **Emotion Matching with Music Instruments**: Link sounds to feelings.

- **Create a "Mood Calendar"**: Track daily emotions.

- **Build a Volcano Model**: Discuss anger and release.

- **Sensory Play with Foil Sculptures**: Mold shapes from aluminum foil.

- **Emotion Role-Play with Historical Figures**: Explore different perspectives.

- **Make a "Feelings Tree" Craft**: Leaves represent emotions.

- **Create a "Story Chain"**: Add to a story one sentence at a time.

- **Build a Model Roller Coaster**: Discuss ups and downs.

- **Emotion Matching with Nature Elements**: Relate feelings to natural items.

- **Sensory Play with Chalk**: Draw and feel textures.

- **Emotion Word Relay**: Race to write emotion words.

- **Create a "Positive Thoughts" Jar**: Collect uplifting ideas.

- **Build a Sandcastle**: Discuss foundations and stability.

- **Sensory Play with Slime and Beads**: Combine textures.

- **Emotion Role-Play with Mythical Creatures**: Explore imagination.

- **Make a "Coping Skills" Toolbox**: Fill with strategies.

- **Create a "Feelings Rainbow"**: Use colors to represent emotions.

- **Build a Model Ship**: Symbolize journeys.

- **Emotion Matching with Facial Expressions**: Mirror exercises.

- **Sensory Play with Gel Bags**: Squishy tactile experience.

- **Emotion Storytelling with Collaborative Drawing**: Take turns adding to a picture.

- **Create a "Confidence Cape"**: Decorate and wear for empowerment.

- **Build a Treehouse Model**: Discuss safety and refuge.

- **Sensory Play with Edible Finger Paint**: Safe for younger children.

- **Emotion Role-Play with Fairy Tales**: Reinterpret stories.

- **Make a "Gratitude Quilt"**: Assemble pieces representing thanks.

- **Create a "Feelings Map"**: Draw paths connecting emotions.

- **Build a Marble Maze**: Problem-solving activity.

- **Emotion Matching with Animal Sounds**: Link noises to feelings.

- **Sensory Play with Cloud Dough**: Soft, moldable material.

- **Emotion Word Poetry**: Write poems using emotion words.

- **Create a "Dream Board"**: Visualize future aspirations.

- **Build a Paper Mache Sculpture**: Long-term project.

- **Sensory Play with Textured Paint**: Add sand or rice to paint.

- **Emotion Role-Play with Robots**: Explore control and feelings.

- **Make a "Hope Lantern"**: Decorate and light up.

- **Create a "Feelings Sun"**: Rays represent different emotions.

- **Build a Model Airplane**: Discuss travel and change.

- **Emotion Matching with Colors and Music**: Combine senses.

- **Sensory Play with Magnetic Sand**: Explore attraction.

- **Emotion Word Crosswords**: Solve puzzles with feelings.

- **Create a "Friendship Book"**: Compile stories about friends.

- **Build a Bird Feeder**: Care for nature.

- **Sensory Play with Bubble Wrap**: Pop and discuss sensations.

- **Emotion Role-Play with Masks**: Hide and reveal feelings.

- **Make a "Calm Down" Bottle with Glitter**: Watch glitter settle.

- **Create a "Feelings Caterpillar"**: Segments represent emotions.

- **Build a Rocket Model**: Discuss aspirations.

- **Emotion Matching with Story Endings**: Predict outcomes.

- **Sensory Play with Sound Tubes**: Explore varying sounds.

- **Emotion Word Ladder Game**: Climb by expressing feelings.

- **Create a "Memory Jar"**: Collect positive memories.

- **Build a Model Garden**: Plan and design growth.

- **Sensory Play with Sensory Balls**: Different sizes and textures.

- **Emotion Role-Play with Everyday Scenarios**: Practice responses.

- **Make a "Coping Skills" Keychain**: Portable reminders.

- **Create a "Feelings Puzzle"**: Each piece represents an emotion.

- **Build a Model Train Set**: Discuss journeys and progress.

- **Emotion Matching with Photographs**: Use images from magazines.

- **Sensory Play with Tactile Letters**: Feel and identify letters.

- **Emotion Storytelling with Finger Puppets**: Small-scale narratives.

- **Create a "Future Goals" Timeline**: Map out ambitions.

- **Build a Lego Emotion Chart**: Visualize feelings with blocks.

- **Sensory Play with Water and Oils**: Observe interactions.

- **Emotion Role-Play with Sports**: Teamwork and emotions.

- **Make a "Strengths Shield"**: Decorate with personal qualities.

- **Create a "Feelings Ladder"**: Steps to manage emotions.

- **Build a Model Bridge with Straws**: Engineering challenge.

- **Emotion Matching with Texture Cards**: Associate textures with feelings.

- **Sensory Play with Sponges and Water**: Absorb and release.

- **Emotion Word Search Creation**: Design their own puzzles.

- **Create a "Family Traditions" Book**: Document customs.

- **Build a Model City with Recyclables**: Discuss community.

- **Sensory Play with Bubble Mixtures**: Experiment with bubble solutions.

- **Emotion Role-Play with Puppets and Scripts**: Guided dialogue.

- **Make a "Courage Medal"**: Award themselves for bravery.

- **Create a "Feelings Chain Reaction"**: Link emotions to events.

- **Build a Model Vehicle with Legos**: Discuss journeys.

- **Emotion Matching with Scents**: Use scented items.

- **Sensory Play with Rain Sounds**: Listen and reflect.

- **Emotion Storytelling with Collaborative Writing**: Group story creation.

- **Create a "Kindness Calendar"**: Plan acts of kindness.

- **Build a Model Ocean Scene**: Explore depths and mysteries.

- **Sensory Play with Textured Balls**: Roll and feel different surfaces.

- **Emotion Role-Play with Historical Events**: Discuss feelings from the past.

- **Make a "Strengths Tree"**: Branches represent abilities.

- **Create a "Feelings Journal" with Prompts**: Guided entries.

- **Build a Model Space Scene**: Discuss the unknown.

- **Emotion Matching with Colors and Temperatures**: Link sensations.

- **Sensory Play with Rice and Funnels**: Pour and listen.

- **Emotion Word Scramble Creation**: Make puzzles for others.

- **Create a "Community Helpers" Collage**: Recognize support systems.

- **Build a Model Mountain**: Symbolize challenges.

- **Sensory Play with Reflective Surfaces**: Explore light.

- **Emotion Role-Play with Animal Characters**: Express through creatures.

- **Make a "Coping Skills" Bracelet**: Beads represent strategies.

- **Create a "Feelings Mosaic"**: Assemble pieces into art.

- **Build a Model Farm**: Discuss nurturing and growth.

- **Emotion Matching with Textures and Colors**: Combine elements.

- **Sensory Play with Sound Bottles**: Shake and listen.

- **Emotion Storytelling with Masks and Music**: Multi-sensory expression.

- **Create a "Gratitude Wall"**: Display notes of thanks.

- **Build a Model Desert Scene**: Discuss isolation and resilience.

- **Sensory Play with Edible Sand**: Safe for exploration.

- **Emotion Role-Play with Superpowers**: Imagine abilities.

- **Make a "Courage Cape"**: Wearable confidence.

- **Create a "Feelings Road Map"**: Navigate emotions.

- **Build a Model Aquarium**: Calming visual project.

- **Emotion Matching with Shapes**: Associate feelings with forms.

- **Sensory Play with Water Beads and Light**: Glow effects.

- **Emotion Word Poetry Creation**: Write and share poems.

- **Create a "Memory Book"**: Collect stories and images.

- **Build a Model Forest**: Discuss growth and ecosystems.

- **Sensory Play with Slippery Stones**: Smooth textures.

- **Emotion Role-Play with Time Travel**: Explore different eras.

- **Make a "Strengths Banner"**: Display personal qualities.

- **Create a "Feelings Bridge" Drawing**: Connect emotions.

- **Build a Model Spacecraft**: Discuss exploration.

- **Emotion Matching with Elements (Fire, Water)**: Symbolism.

- **Sensory Play with Fabrics and Wind**: Movement and touch.

- **Emotion Storytelling with Collaborative Poetry**: Group writing.

- **Create a "Kindness Jar"**: Fill with kind deeds.

- **Build a Model Volcano**: Discuss eruption and calm.

- **Sensory Play with Scented Oils**: Relaxation.

- **Emotion Role-Play with Story Endings**: Rewrite conclusions.

- **Make a "Hope Tree"**: Leaves represent aspirations.

- **Create a "Feelings Mosaic" with Tiles**: Assemble patterns.

- **Build a Model Solar System**: Discuss place in the universe.

- **Emotion Matching with Seasons and Events**: Link times of year.

- **Sensory Play with Light and Shadow**: Explore contrasts.

Tips for Parents :

1. Be Clear and Simple

- **Use everyday language**: Describe activities in ways that are easy to understand.
- **Avoid jargon**: Parents and caregivers may not be familiar with technical terms, so explain concepts in plain English.

Example: Instead of saying "This activity enhances proprioception," say "This activity helps your child become more aware of their body and how it moves."

2. Highlight Benefits

- **Include specific benefits**: Mention how the activity helps with physical, mental, or emotional development.
- **Connect with parents' needs**: Address common parental concerns like improving focus, reducing screen time, or promoting creativity.

Example: "This activity not only helps your child stay active but also encourages problem-solving and teamwork."

3. Use Keywords Naturally

- **Incorporate SEO-friendly keywords**: Use terms like "play therapy," "kids activities at home," "creative play ideas," or "child development."
- **Don't overdo it**: Keywords should flow naturally in the sentence and not feel forced.

Example: "This simple craft is a fun play therapy idea that helps kids develop fine motor skills while having fun."

4. Be Engaging and Positive

- **Encourage creativity**: Use phrases like "let your child's imagination run wild" or "watch their creativity bloom."
- **Use positive language**: Emphasize how fun and beneficial the activity is.

Example: "Building a blanket fort is a fun way to spark your child's creativity and give them a cozy space to relax."

5. Provide Instructions in Easy Steps

- **Break down activities**: Offer instructions in simple steps or bullet points so they're easy to follow.
- **Use action words**: Encourage parents to "help," "let," "guide," or "watch" their child engage in the activity.

Example:

- Gather some blankets and chairs.
- Let your child help arrange the blankets to create a fort.
- Fill the fort with pillows, books, and toys for hours of imaginative play.

6. Make It Relatable

- **Address common issues**: Mention relatable challenges, like rainy days or indoor activities for when kids are restless.
- **Use familiar settings**: Reference locations parents are likely to use, like the living room, backyard, or kitchen table.

Example: "On rainy days, this DIY bird feeder is a great way to keep your child engaged while learning about nature from your own backyard."

7. Focus on Parent-Child Bonding

- **Highlight time together**: Mention how these activities foster bonding between parents and children.
- **Encourage involvement**: Show parents how they can participate in a way that's enjoyable for both.

Example: "Work together to build a marble run using cardboard tubes. It's a great way to spend quality time and encourage problem-solving."

8. Address Specific Developmental Areas

- **Mention specific skills**: Focus on areas like fine motor skills, hand-eye coordination, social skills, or creativity.

- **Link to emotional benefits**: Talk about how activities can boost confidence or reduce anxiety.

Example: "Finger painting helps kids improve their fine motor skills while providing a creative outlet for self-expression."

Made in United States
Troutdale, OR
11/10/2024

24628891R00179